# Families for Tomorrow

This book is dedicated to the wonderful team of people who worked in so many different capacities to make the Congress possible

# Families for Tomorrow

*Papers from
The XVIth International
Congress for the Family*

Gracewing.

First Published 1991

Fowler Wright Books
Southern Avenue
Leominster
Herefordshire HR6 8DE

## Gracewing Books are distributed

*In New Zealand by*
Catholic Supplies Ltd
80 Adelaide Rd
Wellington
New Zealand

*In Australia by*
Charles Paine Pty
8 Ferris Street
North Parramatta
NSW 2151 Australia

*In Canada by*
Novalis
PO Box 990
Outremont H2V 457
Canada

All efforts have been made to trace quoted material included in the various contributions. The Congress for the Family would like to thank individual contributors for assigning to them volume rights in their material.

All rights reserved. No part of this publication may be reproduced, stored in a retrieval system, or transmitted in any form or by any means, mechanical, photocopying, recording or otherwise, without the written permission of the publisher.

© Text, International Congress for the Family
© Photographs, International Congress for the Family, or cited photoraphers.

ISBN 0 85244 172 X

Disclaimer. The views or opinions expressed by the Congress speakers are not necessarily those of the International Congress for the Family UK Ltd, or of the publishers.

Typesetting by Print Origination (NW) Limited Formby, Liverpool L37 8EG
Printed and bound in Great Britain by Billings & Sons Limited Worcester

# Contents

| | |
|---|---|
| **Introduction** | vii |
| 1 *Her Royal Highness The Princess of Wales* | 1 |
| 2 Family—The Natural Institution *HE Cardinal Basil Hume, Archbishop of Westminster* | 2 |
| 3 The Family—a Community of Giving *Rev Lord Jakobovits, Chief Rabbi of the United Kingdom* | 5 |
| 4 The Family—Hope for the Future *Rt Rev Graham Leonard, Bishop of London* | 8 |
| 5 The Harmony of Man and Nature *Dr Seyyed Hossein Nasr* | 12 |
| 6 Nature, Law and the Family *Rev Peter J. Elliott* | 21 |
| 7 The Family and Public Policy *Dr Digby Anderson* | 29 |
| 8 Consumerism and the Family *Michael Schluter* | 34 |
| 9 Family—the Swedish Experience *Katarina Runske* | 39 |
| 10 Feminism, the Family and the Future *Valerie Riches* | 43 |
| 11 Pressure on the Family *Rob Parsons* | 49 |
| 12 'Personal View' from Young Parents *Paul and Helen Danon* | 53 |
| 13 Overpopulation: Facing the Facts *Julian L. Simon* | 57 |
| 14 Population, People, and Environment *Jacqueline R. Kasun* | 65 |
| 15 Contraception: a Scientific Scrutiny *Dr Niklaus Waldis* | 70 |
| 16 Parents and Children: Education in Human Relationships *Mercedes Arzu Wilson* | 77 |
| 17 Natural Family Planning: the Scientific Background *Dr Eric Odeblad* | 85 |
| 18 Natural Family Planning—the Experience of a Teacher *Mrs Veronica Pierson* | 87 |
| 19 NFP—A More Human Alternative *Dr Zhang de Wei* | 90 |
| 20 Cultural Shocks and Social Calamities *Dr Kongolo Mulumba* | 95 |
| 21 The New Medicine *Nigel M. de S. Cameron* | 102 |
| 22 Biological Research: Opening Pandora's Box? *Suzanne Rini* | 106 |
| 23 Seven Wishes for Life *Professor Jérôme Lejeune* | 112 |
| 24 Post Abortion Syndrome: Trauma and Cure *Dr Susan Stanford* | 116 |
| 25 Youth of Today: Commitment to Care *Dr Philippe Schepens* | 119 |
| 26 Education and Alternative Lifestyles *Rachel Tingle* | 123 |
| 27 Drug Addiction: Causes and Cure *Don Mario Picchi* | 128 |
| 28 From Hippocrates to Hypocrisy *Professor Bernard Nathanson* | 132 |
| 29 The Electronic Generation *Michael Keating* | 139 |
| 30 Families Mean Fathers *Dr Patricia Morgan* | 145 |

| | |
|---|---|
| 31 Good Children *Lynette Burrows* | 152 |
| 32 Preteen and Teenage Sex and Environmental Influences *Melvin Anchell* | 160 |
| 33 The Elderly: New Answers *Peter Benton* | 167 |
| 34 Supporting the Family in a Secular Society *Thomas Langan* | 171 |
| 35 Leisure, Youth and Family *Myriam Puig Abulí* | 176 |
| 36 Together for Happiness *Christiane and Guy Scheen* | 183 |
| 37 Europe and the Future of the Family *Archduke Dr Otto von Habsburg* | 187 |
| 38 Family Policies or Social Collapse *Professor Richard Whitfield* | 192 |
| 39 Family—the Way Forward *Rt Hon Angela Rumbold* | 198 |
| 40 *Mother Teresa of Calcutta* | 204 |
| **Biographical Notes** | 206 |

# *Introduction*

The XVIth International Congress for the Family was held at Brighton in 1990. At a time of rapidly changing circumstances the aim was to express a common concern regarding the breakdown of family life and the loss of those values which, learned in the family, make social life possible.

There was also a deep concern for the unhappiness which this breakdown is causing young people and children.

Guatemala, Rome, Madras, Caracas, Paris, Brussels, Madrid, Bonn, Vienna and Zagreb had all previously played host to inspiring gatherings at which men and women of goodwill came together to confront the problems facing the family and to find solutions to those problems.

The family has been described as one of the natural institutions. It has existed in every culture and in every age. The message of the Congress is:

To give encouragement to young people to feel optimistic about family life for the future by presenting practical solutions to the problems they are likely to face.

To help young people and families to be better prepared to understand and overcome the pressures on family life today.

To fill an information gap that exists about the relationship between family life and the principal issues affecting society today.

Christine de Marcellus Vollmer, President
Robert Standring, Chairman & Treasurer
James Bogle, Secretary

# Her Royal Highness The Princess of Wales

We have all had our own unique experiences of family life and I suspect that each of us has our own view of what a family should be. What I have found, both in my own experience and in my visits to organisations which support couples and children in difficulty, is that there are certain common ingredients essential for families of all sizes and types. There must, of course, be love, but love in its most practical forms; commitment to each other, sharing together, self-discipline and some self-sacrifice.

I doubt whether there is any standard formula for a successful family. The family is, after all, the most human, and hence the most imperfect of institutions. Instead, I could only point to those mothers, fathers and children in lonely isolation or in comfortable conformity, who simply do their best with what they have. Their success is measured by the care they have for each other, and I suspect there is no better form of judgement. To all of them, and to all who help them experience the warmth and strength of family life, I offer my support.

You should remember that the very idea of the human family has many different definitions, and perhaps those who depend on it most, the young, the old, the sick and the lonely, can really claim to know its meaning.

# 1. FAMILY – THE NATURAL INSTITUTION

## The Family—Hope for Mankind

*HE Cardinal Basil Hume, Archbishop of Westminster*

At home as well as internationally the family faces intense pressure. As a result its character and role is changing. It is some indication of the depth and extent of the present crisis that many today would seriously question what to most of us would seem self-evident, namely that marriage and family are intimately and inevitably bound together. For some other forms of bonding now claim a parity with that form of family life which is rooted in life-long love of husband and wife. There is such a polarisation of attitudes and generations that family policies have become a political minefield.

No one can deny that a traditional picture of the family has altered more rapidly in the seemingly conservative eighties than, say, in the more obviously non-conforming sixties. The statistics published by the Family Policy Studies centre include alarming evidence of unmistakeable tendencies. In the 1980s the number of children born outside marriage has more than doubled. Living together before marriage has become more commonplace. It is said that in 1987 50% did so compared with 7% in 1970. The future will take us in uncharted territory if, as predicted, one in four children will have divorced parents by the end of the century. Only half will have known what it will be like to be born of married parents who stay together and see their children grow up to independence. The cost in human suffering for these children is impossible to calculate. Psychological insecurity, multiple deprivation, the lack of constant parental love and of adequate and balanced discipline are bound to have serious consequences. Children from broken homes already suffer themselves from greater difficulty in forming stable adult relationships. They are caught in a cycle of pain and uncertainty. Who can tell what might happen to the stability of society itself if such radical insecurity were to become the norm?

We are all part of the problem. As a Catholic bishop I have to face facts and acknowledge that Catholics are as vulnerable as any others to the pressures of contemporary society. Sociological surveys seem to confirm that we are just as likely as our non-Catholic neighbours to suffer marriage breakdown. In fact, on most measurable indicators the outcome of marriages involving Catholics stays close to the national average. They suffer from the same anxieties, have to cope with the same pressures, and share in the same areas of progress we have made in our understanding of the complexities of human relationships. The inspiration the Christian gospel gives has to be translated into practice in the harsh realities of contemporary society. This is no easy task.

Yet this does not change the fact that the vocation Christians accept, at baptism, is that of being a new people of God, a sign of contradiction in the world. This is a mission we are called to at all times. In a special way we are reminded of it and are urged to undertake it in this, the last decade of the second Christian millenium. It will mean that on many of the major moral issues of the day we may well find ourselves confronting many in our society, and not simply conforming to its proclaimed standards. By this, of course, I do not mean that we have endlessly to berate and criticise others. That might make us feel better. But rhetoric, from either the Church or any political body, is simply insufficient. It is our action, our behaviour, that we must examine.

We need, of course, to start from the actual situation people are in, and try to understand with compassion how they got there in the first place. If we respect their integrity and humanity, and show that respect by engaging them in dialogue, we may make some progress both in alleviating distress and importantly in changing attitudes. We need fewer declarations and denunciations. We need to give more attention to the many examples of living, joyous faith and wholehearted commitment to Christian family life. We need to demonstrate in practice that there is a viable alternative to some present-day trends and patterns and one which is infinitely more attractive and satisfying.

I have said on more than one occasion that the soul of this generation will be won or lost over the basic moral issues of life and love. We have suffered serious setbacks recently because of Parliamentary decisions on embryology and human fertilisation. Abortion legislation has been dangerously and deliberately extended. Destructive experimentation on human embryos in their first fourteen days of existence is, I fear, but the beginning of even more drastic assaults on human dignity and the sanctity of life. Human love and relationships have publicly become increasingly trivialised in an atmosphere of sexual permissiveness which almost denies the possibility of exclusive and life-long commitment. Many are not prepared to acknowledge that love requires sacrifice and discipline. They want relationships which make few demands. They simply fail to grasp that, for instance, caring for a handicapped person is as much a privilege and enrichment as it is a burden and responsibility.

Perhaps one of the urgent needs of our time is to deepen and purify our concept of love. And only then may we begin to fathom the secret that lies at the heart of the Christian, and Jewish, faith that everyone is made in the image and likeness of God.

Faith in God as creator and Lord of the universe is, I am utterly convinced, the essential foundation and only guarantee of a genuine understanding and respect for human dignity and humanity itself. That is an immense claim.

Formed by this vision Christians stand for all that is authentically human. I spoke earlier of the battles over the meaning and consequences of life and love. This is where we touch the issues most basic to humanity and it is here that the Church is becoming a prophetic and sometimes lonely voice. It rejects short-term expediency; it clings to a vision of the absolute sacredness of all human life; it defends what is human against the impersonal forces of social and genetic engineering and warns against the dangers of an arrogance which seeks only to exploit and manipulate.

The intransigence of the Church on these issues is well-founded. It is, as I have said, connected intimately with our recognition of God the creator and Lord. Belief in him and commitment to him brings us to our knees in adoration and awe. Heirs of the Judaeo–Christian tradition, we see all that exists as a reflection of the truth, beauty and goodness of God; we acknowledge the unity of all creation as a single outpouring of God's life and love. There can, then, be no created thing which is not sacred nor, in a sense, sacramental—a sign and channel of the abiding presence of the Creator. Human beings are even more privileged. From the beginning, with unparalleled gifts of mind and will, we human beings come closer than anything else to the divinity of which we are image and likeness. Everything human is therefore uniquely precious. Take God from the equation and all is contingent and variable. Acknowledge God and humanity is secure.

The consequence of belief in God has to be a recognition of the special place which the created and the human hold in God's plan. We disrupt or ignore that plan at our peril. This is the theological foundation for the Church's consistent teaching and witness to the sacredness of life and love. That is why we place absolute value on that fundamental instinct of human beings to relate, to love, to form community, to procreate.

We should be under no illusion. Those who have long since abandoned belief in God or have radically different concepts of him, have by that very fact a fundamentally different understanding of what constitutes human nature and the proper ordering of society. It is here that we experience with considerable pain the fragmentation and lack of cohesion present in our society. These radically different concepts result in contradictory approaches to marriage and family life. It is here that the spiritual and moral drama of our time is being played out. It is a drama in which the many actors must continue in dialogue with each other. The stakes are too high to allow communication to break down and strident voices to dominate the stage.

# The Family—A Community of Giving

## *Rev Lord Jakobovits, Chief Rabbi of the United Kingdom*

I belong to the people who first taught the human race that we were all originally descended from an identifiable father and an identifiable mother, that we all derive from a human pair, man and woman, out of whom the human race eventually evolved. I belong to a people that trace their origin to the idyllic couples of Abraham and Sarah, of Isaac and Rebecca, of Jacob and Rachel. In other words we are a people who were born at home, and therefore the entire focus of our national thinking is perhaps best expressed by the collective term by which we have been known since Biblical times: either 'the house of Israel' or 'the children of Israel'. We see ourselves as a family that has a house, a home, that constitute the fellowship, the brotherhood, the family unit of children of Israel.

I am not quite sure that we yet appreciate the depth of the crisis that currently besets the home, and the awesome price that we pay for the alarming breakdown of the family, on a scale that has made the family a disaster area of modern times. Marriage is under siege, and married couples in their relationship to children with a loving home are almost beginning to be an endangered species. The price that we pay is a crippling price in moral terms, in social terms, in economic terms: the results of broken homes in terms of delinquency, in terms of drugs, in terms of AIDS, in terms of lack of output at work, (because people have not got a happy home to go back to at night and recharge their batteries, their cheerfulness, their positive attitude to life). All this cost is colossal, incomparably more than we pay just in medical services. Of course, our society encourages infidelity in marriage, it encourages promiscuity, by public propaganda. I remember the time of the campaign against AIDS, meeting the then Secretary of State in charge, and saying, "By passing around pamphlets dropped into every health store all over the country saying 'Don't die of ignorance, this is a betrayal'. Who dies of ignorance? Ignorance is not a fatal illness. People die because they do not control themselves." Therefore a new focus is needed, in order to ensure that we will not, (as has happened so widely alas) mislead and misguide our rising generation to believe that all the ills of society can be cured by what they call 'safe sex', or pretend that we can ward off the price that has to be paid for undisciplined living and for the belief that all we are here for is to enjoy ourselves instead of believing that we are here to serve, to create and to build.

Something remarkable has taken place in this country and throughout the world over the last few years. A new concept has suddenly seized the whole of humanity, and certainly civilized society, with profound concern, and is now on top of the national and international agenda of nations and of humanity at large. That is the pollution of our environment. A new term like 'ecology' has been invented, and statesmen and stateswomen, international congresses, newspapers, all zoom in on this entirely new recognition that the future of mankind is at risk because we allow our water and our air and our food to become polluted by not taking enough care of our wastes. It is no longer safe to swim in the sea or to drink a cup of water. Lately we have become aware of this, and there are enormous international efforts, national efforts, educational efforts, made to drive this message home, and billions are being spent now throughout the globe to begin taking care of a menace that quietly truly threatens the continuity of human existence. But surely the pollution of marriages, the pollution of relations between husband and wife and between parents and children is at least just as dangerous to the future of the human race? Maybe we can make the subject exciting enough, alarming enough and creative enough in terms of finding answers, to arouse public concern, public excitement, involvement, in an effort to ensure that we recreate the basic building blocks of society which are happy marriages, relations between husband and wife, and themselves and their children.

I suppose that above all we need to try and redress the imbalance that afflicts the whole of our society so grievously, to turn the outlook on the role of marriage, of the home, as the central feature of life, much more dramatically than we have done hitherto. Let me just give you two examples drawn from the teachings of my faith: the Hebrew word for love 'ahava' comes from a root 'yahav' which means to give. What a wealth of teaching lies in just this little bit of etymology. People often look upon love as what they can get out of life and not what they can put into life. We believe that young people have to be trained to realize that real loving means what you are prepared to give to your partner and not to demand from your partner. Let me express this in another wise saying taken from our ancient writings, the Talmud. It tells us there that if a young marriage breaks up, then even the altar in the Temple sheds tears. Why the altar? The reason is that if a young marriage breaks up, it is somehow because neither side was fully prepared to make some sacrifice for the sake of the partner. And what is the symbol of sacrifice? It is the altar. Therefore the altar failed to teach its message. There can be no happy marriage without the preparedness to give away something. I am, like my wife, the eldest of seven children. I well recall, that when in our childhood we got a bar of chocolate, before I got my share, I had to give away six shares to my younger brothers and sisters. That lesson is not learnt by most of our children—that before you enjoy something you give something away, and you share it. The result is that being only single or two, the whole world rotates around them, and since they have everything, they enjoy nothing. You ultimately enjoy only what you have struggled for, what you have fought for and what you have gained as a result of effort, and what you get for nothing is worth nothing.

Let me conclude with a little experience between a mother and children, that happened not so long ago to the eldest of our daughters. She is today the mother of eight, a young mother and an extremely active mother in the community. She went shopping in one of these huge supermarkets with two of her children, aged three and four, and suddenly heard the public announcement system calling for the mother of Ephraim, who has been lost and is in the 'lost-

and-found' department of this huge supermarket. She looked around and her Ephraim was missing. She got the shock of her life, and panic stricken, she rushed around with the other child asking for the lost-and-found department. She walked in there fearing to see her child in tears. But she saw her Ephraim playing happily, and he looked up and said, 'Hi, Mummy, have you been lost?'

I think that the problem today is not that the children get lost, but our mummies and our daddies get lost. If we create the right parents with the right sense of commitment to the enrichment of life, the sanctification of life, the ennoblement of life, our children will not be lost. Our children will be regained and will become that joy in our lives that will make all our problems in society, grim as they may sometimes be, more easy to bear. We will know a generation will be following us that will be inspired by values that will ultimately bring the blessing of fraternity, of brotherhood, of belonging to one large family and seeing in each human being a brother, a sister, having that relationship because we all acknowledge that we are the products of a common Father in Heaven.

# The Family—A Federation of Trust and Love

## *Rt Rev Graham Leonard, Bishop of London*

In seeking to respond to the enormous pressures on family life today, we have to be both realistic and compassionate. We have to be realistic in recognising the nature of human beings and the nature of the created world in which they are part and within the terms of which they have to live. We have to be compassionate in caring for people as they are, not as we would wish them to be. In these days, particularly in this country, it is so often assumed that if you have standards you will seek to impose them without compassion and apportion blame to those who are not personally responsible for their situation. On the other hand those who do have standards often assume that to accept people as they are and do what is possible for them in their situation involves a denial of those standards. In fact, both realism and compassion are needed. If both are not evident, then there is no hope nor creativity. A doctor who is seeking to heal must first make a judgement about what is wrong, a diagnosis, on the basis of which medical care will be given with compassion which takes account of the patient as a person. Both diagnosis without care and care without diagnosis are inadequate to bring healing.

I would also like to emphasise that I speak as one who is not only a professional Christian but who holds office in the Church. But I do so not only without apology, I do so with confidence and for this reason. I believe that the Christian Gospel, springing as it does from the actions of God the Creator, reflects and makes possible of fulfilment the true nature of man as he is created in the image of God. As the scholastic tag put it succinctly: 'Grace does not destroy nature but perfects it'. The point I am making is that in speaking about the nature of man I am speaking about what is common to all and which expresses Christian belief.

The human person is a highly complex psychosomatic unity who is an integral part of the physical world yet who is capable of transcending it and reflecting upon it. He has to learn to act as a unity of mind, body and spirit. While made in the image of God and capable of entering into personal relationships, of loving, of creative activity, of appreciating beauty, of knowing what is right, he is also very much part of the physical creation. He cannot, unless he is false to his nature as a human being, try and act as if he were free to make his own laws about the way creation works or expect the physical world to adapt itself to his desires. In fact, we all try to do this to some extent, as Dorothy L. Sayers used to remind us when she wrote of the way in which, having failed to look at the indicator at the railway station and finding ourselves going in the opposite direction to that we intended, mutter 'wrong train'. As she points out, there is nothing wrong with the train which is 'a perfectly good train, proceeding on its lawful occasions to the destination appointed for it by a superior power. To be sure, it has a wrong passenger, who has nobody to blame but himself'.

As part of creation, we are subject to its laws. I accept that logically it is not possible to argue from 'is' to 'ought' but I do believe that the way we behave morally must reflect and be congruous with the way the physical world works. One powerful reason for the present deplorable situation with regard to the family and family life is, I believe, that we isolate our physical affections and instincts from ourselves as persons and try to ignore the effects which our physical actions have upon our ability to act as morally responsible persons.

To speak of moral laws or standards often leads to a charge of being 'authoritarian' or 'legalistic'. But no one calls a scientist 'authoritarian' or 'legalistic' when he tells us that carbon monoxide is poisonous because it affects the red blood corpuscles. What he is saying is that it is part of the given-ness of creation and expresses a truth which we accept or reject at our peril. The fact that someone may choose to ignore that fact does not alter or abolish it. Nor does the fact that someone may use it wrongly to destroy himself. Indeed we would regard it as reprehensible and culpable if a scientist were prepared to modify what we knew to be true to fit in with someone who sincerely but mistakenly believed it beneficial to inhale it.

Moral responsibility in the sexual sphere must be based on the nature of man as created in the image of God. 'Male and female created he them'. It is in the complementary exercise of their distinctive roles that men and women can be fulfilled, whether in family life or in society as a whole.

It is through the body that a human person is set in relationships which have then to be lived out at the personal level. I say 'set' because the first relationship is that which is given to us without our consent, namely that of being our parents' child. The relationships which we have to our neighbours are partly given and partly by our own choice. In marriage, the relationship which we have to our husband or wife is that which comes from deliberate and free choice. It is a relationship which requires the unity of mind, body and spirit in a very particular way in that the physical commitment of sexual intercourse is accompanied by acceptance of the responsibilities which can be expected to flow from the union. It differs from fornication in that in the latter the physical union is not accompanied by that commitment of the will. It differs from adultery both in that respect and in that there is infidelity to the life-long commitment, the fear of which alone can be very destructive of the true relationship of love. Further, it is that union of mind, body and spirit which provides the context in which the responsibilities of marriage in respect of the couple to each other, to their children and to society can be fulfilled. A marriage in which the sexual element is allowed to predominate at the expense of the commitment of heart and will, is as much a parody of marriage as is that attitude which sees it as a purely private affair which is no concern to society.

I am well aware of the new factors in our time such as the reduction in child mortality, the availability of contraception, labour saving devices in the home, the cost of housing and so on, which present problems in determining the pattern of family life and in securing stability. If they are to be faced and the right solution to be found, it is vitally necessary that the moral element is restored to our thinking about the family.

In particular it demands the recovery of the oft-derided but fundamental moral virtue of chastity, which, based as it is upon the nature of a human person, embraces human sexuality and sees it as being fulfilled in relation to heart and will. Chastity reflects the true characteristics of man and of the integrity of the human person. It reflects the fact that man is designed to act in one piece, mind, body and spirit and that commitment of our body to another person must be accompanied by commitment to mind and will in an entire and permanent union. Allow our bodies to be detached from our heart and will and we become slaves to our bodies—at the mercy of our passions.

Chastity reflects our nature as social beings, capable of loving and living in mutual dependence, which requires fidelity and trust-worthiness. Infidelity, by contrast, springs from that self-centred attitude which abandons others when they no longer serve our purposes, and which itself springs from treating others as if they were but for our benefit and use.

Chastity reflects the nature of man in that, while recognizing the goodness and power of our emotions, it prevents us from being locked in their tyrannical grasp. The marriage bond, for example, can set us free to love for it binds us at the moment when things are difficult and spurs us to overcome the problems and strengthens the union, whereas a temporary relationship depends upon the partners keeping emotionally up to scratch all the time. When emotion wilts there is no spur to love.

Hence chastity defeats the evil of children being made to suffer for the emotional vagaries of those who are supposed to give them the love and security in which to grow. Chastity enables us to love our neighbours and binds society, for the chaste person is one who can be trusted with her neighbour or his neighbour's wife, without fear that he or she may snatch the one or the other for themselves.

By chastity that pair-bonding between a man and woman which is part of human nature, is elevated above its biological function to be the means by which the partners can learn to experience that true love which is of God.

It is by chastity that our sexual instinct is disciplined and directed in such a way that it becomes the instrument of our highest instincts of love, fidelity and integrity, whether by the exercise of that instinct within marriage or by the consecration of its power so that its energy is used in the exercise of our personality to other good purposes.

Such are some of the ways in which chastity reflects our human nature. I could develop its understanding further and try to reveal how, in Charles Williams' words, it can bring a 'very high and particular joy' and how that joy can be even greater when it is given to God in Christ from whom it comes. I must be content to affirm, again in Charles Williams' words, that it is part of that obedience to what he describes as the general principle of things—'to the way we are made—to what we are as human beings and to the fact that discipline is the way to freedom and joy'.

For those who attack chastity, it is a self-evident truth, which, for them, it is criminal to question, that sexual activity is an absolute necessity for human beings without which their lives are maimed and deprived, a notion which is not only shown to be false by the observation of people throughout history, but which confuses sexual experience with the disciplined exercise of the energies of sex in obedience to love.

I must say something about the situation in this country where the situation is particularly grievous and where recent legislation has done much to undermine—no, honesty compels me to say remove—the moral element in marriage. In 1966, the Law Commission considered one aim of a good divorce law to 'buttress, rather than undermine the stability of marriage'. In 1988, the Commission, with a partly new membership, published further proposals which not only seem to abandon that aim but rejected 'the view that the law must provide a moral framework for marriage'. It did not agree with the Prime Minister that the extent of family breakdown meant that the very health of society was at risk and considered that the number of divorces did not, as is sometimes alleged, indicate a fundamental weakening of the fabric of society. It did, however, weakly admit that 'divorce law does have some bearing on the social climate' and that it may be 'that less restrictive divorce laws contribute to an increasing disposition to regard divorce not as a last resort but as the obvious way out when things begin to go wrong. If so they may have contributed to some extent to the increased rate of marital breakdown'. I read the Report with growing concern and as one who has to try to deal with some of the distressing results of marital breakdown, particularly in respect of children, wondered what kind of ivory tower the Commissioners were inhabiting. My concern has been increased by the way in which the House of Lords I have heard Law Lords arguing that legislation must reflect the social outlook of the day. For this reason I hope that whatever this Congress achieves and I hope it will be much, it will not only help to prevent further legislation which undermines family life but will help to bring about that restoration of the moral element in our divorce and family legislation which is so urgently needed for the sake of all members of our society.

# The Harmony of Man and Nature

## *Prof Seyyed Hossein Nasr*
## *Professor of Islamic Studies, Georgetown University*

There is a crisis in the relationship between man and life itself. (When I speak about man I of course do not mean the male but the human being)

This is reflected first of all in all the tragedies we see in the destruction of the cycle of life around us: the ecological crisis, the death of a large number of animals and plants which we look upon as if they mattered little. Only in the last few years have we finally tried to do something at this late stage of human history about this tragedy, caused by modern man's special relationship with nature which is no longer one of care and responsibility, but one of rape in order to satiate immediate desires as if a man were dealing with a prostitute rather than with a woman to whom he is married and to whom he is responsible for the rest of his life.

And the crisis of nature is also the crisis vis à vis life. It therefore penetrates not only into the world outside where life manifests itself in the form of animals and plants, but also within us, within the human being. There is a crisis of the meaning of life within *us* by the very incubation of life and its destruction—the murder of life at various stages all the way from the time of its inception to what takes place on our streets in or cities throughout the Western world and now more and more in the so-called third world.

The crisis of life is combined with the destruction of the relationship—the normal and harmonious relationship—which always took place between man and nature and which was always taken for granted.

Today in modern society, the movements for the preservation of life, and for the environmental concerns seem in the eyes of some people to follow two very diverse and different directions. Politically these two groups often at times stand opposed to each other. But I wish to show that this in fact is a false and illusory way of looking at this problem. The problems of life, whether within us or within human society, and within nature, are really the same.

The first question is therefore to ask is 'How did this crisis come about?' Let us not fool ourselves here. A large number of people dealing with the ecological crisis and with the destruction of the harmony between man and the environment are in fact people who have been torn away from religious morality. They have lost the sense of the sacred and having desecrated nature for several centuries, now lay the blame upon the feet of religion itself. How often have we heard at conferences on ecology that everything is the fault of the book of Genesis and that it is Judaism and Christianity which are responsible for the destruction of nature and the natural environment by modern Western civilisation? Usually Islam is included in this equation, although when one speaks of the Judaeo-Christian in the West these days, the third member of the Abraham family, Islam, is left out. But in this context at least, Islam is also included with Christianity and Judaism as being responsible for the crisis of man and the environment.

But we must seek a bit further for the causes of the crisis.

When Christianity spread into the Mediterranean world it had to deal with a great problem of idolatry in the form of worship of the cosmos, the natural world. This form of naturalism forced the early Christian thinkers to draw a very sharp line between the realm of religion, theology, and the realm of the cosmos, cosmology, and to show very little interest in a religious cosmology. This attitude in the early Church fathers was not total, but gradually created a situation in which many people felt that the role of religion was not in fact to provide a theological explanation of the world of nature but a theological explanation of the meaning of human existence and morality and ethics. This of course was correct, but no religion can remain without a religious interpretation of the natural world. Therefore as Christianity developed, not only to become the religion of salvation at the end of the world (which the first century Christian expected soon), but also a religion destined to save a whole civilisation and to create a major world civilisation, certain Christain thinkers did have to pay attention to the significance of nature. They included Maximus the Confessor and Dionysius, and Origina (the Scottish or Irish writer living during the 9th and 10th centuries, who wrote about the sacramental view of nature which wasn't very far from being totally absent from Christianity). Maximus the Confessor, wrote that 'If everything is not a sacrament, then there is no sacrament. And the sacraments of the Church only emphasize something divinely ordained in which all orders of nature participate in the sacramental quality which issues from the Christic presence.'

Here I speak in purely Christian terms because I am quoting, practically verbatim, but these views are also to be found in other religions including Islam, in which the presence of God is not limited to the rites—what the Christians call sacraments—but also to the world of nature.

The ideas of St Maximus and others, however, became gradually eclipsed with the rationalistic constructions of the 13th and 14th centuries when scholasticism to a large extent took over and the sacramental view of nature became somewhat lost, although in the great doctor St Thomas, the emphasis on the forms of nature still preserved a relationship between the world of nature and the world of theology.

With the advent of nominalism and rationalism in the late Middle Ages, this view became gradually further alienated from the mainstream of Western European thought, and with the coming of the Renaissance, Western man felt that he had rediscovered nature (as we see in the paintings of the Italian Renaissance) but at the expense of a nature which was no longer within the Christian universe. Hence a secularisation of nature set in, which with the humanism of the Renaissance, has finally led us to the impasse that we see today.

These things all seem very very far-fetched. What do the landscapes of Michaelangelo Boticelli have to do with the death of the seals on the shores of England two years ago or with the drilling of a hole in the ozone layer? But they are very far from being unrelated. Discovery of nature in the European

Renaissance followed by the love of nature did not take place within the theological and sacred universe of Christianity. Some of the people of course who wrote were pious Christians—but their love of nature, their view of nature, was in a sense 'pagan'; it was not within the Christian synthesis which had dominated European civilisation for such a long time. Therefore, as a result of this, the love of nature and the expression or the sense of the sacred, were gradually separated in Western Europe.

This was the first important step in the crisis that we now face in its full fury in the later part of the 20th century. The first step was the loss of the sacred. That is, the sacred became limited to the sacraments understood as to the Eucharist and to certain objects: icons, going to church, to the spaces within the beautiful cathedrals created before the architecture itself became more or less secularised. The idea of the sacred being everywhere was gradually lost in the scientific and philosophical world of the 16th and 17th centuries, with European philosophy declaring its independence of Christianity, and in the Scientific Revolution of the 17th century with the creation of a science which explicitly denied the possibility of the study of the sacred as an object for science. Science went on its own way, declaring the independence of itself and of the natural order from any order beyond itself.

So the loss of the sacred was followed by the gradual secularisation of nature. Any sacred view of nature was viewed as being magic—magical, even unChristian. A number of Christian theologians, especially with the rise of Protestantism (although Luther himself was very much interested and loved nature) went back to the early position of the Church, considering any sacred love of nature as being a kind of idolatry. For a while there was a divorce between religion and science in the West, which is so well expressed in the famous trial of Galileo. The poor Cardinal Bellarmine who is blamed in the text books as representing bigotry, was in fact right, and Galileo was wrong. Galileo said that the function of the church is to lead men to heaven, not to study the heavens scientifically, which is for scientists to do. And he was totally wrong, because once that happens, then the study of the heavens and the study of the earth becomes a study totally divorced from what is man's end, namely the relation to the sacred, and leads to the unparalleled crisis which we are facing today.

The secularisation of nature soon led to what is called the mechanisation of the scientific world view. That took place mostly in this country through the great genius of Sir Isaac Newton, The *Principia*, expressed for the first time the scientific attitude towards the world and the creation of a world view in which the whole of the planetry system, and by extrapolation, the whole of the cosmos, was seen as a great clock, whose laws were now solved by the Newtonian equations. This world view appeared as a great triumph of the human spirit, and in a certain sense it was. But it was the quantification of nature. Nature became pure quantity, and the role of the physicist, who now was the new priest of the new civilisation, was precisely to calculate these quantites and laws and mathematically determine the motion of this great clock.

The mechanistic view of the world was too successful to be cast aside and its success was not only in its internal theoretical success, but in the fact that it promised power. It was another Englishman, Sir Francis Bacon, who changed the whole goal of knowledge, of organised knowledge which we call science, by saying that the goal of science is to gain power, and not to perfect the soul as St

Thomas or St Augustine, or large numbers of Muslim writers would have said. Henceforth, science of course became the instrument for the gaining of power, and therefore became wed to very powerful economic incentives and forces which were then nascent in Europe (in both Italy and northern Europe) and gradually led to the Industrial Revolution and the unbridled passion with which one part of the human race, that is Western Europe, and mostly North-Western Europe, set about to conquer the world, not only politically, but also technologically.

There was another element from the Renaissance which we must mention, for without it the destruction of the harmony between man and nature can never be understood. And that is the rise of what is usually called humanism. By humanism here I do no mean Christian humanism, or Islamic humanism, or Jewish humanism. I mean the kind of secular humanism which set man as the ultimate criterion and value and the ultimate judge and determiner of meaning. This kind of humanism, very strong still in Western civilisation, set the empire of man as the final and ultimate arbitrator—the ultimate value. It substituted what Christ called the Kingdom of God by the kingdom of man. It was Christ who had said that the Kingdom of God is within you and 'Seek ye first the Kingdom of God, and all else shall be added unto you.'

The Kingdom of God became the kingdom of man and as a consequence man gained for himself a totally disproportionate evaluation of himself. Other human beings, from Aztecs and Mayans of Central and South America, to Persians and Indians and Chinese and Africans, are also human beings: they also have a kind of humanism in the sense that human life is valuable, human emotions are important, they are as selfish and egotistical, as good and as bad as Europeans, as Americans! Human beings are human beings everywhere. I'm not trying to differentiate between them in that sense, but to say that this kind of humanism 'absolutised' the human state. Everything was sacrificed to the altar of the human state. And the first thing that was sacrificed was God. God and the transcendant became secondary to human interests and human interests became limited to terrestrial interests. Christian humanism or Islamic humanism was also interested in human welfare, but it saw humanity in its totality including the after-life, including the immortal soul which is the concern of religion. This new humanism saw the earthly abode of man as being his ultimate abode; man became a totally earthly being and his welfare became absolute. You see this debate coming out every day today in newspapers. When in order to feed 2000 stomachs in Oregon you tear down a whole forest which could destroy the whole ecology of North-Western United States, you are again applying this: the economic welfare of 2000 people is more important than a whole part of nature which could destroy forever many species, not to mention the incredible consequences for man himself. This short-sighted view of human welfare became so absolutised that not only did it sacrifice God Himself to the altar of terrestrial man's rule and terrestrial man's view of himself, but also sacrificed the whole of the natural order.

Henceforth, all animals and plants were seen only as creatures, objects to be used by man, but not by man as a saint who would pray for the animals as St Francis of Assisi did, but as essentially a devouring animal whose needs are infinite and whose means of acquiring whatever he wants now become more and more brutal and more and more forceful. It was from this background that modern man gradually succeeded in first of all conquering the rest of the globe, in making use of the oxygen, of the waters, of the resources that really belong to the whole of the world, and in bringing about an environmental crisis in which the rest of the world had only an indirect and passive share.

It is very important to remember this when we talk for example about population control and we say 'if only those Chinese and Indians and Bengalese and Egyptians could stop producing so many people everyone would breathe a better air; there would be no acid rain, and all the rivers would be fresh and everything would be fine on the surface of the globe'. How false this view is! Every person who is born in the advanced industrial nations has an impact upon the environment which is several hundred times more than the impact created by those poor people whom Mother Theresa takes care of in Calcutta, or even people living in fairly well-off conditions in the Middle East or other parts of Asia and Africa and South America. It is very important to remember this and to remember that in fact the conquest of the rest of the world was made possible by looking upon nature as an IT, as an object to be used and devoured without any interest whatsoever in the rights of the life of nature and made possible by the complete and ultimate secularisation of the whole of life. The last step was the secularisation of sexuality. When Europeans were conquering the rest of the world in the 19th century, sexuality in the West still had something of its Christian meaning within the family. We always talk about prudish Victorian Englishmen and women—that seems like 2000 years ago, yet was only less than a century ago. It was the last thing that was left that could be in fact trivialised by being taken out of the context of the sacred, and it is precisely this final element of human life—the last thing that man had which he could destroy and trivialise—that has brought on the family crisis.

In order to bring back the meaning of life (including sexuality and the significance of the family) one has to regain the harmony between man and nature, and the life of nature which also penetrates into us. It is not only our biology but it is life itself. To do that one has to regain the sense of the sacredness of nature—the sacredness of life—and the sacramental quality of life and of nature. One cannot separate the two. One can no longer say—all right, human life is sacred but the life of those cats and dogs and horses and racoons and birds of prey are trivial and not important. The whole chain of life is interrelated and this is seen in the teachings of Christ; it is seen in the Koran (the sacred scriptures of Islam) and in all of the other celestial religions of the world—the revealed religions of the world. The sacramental view of nature has to be regained.

How does one regain it? To regain the sacramental view of nature one has to regain a sense of the sacred. And in order to regain the sense of the sacred, we have to first of all understand what is the sacred.

Today as we live in the latter part of the 20th century, many people have no sense of the sacred—what is the sacred? They say it is a term that is a fetish for all of these other terms that anthropologists have invented in order not to study religion seriously. It is a sociologically determined attitude.

But in fact the sacred is an ontological reality; it is an inate part of the being of things in the same way that the rose smells sweet. That is not a sociologically defined sense. Anyone with a sense of smell can smell the sweetness of the rose and anyone who has the sense of smell of the sacred can smell the sacred. Unfortunately the sense has become atrophied in certain parts of the world including, of course, what was once the cradle of secularisation and modernisation, Western Europe and America. Therefore one has to go back to the beginning—what is the sacred? The sacred, *sacrum* in Latin, from which the English word comes is very difficult to define, like all primal terms. Its like saying—what is beauty? What is reality? What is God? It is difficult to define. But it's not impossible—the sacred is really the eruption or manifestation of the eternal order in time of God and the spiritual world in the temporal sequence and world in which we live. It is not wholly of this world, but nevertheless it permeates this world. Everything has a face turned towards the sacred, because everything is created by God and ultimately returns to Him; not only the human beings, but everything, finally returns to God. The writings of the early Christian thinkers and theologians attest to this.

Now the sacred is available everywhere, and yet it is not available unless we submit ourselves to the major messages of Heaven which God has sent us precisely because we are not able to swim up the current by ourselves; we need Divine help. Therefore religion is necessary as the conduit for the discovery of the sacred. I don't mean only one religion (I am not a Christian, I am a Muslim, but I believe in the truth of all religions that come from Heaven). I believe that in the West, although you have not the penetration of other religions and interest in other religions, essentially the major religious force is still Christianity, and it is a revival of Christian values that in fact is the only way of salvation for the present day Western civilisation on both sides of the Atlantic. It is religion which makes accessible the possibility of the regaining of the sacred. That particular and more limited version of the sacraments (the sacraments in which devout Christians still partake) is precisely the key which enables the human being gradually to be able to see the sacred in all things. The first thing that is to be done is therefore to rediscover God, to rediscover the origin of religion. This is very difficult, and the reason why is that much of religion—the religious message in the West—has become covered by the dross of centuries of battle against rationalism, against secularism, a gradual receding of the theological forces to the extent that there are many theologians in the West who are in fact not theologians at all. In the Eastern Church, the word 'theologian' means to have the '*theos*'—God—dwell in you, a very exalted position. In the West even the more limited meaning of theologian as understood in the past is now so diluted that there is many a physicist who is a better theologian than many professional theologians. Theology has been receding with an inferiority complex for some time in order to placate the forces of rationalism and secularism. There is no need for this. All one has to do is to see the castle made of cards of modern science and rationalism falling down with the wind of the 20th century, to realise that the theological task is much more serious. What is important is to return to the principles of the rich tradition of Christianity and to be able to provide once again the metaphysical and theological response which the modern soul and the modern mind require. In addition to the return to God, essential in order to regain the sense of the sacred, it is also necessary to rediscover the spirit.

This is a vague term in English but let us use the Latin '*spiritus*', which is used to refer to the Holy Spirit, but also to that which comes from God, the world of the Spirit—that which is the deepest level of the human soul.

To be man is to believe in God.

Man is made in the image of God as both the book of Genesis & a tradition of the Prophet assert. To rediscover the reality of the spirit may seem somewhat more difficult, because the modern scientific world-view has become so dominant as to make anything which does not fit into its world-view appear to be unreal.

What has to be dismantled is not science, but the scientific world-view as a monolithic and monopolistic interpretation of God's creation, a murderous (I cannot use any softer term) way of looking at the world. If we are able to see through this world-view then perhaps we will be able to find a place in the world for the manifestation of the Spirit. How many of us look during a starry night at heaven and see anything else but masses of protons and electrons moving in whirlwind throughout space? And how fooled we are by big and small telescopes, thinking they are going to reveal to us the secrets of the universe, as if the secrets of the universe could be purely brute facts. Those facts are very interesting. These are not bad intellectual preoccupations, but that is not what the mystery of the univese is. The mystery of the universe is the mystery of existence. It is this which needs to be seen and to be felt once again. And if that were done we would see the presence of the Spirit, not only within us, not only within saintly men and women, but also within God's creation and through that perhaps to re-establish the harmony of man and nature.

How silly it is for human beings to claim to be the author of life. We can never create something. Creation belongs to God and life belongs to Him. We have it on a borrowed term. As human beings we are aware of it, and we should develop a philosophy vast enough to be able to understand the mechanistic and post-mechanistic views of modern physics without destroying the meaning of life and the meaning of the rhythms of nature, the laws of nature as coming from the divine origin.

This harmony between man and nature which I hope will be created through the regaining of the sense of the sacred, must also entail the harmony between the two basic forms of life, namely man and woman. There is a very great mystery as to why God created nature in this way. Why is there this polarity? Why is there sexuality, not only among us, but also among other animals, and also certain plants? I think the answer to this has been provided very amply by the traditional philosophers and theologians in both Christianity and also in Islam and other religions. The man–woman distinction is not an accident. The male and female natures are complementary, they are not identical and they are not to be reduced to a least common denominator—egalitarianism—which would destroy the beauty of God's creation and certain particular qualities of a divine order which are manifested in the female or the male.

One of the consequences of the loss of the harmony of nature is the loss of the harmony between the two sexes. The alienation of men and women from each other, is I believe, a consequence of the loss of this larger harmony. And this larger harmony which has been lost, namely the harmony between man and nature, is also due to the loss of course of the harmony between man and God.

The human being, the human state, can never be at peace with itself unless it is at peace with God, and it never can be at peace with nature unless it is at peace with itself. No humanity which does not have inner harmony can hope to have external harmony with nature. That is why so many of these ecological movements today, although based upon wonderful intentions and correct emotions, do not get very far precisely because they are carried out without trying to create harmony within oneself and harmony with God. The hierarchy of harmony with God, harmony within and harmony without, cannot be broken by governmental edicts and laws and economic reforms by whatever kinds of social engineering we try to foster in order to solve social problems. Those are really cosmetics. (The word cosmetic itself shows profoundly what has happened. Today cosmetics are cosmetics—the way I just used it—originally it meant to become cosmos-like. The word cosmetic is related to the word *cosmos*. When people painted themselves in the jungles of Guatemala or in the middle of Africa or Australia, they were re-establishing this harmony within man and nature.)

There is therefore no harmony possible between men and women unless that harmony is found in God. The more industrialised, more modernised societies become, the greater the alienation of the sexes, leading to deviant sexual practice, to all kinds of diseases, and to the break up of families. The male and the female complement each other in God and in the Spirit, in the state of perfection which belongs only to God and the spiritual world. Without that the male and female are left on their own and they vie with each other for completion and at the same time for complementarity without ever being able to fulfil this in a complete way. There are of course exceptions to this case, for sometimes great love can be created between two beings of opposite sex without a conscious awareness of the Divine, but even that is divine because all love ultimately comes from God. All great love is a divine gift.

Without this sacramental view of nature one could say that modern man has really nothing to do. We are wasting our time on the surface of the earth. What are we living for? So we have no poverty, everybody's healthy, everybody lives 120 years, and so forth and so on—so what?

Man was originally conceived as a pontiff. You still fortunately have this title in the Catholic church. The pontiff is the bridge between God, Christ and the world and the church. And in a more general sense, all human beings, if they live fully to be what God created them to be as women and men, must be pontiffs, must be bridges. We cannot fulfill our function in this world without being a bridge. The world of nature needs us as channels of grace. We are like windows in a dark room through which the light of the Spirit shines. Without that grace, nature suffocates, and no matter what we do with engineering we are not all going to be able to stop that suffocation. I think that what we have done to the globe in the last hundred years is a perfect testimony to this metaphysical truth expressed so lucidly by so many great writers in the Christian, Islamic and other religions. The prayer of St Francis of Assisi was not only sentimental; he was acting as the *pontifex* when he was addressing the sun and the moon and when talking to the birds. In order to be fully human we must be able to perform this function of acting as a channel of grace for the world of nature and for the whole of life which we carry within ourselves, and by virtue of which we are able to speak to each other, to breathe and to enjoy God's bounties. Not to allow this grace to flow through us into the world of nature, is not only to destroy the world of nature, but also to destroy human life. It is very late in human history and we are beyond the point of diplomatic platitudes and niceties; we *really* have to take the bull by the horns because if we do not do so we will have betrayed the trust of the covenant which we have made with God as human beings. The destruction of the earth, the destruction of life, the destruction of the family which is based on the sacredness of sexuality, on the sacredness of human life and all forms of life, all of these are as a result of our having ceased to fulfill our functions as a bridge between heaven and earth, as the original and the authentic *pontifex*.

Let us pray and hope that a major step will be taken to rediscover the sense of the sacred and through it the harmony between man and nature.

# Nature, Law and the Family

## *Rev Dr Peter J. Elliott*

When we talk of 'Natural Law', people imagine we are referring to the laws of nature, such as gravity, but this is not so. We are talking about that *moral* law which belongs to the basically unchanging nature of the human person within a created, ordered universe. By the terms 'natural law', we describe an innate moral code built into us, a moral law engraved within the nature of every person. Each of us has the capacity to know that good ought to be done and evil avoided, according to the dictates of right reason. This moral reasoning takes the form of a sense of what is right or wrong, our conscience which tells us that this ought to be done or that this ought not to be done.

Before I relate the Natural Law to the family, I must make an ecumenical observation. As a priest working in the Vatican, I represent the Catholic tradition which maintains belief that God has created us with a basic capacity to grasp the Natural Law and, furthermore, that not only individuals but society as a whole should be ordered and guided by it. I realize that some other Christians from the Reformation tradition are not so confident in the role of Natural Law because they see human nature in a less optimistic way than Catholics do. They argue that, while there is an unchanging moral order, a capacity to discern what is right or wrong within human nature has been severely damaged, if not destroyed, by original sin. They regard the Catholic preoccupation with Natural Law as a hearkening back to classical pagan philosophical ideals, when all we need is the Law revealed in specific commandments in the Bible.

However, I believe that in practice we do not really disagree. In the Letter to the Romans, Saint Paul himself outlined Natural Law in describing those who do not know the revealed commandments: 'When Gentiles who have not the law do by nature what the law requires, they are a law to themselves, even though they do not have the law. They show that what the law requires is written on their hearts, while their conscience also bears witness and their conflicting thoughts accuse or perhaps excuse them on that day when, according to my gospel, God judges the secrets of men by Christ Jesus.' (*Romans 2: 14-16*).

This moral law of nature written on our hearts does not 'work' automatically. In that sense, it is not the same as the non rational physical laws of nature, such as gravity. We are weak, fallen and sinful. We do make mistakes and we find it hard to work out exact applications of the Natural Law in certain areas. This is why we need grace and Divine revelation to guide and sustain us and to form our consciences. But we still know that there is right and wrong, that there is an objective moral order, as real and abiding as the physical laws of the created world in which we live.

Natural Law, being universal, is an ethical meeting-point for all people, regardless of race, religion or politics. When we see the essential role this universal moral law plays in family life and in the family's place in society, the importance of this meeting-point will become clearer. Every issue and possibility raised at this congress is a response to principles of truth, justice, goodness, Natural Law principles which bring us together in deep concern for the families of today, that we may build families for tomorrow.

## *The nature and rights of the family*

The crisis in the family is ethical—ultimately spiritual. It is always centred around the perennial human choice between doing good and avoiding evil or of conforming to the decadence around us. This is why the Ten Commandments are largely family laws. Read them for yourselves and see how God has revealed specific family applications of that law engraved on our hearts, our stubborn and often hardened hearts as Moses knew so well. But God created us in his own image and likeness and in the moment of creation presented the first bride to the first bridegroom, therefore his Law for us is largely a family law. It proceeds from his eternal Nature into our created nature. As persons we participate in his Eternal Law through the law of our rational moral nature. Yet through biology, sexuality, gender, it is natural to us as embodied persons to be formed in families and to form families.

As the natural and primary society of persons, the family is subject to the Natural Law. This begins with the bond of marriage which creates a new family. It proceeds into the procreation and raising of children, and then through the various phases and changes of family life and structure.

The transmission of human life is thus an important area for us to seek to discern how good is to be done and evil avoided. This explains why my own Church takes a stand on a particular application of Natural Law. I refer to the famous reaffirmation of a Natural Law morality in the rejection of contraception, sterilization, and abortion in the encyclical letter of Paul VI, *Humanae Vitae*, July 25, 1968. This teaching was repeated in more personalist way by John Paul II in his magnificent exhortation on the family, *Familiaris Consortio*, November 22, 1981.

Whether or not you agree with Catholic teaching in this critical area, you may agree that individuals, families and society in general are suffering the conseqences of destructive interference in the personal and sacred process of transmitting human life. When you break the law of gravity, you break your neck. When you break natural law, you break the family. Consequences do not determine what is right or wrong, but they do help us to discern how the moral order works, and that is as inherent in creation as gravity. This also explains why a modern method of natural child spacing is part of family life, discovered, (I am proud to say!) by two Australians, Drs. John and Lyn Billings.

But the tradition I represent, is not only concerned with specific moral applications of Natural Law. Human rights are a major theme of the Church in the age of John Paul II. His concern for human rights rests securely within the social teaching of the Church, which is based largely on Natural Law. Where there is an inherent natural moral order there are rights which are equally natural and inalienable. If the human person is a moral being, if moral laws are as inherent as the laws of nature in the environment around us, then in justice, duties and obligations set up inalienable rights.

Individuals have natural rights in the ordered society which ought to reflect Natural Law. But, 'no man is an island', and individuals are born into and formed by a family. Therefore this natural primary community has its own inherent rights. It is time we heard more about the rights of the family and a little less about the rights of the individual.

In 1983, to secure and proclaim family rights, the Holy See published *The Charter of the Rights of the Family*. In reading this document, you find a statement of specific natural rights based on Natural Law, rights arising from the nature of the human person living in the first natural community or society, rights arising from being married persons and especially the inherent rights of parents. But what the reader of this Charter immediately sees is the way these rights are disregarded, even denied or scorned in the kind of secularist societies developing today. The crisis in family rights thus takes us into the inner crisis of the family. Why should Johnny obey his parents when they have been abolished? Of course Sue can go on the pill or have an abortion without telling mother, because mother no longer exists when Sue makes these choices.

## The crisis of ethics and law

In the light of Natural Law and family rights, we look at the prospects for the families of the future with alarm. We can first discern what is happening in a negative way, by understanding the destructive and nihilistic power of the alternative philosophy to Natural Law. This is known as *legal positivism*, which may be described as the state or society determining what is right or wrong by passing laws. What is right is what is legal. What is wrong is what is illegal. The positive or negative force of law is what determines an act to be moral or immoral, or 'appropriate' or 'inappropriate', according to the language of those who promote legal positivism.

Let me give some topical examples. Abortion is right because the state says so. You can experiment on embryos because Parliament allows such acts. A deformed foetus may be aborted up until birth, because the law seems to allow for this. Jews and gypsies are not human beings according to the law and may be sent to the gas chamber. You note how I have deliberately linked Nazi Germany, epitome of legal positivism, with our current social situation. This is our tragic and dangerous dilemma.

In times past, even in the recent past, a sense of what was right and wrong, always right and always wrong, permeated society, maintained by religion, or by a respect at least for the moral value of religion. This Natural Law ethic was reflected in laws and in attempts to reform unjust or draconian laws. Now that has gone.

Human rights cannot be innate and natural once legal positivism is in control. Under legal positivism, human rights are granted—or taken away—by the state or society. I add the word 'society' because 'social consensus', or what is claimed to be majority opinion, is the usual justification for legal positivism. Of course in the legal positivist society all sorts of individuals and groups gleefully scramble for their 'rights', like the survival of the fittest at a bargain sale. But these rights are not deemed to be real unless the state says so. There is a hideous moral gulf between the Nineteenth Century struggle to free slaves, based on Natural Law principles, and the struggles to legalize abortion, vice and perversions, justified by an alleged social concensus. It is assumed that what was once wrong is now acceptable and what was acceptable is now wrong. Asserted rights over one's body or fertility and the sovereignty of sexual pleasure are allowed to destroy the natural right to life and to undermine the right of natural sexuality.

Remember the famous 'new morality' of the South Bank theologians, nearly thirty years ago? That was an attack on Natural Law morality. It was the revisionist morality of clever and rather nice religious people who thought they could discover right and wrong for themselves in each different situation. They told us that 'modern man has come age'. They were in fact using a familiar historicist argument against unchanging human nature and the objective moral order. They said that human nature changes and therefore morality evolves, and that is the end of Natural Law which says that basically human nature is the same and the objective moral order remains the same. In practice, apart from initiating a disastrous descent into 'loophole morality' in the moral theology of the major Churches, their 'new morality' assisted the triumph of sociology over ethics, of public opinion over what we know, deep down in our consciences, to be truly right or wrong.

But *what* does society say? Is it society which really determines morality and hence law, or is it well-organised pressure groups? Is it not the so called social concensus simply organized by those who determine mass media policy? The tyrants whose word is law today are not emperors or dictators but the unseen ones who decide the relentless anti-family immorality of much of the media. Furthermore, the logic of social consensus reinforces itself. If one were to do a door-to-door survey simply asking whether abortion is right or wrong, many of the responses would run like this, 'It can't be wrong can it? After all it's legal now isn't it?' And you would get the same answer from Beryl in Battersea as you would from Cynthia in Knightsbridge.

What does this assault on a Natural Law morality do to the family? It destroys the family by ignoring the rights of the family. This may best be explained through the example of no-fault divorce. By removing fault from divorce proceedings, you render divorce simply an agreement to separate or the decision of one partner to depart. By making divorce easy you strike at the created reality which causes the family to exist, marriage; you subject children who are meant to enjoy the security of that bond to the caprice of individuals, and as is evident in my own country, you leave divorced women with children in difficult circumstances. In the midst of personal anguish we must ask where are the rights of the family once the marriage contract becomes easier to break than a time-payment contract for the new TV.

## *Abolishing the family*

Therefore, looking deeper at this threat to family life we can discern that it is a denial of the very existence of a natural community called the family, which is the fundamental dynamic cell of society, an organic community which is good and which should be defended. However, we are not idealizing the family as we defend it. G.K. Chesterton, who wrote extensively and prophetically on the family, once remarked: 'When we defend the family we do not mean it is always a peaceful family; when we maintain the thesis of marriage we do not mean that it is always a happy marriage. We mean that it is the theatre of the spiritual drama, the place where things happen, especially the things that matter. It is not so much the place where a man kills his wife as the place where he can take the equally sensational step of not killing his wife.'[1]

By removing moral responsibility from a bored or unfaithful spouse, an easy divorce law is saying that this is not a moral matter because the smallest community formed by the marriage bond sets up no moral duties or obligations which should be reflected in particular laws. The spouse who is inconvenienced by the community formed by marriage can abandon that community. It follows that children can also walk out of the home, if they wish. Because its natural base no longer holds, the whole of society is now centred around the convenience or comfort of an individual. It is the triumph of the 'imperial self'.

This denial of the reality of the natural community formed by marriage helps explain the curious redefinition of the family as a 'household', that is as any group of people living under one roof. Any association of individuals is blithely called 'family', regardless of relationship, marriage, gender or sexual inclination. One is reminded of the evil Manson 'family', for the devil parodies and inverts that which is innately good and natural. On the level of political philosophy in the redefinition of 'family' we can perceive extreme liberalism even nihilism, where the individual is the measure of all things. This godless, self-centred individualism envisages society as a collection of individuals, wandering through a series of ultimately pointless and expendable 'relationships'. At a more fundamental philosophical level, making words mean what we choose them to mean draws us into the web of a sceptical world-view—we can never know a rose but only play games with words, with the name of the rose.

On a broader social level, the rights of the family are central to a contrast between different visions of society. Using familiar British reference points, it could be argued that we are still involved in a struggle between two minds: Edmund Burke, who saw society as made up of natural societies such as the family, and Thomas Hobbes, who saw society as made up of compitetive, and rather nasty individuals to be regulated by the supreme state authority. Burke had an awareness of Natural Law ethics, of divine purpose within society conceived as an organic and natural order. Hobbes denied the existence of Natural Law. For him, the state determines what is right or wrong in regulating relations between rather brutish and competitive individuals, who left to themselves would destroy one another. Hobbes was a father of legal positivism and he seems to be winning today.

Unfortunately, Hobbes was one of the fathers of modern totalitarianism, because, in his system, the state ultimately controls all individuals and groups. On the other hand, as they know so well in Eastern Europe, the family is the centre of true liberty. Chesterton also said: 'The family is the test of freedom; because the family is the only thing that the free man makes for himself and by himself.'[2] The totalitarians, whether old Marxist or fascist, or new consumerist, must break the family. Why? It is the natural citadel for free men and women confronted with the diabolical demand—that you must surrender your very self in return for a secure place in our system and the share of the booty which we will allot to you.

## Family politics

How can the family meet this challenge? At the level of society in general, by engaging in family politics. Today we desperately need a family politics to tackle issues such as easy divorce, discrimination against married people, equating common law unions or homosexual alliances with marriage, the denial of parents' rights in education especially sex education, artificial control of population growth, the intrusion of pornography into the home through the media, ignoring the rights of the father in disputed areas where radical feminism has abolished him. But these ethical issues must not be only the traditional family 'reacting' to social engineering. There must be positive initiatives to advance and secure the innate goodness of the family, for example, a living wage for parents, taxation in favour of the family, incentives to encourage mothers to stay in the home, the promotion of a positive and healthy regard for childbearing, and child-rearing supporting small family businesses and enterprises.

It goes on and on, this family politics. Unfortunately we have to face the fact that much of it is a struggle to reverse years of accumulated discrimination against the rights and the very nature of the family which delineates those rights.

Because the natural society of the family is formed by procreation, family politics must be concerned with the sanctity of human life from conception until natural death. If you think the pro-life movement is only about saving unborn babies from the abortionist and elderly folk from a lethal injection, think again. It is a family movement. All its moral issues have a direct impact on family life. That unborn infant, that elderly person, is first and foremost a member of the basic living cell of society, and it is within some form of family that the life or death decisions are made. When death is chosen, part of the family dies. We choose life. The pro-life movement epitomizes the essential unity between the family and Natural Law ethics. Let us work for the day when every pregnant woman can walk down the high street with joy, the mother of hope treated with respect because she embodies trust in the families of the future.

Through family politics you are also called to be involved in struggles to renew society, for example: maintaining Sunday as a day of worship, rest and recreation, securing each neighbourhood as a peaceful family space, seeing that environmental issues serve the family, protecting, healing and supporting the poor family, the aged and handicapped at home. In the light of these concerns which find their place at this Congress, it is clear why family politics can emerge as the wave of the future. But sound family politics is not merely a string of causes to make life at home more cosy. It must be based on the fundamental struggle to make law and social policy strongly support every marriage and every family. It will be a struggle to reassert Natural Law as God's gift of freedom and that is the critical spiritual struggle for true freedom in the Europe of the future.

## Renewing family life

However, family politics is only part of the answer. It is so easy to run around trying to convert others while ignoring one's own soul. Remember Dickens' character Mrs. Jellaby, so concerned about children in distant missions abroad that she let her own children fall into neglect and ruin. The recovery of what is natural and good begins at home. It is not for me to lecture you on what needs to be done. All I can request is a thorough examination of conscience concerning life in your own home. From Natural Law and natural rights flow moral obligations and responsibilities. Consider, for example the duty of parents to love their children with the gift of their time, which should flow from the noble and attentive self-giving love between husband and wife. Only free men, women and children can give themselves in love in the freedom of their home.

Unfortunately, the insularity of the modern family is one major obstacle to the moral and spiritual renewal of the natural and good community in the home. For example, the obsessive privacy of the selfish society can shrivel up the family. It is one thing to tell busybodies trying to rescue your children from your religious formation to 'Keep out and mind your own business!' It is another thing to avoid other families, to try to 'go it alone', when what we need is a family-to-family ministry. The family itself transforms the selfish society by making a commitment to other families. You will have the opportunity to make that commitment through the various associations you meet here in these days of work and celebrations. This solidarity of families with one another is a ground for hope.

We must first defeat our own pessimism. Let me speak honestly. I frequently travel between Europe, Australia and the United States. I work in perhaps the best vantage point in the world. Constantly, in your country and mine, I find a terrible pessimism concerning marriage and the family. Faced with the tragedies of family life today, there is a tendency, even among Christians, to take the broken home, the single parent and say, 'Well, this is the norm today. We're not going to change this trend and we should build all family policy around these hard cases.' But the truth is otherwise.

While we must stand in solidarity with the family which suffers, there are thousands of good, healthy families out there. They are trying to live as communities which are natural and good, essential cells in a natural human society. These families are the 'norm'. Your family striving to find happiness in doing what is right is the 'norm'. What is good and true and strong is the 'norm'. This is not idealism. This is healthy realism based on the Natural Law. It is a call to trust the family, to be confident in the resilience and innate goodness of the little community of life and love. It is a challenge hurled back at the godless state and the godless society which can never tolerate that sensible principle of subsidiarity, that the small groups can usually function better than big business or big government. This realism is the ground for hope for families called 'to become what they are.'[3]

The path ahead is glorious. It is not a nostalgic return to the past. We can never go back to Eden. That way is barred and the angel stands there with fiery sword forbidding entry. No, we must take a higher and humbler path, across the hills of time, guided by the glimmer of eternity to a small village and a little home where God Himself rested in a gentle mother's arms and played beneath a foster father's loving gaze. If the 'future of humanity passes by way of the family'[4], we must first find our way home to Nazareth.

**Notes**
1 G.K. Chesterton, 'The Home of the Unities', in *The New Witness*, 17 January, 1919.
2 Ibid.
3 Pope John Paul II, *Familiaris Consortio*, 86.
4 Ibid., 17.

# The Family and Public Policy

## Dr Digby Anderson

What is it that we should fear above anything else, at least on this earth? Not war, there is something worse than war. Riot is in a way worse than war. War has an order of its own, and riot is the breakdown of order. But even riots, (and we sometimes see riots on our television), are a breakdown only in legal order and they don't, thankfully, last long. What we should fear above everything else is the loss of fear in society, a total breakdown in order. This ultimate nightmare, is that individuals act totally unrestrained, not only by the law, but by habit and common values. It is the ultimate nightmare, because in it society ceases to exist.

Society, the orderliness of our society, this is the achievement of centuries of living together. So it does not make sense to ask what produces an orderly society. The important question is what sustains it, what keeps it going, what is it that passes on the common values, the patterns, the behaviour, the loyalties, the common language, even the ways we agree to disagree. What stands between this and anarchy? It is not principally the law and the government. Law only works when people have already some measure of social cohesion. No government has the resources to induce entire generations into being orderly adults. The huge task of keeping the bulk of society going, reproducing the habits, the values of a civilised society, is done by less formal forces, and the most important of these is the family.

This is textbook material, but it is necessary to say all this, this which would have been common sense to any other generation. Because there are those today who portray people who have an interest in the family as indulging in some sort of idiosyncratic hobby or obsession—moralists, they call us. 'Fine', they say, 'If they think the family is so important, let them live in families, campaign for families, but not impose their ideas on the rest of us, who are more interested in trade unions or the ozone layer, or who just want to be happy individuals'. But the family is not an optional interest, for moralists or for anyone else. It is not something that individuals or political parties can consider being interested in as they might consider taking up the cause of the Channel Tunnel or physics in school. For without the family there are no trade unions or indeed organised opponents of trade unions. There is no understanding or organised attitude to the ozone layer, no physics, no school, no Channel Tunnel. Quite simply the family, in stability and strength, is of a quite different order to all these other important questions. It is a matter which is fundamental and for all.

You can see all this if you approach it in another way, for we are beginning to glimpse the sort of social problem which arises when family formation is impaired. In Britain today over two thirds of children born to teenage mothers are illegitimate. The divorce rate is the highest in Europe and its rate of increase has overtaken that of the United States. These divorces, against all the promises and predictions of divorce reformers, include more and more young children. In inner city areas one child in three is being brought up without a father. To the agony these developments cause to individuals, to children, the fathers and the mothers, must be added the social cost. *Today* newspaper reveals that the cost of keeping a single parent family on State Benefit till the child is sixteen is £100,000 of public money. The total of all those costs is somewhere around £3.9 thousand million pounds a year, spent on single parent families, taken in taxes from often two-parent families struggling themselves to make ends meet. This same amount of money could have gone to hospitals or the care of children whose plight, (unlike that brought on by promiscuity or divorce) was caused by the death of a parent or some other unavoidable cause. There are also social costs in crime, increasingly associated with the legitimacy of divorce and other forms of 'decision parenthood'. To that we must add the sufferings from promiscuity-related Aids and the poverty caused by families incompetent of managing budgets, a poverty again not only a problem for those immediately concerned, but for all who contribute to the public purse.

Do not be persuaded by those fag-end of the thinkers for the 1960s, that tell you that each of us has a right to do their own thing, that decisions about relationships are a private matter. Such decisions have public consequences, and costs to other people. They cause changes in the health of society, especially in crime, which has its own victims.

So the health of the family is a matter and a concern for all, a public matter, because its ill-health has consequences and costs for all.

But, be careful. Do not overdo the current tribulations of the family. To exaggerate them plays into the hands of those who hate the family and claim that it is already dead, and yet society seems to be living reasonably well. It must be soberly restated that the majority of children are still brought up by two parents, their own biological parents, and those parents stay together. The majority increases still further if we include parents, who although they subsequently break up, form their families, with the considered commitment to stay together permanently. Homosexual couples raising artificially produced children, and voluntary single parents, (deciding beforehand to embark as single families) and other deviant forms, are the minority, the extreme minority. Recent American research argues that the number of homosexuals is far less than has been thought since the Kinsey Report—under 4%, not the 10% that is so often advocated. It also finds that chastity, defined at least as fidelity to a married partner, though admitting of premarital sex with that partner, is the chosen path of the majority of Americans.

The traditional family is still then the norm, both statistically and in the expectations and attitudes of most people. It is, in both senses of the word, normal. This should be insisted on. It matters, for example, when advocates of abnormal family forms argue that these are the so-called families and that they should receive as much assistance, from the government as normal families. It matters when they want education about parenthood to be neutral, as between different types of what they call the family. So certainly proclaim the problems of the family today but don't overdo it. The normal family is still the norm! Another reason for not overdoing it is that the troubles of the contemporary family are nothing to what would happen if it really did break down. That is the reason for insisting too on the nighmare. There is far, far worse to come if the decline in family standards is not halted. So care needs to be taken about the true situation.

What steps, then, could be taken to halt this decline? There is a limited amount that government can do to restore family cohesion and effectiveness. Family life is a matter of values, the formation of habits and education. It is much more important what ordinary men and women and bodies such as the churches do than what politicians do. Nevertheless, there are four broad ways in which a government should try to help. First the law. Divorce has been made, not only easier, and faster, but it has also had morality and increasingly the note of fault removed from it. It has been made an administrative arrangement and indeed a partner can be effectively divorced without consenting, when he or she has done nothing to contribute to the breakdown, or alleged breakdown of that marriage. There are proposals that the Law Commission can make divorce yet faster, yet cheaper, yet easier, and yet less painful. Those, of course, should be resisted. It is time to make divorce exceptional, it is time to make it hard, it is time to make it costly and it is time to place back in it the ordinary person's understanding of morality, for of course it is a moral matter. Progressive people always say that one cannot turn the clock back. But whatever you thought of Mrs Thatcher and Mrs Thatcher's economic policies, there is absolutely no doubt that the lady showed us that you can indeed put the clock back, and for that at least, we should be grateful. What is going on in Eastern Europe at the moment is nothing less than putting the clock back. It is sociological nonsense to say that it cannot be done. It is being done all the time.

Another area of the law in which the government is concerned is the age of majority. It used to be sociological textbook material to say that the more complicated a society was, the longer it took to grow up and become an adult member of it. It is fairly easy and fast to acquire the competences to act in a primitive society, but a highly technological society requires a long period of preparation, when one is neither a child nor yet an adult. Every bit of sociological evidence points to a need to raise the age of majority and not to further lower it. That should be an interest of government however politically impossible it may seem. It is, for example, possible that, before actually changing the law, one could at least look at the subsidies which erode parental authority in higher age teenagers.

The government is also concerned with funding various associations, including the family, through its tax system and through its welfare system.

The family is a matter of decisions. People make decisions: to marry, to have children, to have children outside marriage, to desert a spouse or their children, to enter deviant relationships. These decisions are taken in the light of various pressures, various costs and rewards, not only financial but concerning the attitudes of other people. The government must make sure, while helping those who are already in need, that their various tax and welfare benefits do not send the message which in any way makes those contemplating, for example promiscuity, less frightened of any consequences. It is not sensible to give away money which attract more people into those situations. Whilst people do not actually calculate their way into single parenthood, they do see other people engaging in behaviour which was once unthinkable, and somehow making out not so badly after all. It is that example, not the calculation, that government benefits can engender. There are divisions amongst sensible people about how far the government should go in making faithful marriage a financially rewarding state, but what it must never do is what it was doing recently: actually providing tax incentives to co-habitation and conception out of wedlock, particularly via Capital Gains Tax and double-mortgage Income Tax relief.

The government should also look at a combination of law and social benefits. It is already looking at toughening the law which underwrites the contract implicit in wedlock and in a family. When people get married they form an implicit contract to look after each other, and when they have children to look after them. The government has proposed to chase errant fathers who are not supporting the wives and children that they have deserted. It could go much further. Societies such as West Germany or Switzerland who take family policy more seriously, actually underwrite the obligations in family life whereby even uncles and sisters and brothers can be held legally and financially responsible for the needs and welfare of each other. Children when they become adults can contribute to the welfare of their elderly parents. That again is simply the system of subsidiarity, that the State should not meet needs which the family not only can meet but has an obligation to meet. Next, the State is engaged in education. 93% go to government-funded or government-run schools. It is therefore crucial that the curricula of these schools, whether they teach orderly values and family values and skills in parenting or not, (and perhaps it is safer that some of them should not and that this should be done at home) should not be permitted to subvert family values. It is time for a much closer monitoring of what goes on in schools under the heading 'Education in personal relationships' and 'Health Education'. It is also time to insist, although we do not necessarily have to say that this is desirable, we just have to recognise it as a fact, that the burden of home-making and looking after children falls more on mothers than it does on fathers. It is therefore quite crazy to talk of a gender-free curriculum in schools. As long as girls are going to grow up and become mothers and look after children, their education and their curriculum should take account of that fact and should be slightly different from that for boys.

Lastly, the incentives which encourage people to behave in certain ways and discourage them from others are not all financial or legal. In any society people seek the approval of others, are worried about public shame and stigma. The progressive mind does not like stigma very much, but I and also most sociologists, until very recently, would maintain that unfortunately that is necessary. It makes for an orderly society. We must make clear that certain acts, such as fathers deserting their wives, children and responsibilities, are despicable. Fear of ridicule, gossip, exclusion, those things are the social cement which keep fallen men and women on the straight and narrow. We need more of that sort of unpleasantness in our society and less neutrality in the face of anti-social and anti-family behaviour. Here, too, the government can help, for its laws and policies do more than just alter laws and situations. They help set standards. But even more can be done by non-state and community organisations, such as the churches. This government's record on the family is not good. Neither is the opposition's. But neither of them are so culpable as my own church, the Church of England. A Church in which in all the massive pages of *Faith in the City*, so taken up with political solutions to social problems, there is nowhere an identification that the family is the principal source of welfare in society. A Church which has gone along, even encouraged, easy divorce to the point of pushing through Parliament recently laws to allow divorcees as priests, a Church which cannot bring itself unequivocally to condemn anything in moral terms except, of course, Thatcherism. And I say this as a member of it.

So, the family is not an optional interest for moralists, but the care of anyone who wants an orderly society. The family is deeply in trouble today, but it is still the norm. The family is able to be helped by turning back the clock on divorce law, on the age of majority, by more helpful social security and tax systems, by state school curricula changes and by example. But most of all, it is in need of support of the churches, of voluntary groups and the commitment of ordinary men and women and their values. You must speak up, even if it means unpleasantness. Otherwise, it is the nightmare, perhaps not for us, but for our children's children.

# 2. THE FAMILY UNDER PRESSURE

# Consumerism and the Family

### *Dr Michael Schluter*

Did you know that the average American spends 1½ years of his or her life watching advertisements on the television?

Of course, British people are not nearly so extreme. We only watch 5 hours a day on average of TV and we only have 6 minutes per hour of adverts if you average it across the channels, ½ hour per day, 8 days per year.

Do these ads influence us?

The story is told of the chairman of Unilever who said he knew half of his spending on ads was a complete waste of money. The only trouble was he didn't know which half!

Of course, the other half is *not* a waste of money.

Even British people are bombarded with hundreds of messages from the advertisers each week.

According to a recent advertising agency report, the goals of the younger generation as they become adults will be to have more money and more luxury goods. What is that if it is not *consumerism*?

So I am defining consumerism as 'the pursuit of more money and more luxury goods'.

I want to persuade you that in a fundamental sense, consumerism undermines and destroys families. But before I argue the case, two caveats:

(a) I am not suggesting we should abandon all our consumer goods and material possessions and go back to a primitive village existence. I have lived in Indian villages and life there for the poor is both uncomfortable and precarious. No modern medicine, no clean water and no electricity. It's not as idyllic as you might imagine!

(b) Secondly, speaking of families, I am not just speaking of the western nuclear family—mum, dad and two kids. Families in my talk today refers to all those related by blood, marriage or adoption. It includes the wider family as well as the household family. Adult brothers and sisters. Grandparents. Aunts and uncles. Cousins and distant relatives. *Open not closed. Inclusive not exclusive.* For each of us how the family stretches out differs. But we need this *open* and inclusive idea of the family. Not a closed and inward looking concept.

Dr Michael Schulter 35

So, I do want to argue that consumerism—the pursuit of more luxury good—attacks family relationships and family solidarity at three key points.
— TIME
— STRESS
— VALUES

I tried to make it 'TSB', but I hope you will still remember it! Lets consider the mechanics by which this takes place.

## Time

Family relationships need TIME. It may seem obvious, but it needs saying. They need what my wife calls quantity and quality time. *Quantity time* is just being around. It's important for peoples' security. Just being there helps children in particular to feel they belong somewhere. They probably pick up values mainly during quantity time. *Quality time* is important for peoples' sense of worth. Just by observing it is as we give people, and again especially children, our exclusive attention that they feel valued.

Consumerism takes time and often competes with the family for time.

An example of how this takes place.

To get more luxury goods you need more money and to get more money people spend more and more time at work. So:

(a) Men are doing more overtime among all income groups. (Average hours of manual workers have gone up from 42 hours to nearly 44 hours per week)

(b) More women are going out to work and working longer hours. Since 1980 we are working longer hours and the executive input rises as well. That in turn increases the strain and stress.

(c) Teenagers are increasingly looking for holiday work and weekend work. Of course, there are a host of reasons for these developments:
— You are paying a mortgage and the interest rate goes up. Rather than sell the house at a depressed price you look for ways to increase your income.
— You are a married woman with your children now all in school. You want to use your nursing, journalistic or administrative skills or whatever your training was, or you are bored at home, so take a part time job, and so on.

I am *not* saying that working long hours are wrong! In a small survey we carried out from the Jubilee Centre in 1987, we found that where there were multiple debts,
— in half the cases there was marriage breakdown or divorce *plus*
— extensive evidence of child abuse. NSPCC found the same. Ordinary people would knock kids about through worry caused by taking too much credit.

*Credit can seriously damage your family*. Yet we have unrestrained promotion of credit. I am delighted that Mr. Major is telling the banks that this has to stop. But I have a message for Mr. Major: 'when banks and other financial institutions are fighting to keep their market share, as they must, it will take more than words to hold them back from promoting credit!'

## Values

Here we are approaching the nub of the issue. The most subtle and the most vicious, attack by consumerism on family relationships—both in the home and in this wider family—is at the level of values—what we hold to be important, and how we define who we are.

What do you think is most important?—to have healthy happy relationships at home, or to be wealthy?

Would you rather be in a large house with a big car and a marriage on the rocks—or be in a small house with no car and be happily married?

What matters most to you?—relationships or possessions? Or, to use Jubilee Centre jargon—are you a *relationist* or a *materialist*?

For those of us who are Christians it is important to realise that Jesus was above everything else a Relationist. He defined what mattered in life by the first two Commandments:

> Love God with all your heart and mind and soul
> Love your neighbour as yourself

Love is about the *quality* of relationships. Jesus is saying that it is relationships which are the really important things in life. This has implications across all parts of life. You have heard the expression LDS—Less Developed Country. But how do we define less developed? Is it the materially poor or the relationally poor?

When we vote for a political party do we look only at economic growth or the relationship consequence of the policies they are proposing?

It is hardly surprising that for relationists, family relationships are of supreme importance. The very word 'relationist' has within it the very word 'relation' which can also mean 'relative'. Our relatives—spouse parent, child, brother, sister—are for most people the closest and deepest relationships they will ever have. They are also generally the most demanding.

Families can only thrive in a society where the outlook of the majority of people is Relationist and not Materialist. But in Britain today we seem to become more and more preoccupied with the headlong pursuit of luxury goods.

*So where is the push for consumerism coming from?* Primarily from advertising and the media from which we receive hundreds of messages each week. Advertising is selling dreams. This is how Mike Starkey puts it in his book 'Born To Shop' (published by Monarch)

> 'What is being sold is not a mere product, but an image of yourself—transformed, beautified, more confident, happy; not insecure, unstriking to look at and unfashionable in dress. For this reason, advertising has to create dissatisfaction and play on people's universal sense of personal inadequacy. The reality of your life is unpleasant, you are told, but with this one purchase it can be transformed. Your job is mundane, you have spots or dandruff, you are surrounded by screaming toddlers, you feel an inner loneliness—but you too could be an odour-free, head-ache free, spotless, constantly stimulated piece of seductive humanity'.

Many of the values implicit in advertising are blatantly anti-family. You remember two of the worst—'It takes the waiting out of wanting' 'Give yourself the holiday you deserve'—it is an appeal to instant self-gratification to the exclusion of all else.

So there is a struggle going on about values. On this hand, religious life, especially Christian belief in this country—and those committed for environmental and other reasons to a Relationist vision of society. On the other, the multi-billion pound advertising industry. There is no doubt in my mind which side is winning at the moment.

## Conclusion

If we believe in families as being important, what can we do about it? Here are my four very practical suggestion of what *you* can do:

1. Guard your affections for they influence everything else in your life. Watch out for what you give your time to, what you think about and how you set your priorities. Commit yourself to be a Relationist if you care about your family. Then explore its implications for public policy.
2. Remember that family communication time really *matters*.
Meals together.
The school run.
The Sunday family walk.
Just sitting around the table talking.
It means turning off the TV. Give priority to quantity time as well as quality time at home.
DON'T LET YOUR HOME JUST BECOME A MULTI-PURPOSE LEISURE CENTRE!
3. Be very careful with consumer credit. Remember that CREDIT CAN SERIOUSLY DAMAGE YOUR FAMILY! None of us can assume all will go well in the future. It is presumptuous to believe that life is all sweetness and light. Most credit involves taking an unnecessary risk. The issue goes beyond credit in itself and will not resolve the problems of the family without a fundamental reappraisal of the whole system.
4. CAMPAIGN! Do you remember the old slogan:
     *'Don't just sit there—do something'*
Raise the issues, argue the case! Don't impose, but rely on the force of argument as we apply the commandment to love our neighbour.

The only hope for Britain in the 1990s relies in putting Relationist and family values back into public policy by all of us who care about them getting actively involved, locally and nationally. Campaign with any of the Relationist groups—Family and Youth Concern, SPUC, Life, Care, Keep Sunday Special, Credit Action, National Viewers and Listeners... Also join THE SEVEN HOUR CLUB—and commit yourself and enrol your family in limiting your TV viewing to a maximum of seven hours a week!

No political party in my view at present is giving any priority to family and relationist concerns. And they won't until they realise there are enough voters who care about them.

We need pressure groups to protect our physical ecology. We have lots of them. But how much more do we need pressure groups to protect our social ecology. We have few of them and they are not as strong. So my plea to you all is not to sit on the sidelines. Become a player. If ever there was a time in the history of our country when we needed action, it is today.

# Family—the Swedish Experience

## *Katarina Runske*

I come from Sweden: I was born almost on the Arctic circle. If things were different I would have stayed. There is plenty of space and clean air for the 8 million inhabitants. We have wilderness, lots of lakes, high mountains and a long marvellous coast with hundreds and hundreds of small uninhabited islands. Sweden has not been at war since 1809, we speak one language, we have one religion. Several of our industrial products are well known all over the world. Who has not heard of the Volvo cars and the Orrefors crystal? Our country has been a stable part of the world until recently.

So the Swedes have every opportunity to live in a paradise. Sweden has been a model country for the rest of Europe. But the current developments you find in Sweden you can find elsewhere too.

For me the word 'family' means the form of married life between two persons who want to live together and to raise their children within their marriage: no more no less.

So what is the situation for this ordinary family in Sweden? The answer is simple; it is almost impossible. Of course it did not become like that overnight. It came creeping on to us like it does in all countries. In Sweden it goes back quite a long way. I would say it started around 1930 when Alva and Gunnar Myrdal—a very famous Swedish couple, they both got different Nobel prizes—wrote a well-known book called 'Crisis in the Population Question'. This is how they describe a housewife. I quote from page 249: 'It is still possible for weak, stupid, lazy, unambitious, and otherwise lesser equipped individuals to remain and make their way within the domestic work, both as housewives and as servants. And for the rest prostitution is always available.' That was when it all started. And so in the name of equality women started to compete with men. Many functions today are now taken over by women. But the worse thing is that women fight against women. The ones working outside their homes cannot accept that we wanted to stay inside and continue to look after our children. They don't respect us, or our decisions.

The late prime minister Palme—who was assassinated two years ago—proclaimed the housewife officially dead. His Minister of Equality said that housewives belong in a museum, and a large daily paper proclaimed housewives as traitors.

After giving us this bad reputation it was easier to start to take our rights away. It was said that no one wanted to be at home. Today that is still a lie. The fact is that 86% of women are working outside their homes. More important is that 83% would *like* to work in their homes as housewives but can't afford it. That is the reality of Sweden today.

It took about 40–50 years to achieve this situation. Slowly, one step after the other, all family rights were taken away. It started in the legislation. We now reached a point where the word 'family' is no longer in the lawbook—the Swedish code. We exist as households, and households can be two women living together, or two homosexuals. The Swedish 'Organisation for Sexual Equality' is now demanding that the law gives homosexuals the right to marry.

Parents' rights are not even in the constitution.

These family and education policies in Sweden are clearly against the Human Rights as expressed in the second clause of the first amendment to the European Convention on Human Rights of Nov. 4th, 1950. This clause says that the state shall allow parents to choose the form of upbringing for their children. Swedish politicians talk very loudly about human rights in Chile and South Africa, but some basic rights are overlooked back home.

Very few people, realise the problems with the legislation because the main problem is the family's economy. It is impossible to live on one salary in Sweden. The taxes are so high and the welfare system so complicated that those who want to stay at home are still forced to find a job outside.

The Swedish tax system is the main tool for the equality-family policy and that system is built on the assumption that all grown-ups support themselves and the State looks after the children. No tax-reductions are allowed if you have a large family. Costs for the duly approved day-care centres are often so low that it costs more to feed a child at home. Children's allowances are paid by the State and the parents pay about a quarter of the cost for a child. A Swedish worker earns about 110,000 Skr/year (about £10,000).

If he has a spouse working at home and two children, he must earn about 170,000 Skr in order to reach what we call a minimum standard of living. The ordinary worker can evidently not make it. Nor can most white collar workers, college teachers, professors or engineers. The welfare system is like a big net around us. It takes care of everything. Of course nothing is free, so 67% of the GNP goes to—the public sector. To keep the image up Sweden borrows money abroad, and our grandchildren will have to repay.

Out of 4.3 million households 1.4 million are living on or below the poverty line, which means they have to get support from the state to exist. The families might get money for housing, clothing, and so forth. To get the support you have to follow certain rules. So they keep us in the net. If the welfare system is going to pay you or help you with the rent of food, both parents have to be working and the children have to visit a daycare centre. That is a commitment so you have to make your choice: both parents working and you get the support. To me that is blackmail. It would cost the state less to have a mother at home since the cost for one place is subsidized with about 60,000 Skr/year by the State and municipality combined. Thus the cost for keeping two children in a day-care centre is as high as an average worker's salary. So the money is there and given to the 'approved' day-care centres. All private alternatives have to follow the State rules to get money. The family who wants to raise their own kids get nothing of the subsidies. Nor does a family who would have preferred to put their kids in private day-care: maybe belonging to the church or a Montessori group, etc, where the risk of socialistic indoctrination would be less.

The latest statistics on marriage I have are from 1986: 37,000 married and 19,100 divorced.

101,950 children were born and from that number 49,300 were born to unmarried mothers. That is 48.5% of all births. 33,100 abortions took place and in 1987 the figure I have was 39,000 abortions.

The divorce problem in Sweden is a bit different from other countries. People divorce to be able to live together. This might seem odd to you, but the reason is simple. The welfare system looks after divorced people so much better than married ones. So people use this, and they divorce just on the paper and then they can live together and have a mother at home. That is also the reason why people do not marry or do not work full time. If you stay below a certain level of income you get support by the State. We learn how to cheat to survive.

The one who stays at home has no status or rights whatsoever. The housewife gets no pension or support in any way. All rights are given to those who work outside the house. For them there is money for everything. They get 30 days paid leave each year to look after their child when it is ill. That means for me with three children that I could be away for 3 months and then my paid vacation 5 weeks and I would probably get extra leave if I asked for it. I even would get paid for the time it needs to train my children to go to the day care centre. So I would get a pension, sick leave and other facilities. As a housewife I get nothing, not even respect from my fellow sisters.

Something must be wrong in a society when 83% want to stay at home and yet 86% have to work and the cost of the day-care centres so high. Maybe the reason is to be found elsewhere.

Sweden's Social Democrats now intend to make a compulsory law that *all* children will have to attend a day-care centre. In their party programme they mention the year 1991 and the Social minister said recently that he wants to offer a place to every child from 1.5 years old.

What are these centres like? They seem to grow like mushrooms from the ground everywhere! They are nicely equipped with the right toys, the right staff with the right training. The children eat high-fibre, healthy food and are taken on outings to different places chosen by the staff. Who do you think you are to deny your child all this? Is your kitchen table really better than the one at the day-care centre?

All the women's organizations tell the same story. Every woman, they say, should have her own money and not have to depend on a man. 'Are you just an appendix to your husband?' is a very common question. To stand all this you have to be very strong, and your children too.

It is tempting to leave your children to someone else and take a job and suddenly get respect and a salary.

It takes some time until the effect is visible in the society. Suddenly you come to a stage where the roof falls down, and then it is too late.

We have research in many fields today and they all show the problems from which our children and youngsters suffer. We should ask the children how they feel about being left every day. A professor pointed out that every fifth child suffers from psychological disturbances and every fourth from anxiety and fear. He gave reasons for this: the increasing amount of working women, the divorces, and the moving from the country to big cities. Another professor from the Stress Research Institute notes that every third child who passes the compulsary 4 year old medical examination done by the authorities suffers from psychological disturbances. This doesn't mean teenagers with love problems, it means small children, 4 years old.

We know that in Sweden over 120 children commit suicide every year. We know that small children get ulcers.

We know that small children at very low ages use drugs and alcohol.

We have statistics for it all, and still we do nothing.

We have severe problems in our schools. An increasing number of children leave school after nine years without knowledge of reading and writing. The teachers complain that they have to spend so much time teaching the smaller ones how to use a knife and fork, button a coat etc.

Violence in our schools has also turned into one of the big problems and one that it is hard to eliminate. But of course we know that many children spend all their free time in front of the TV and video. And the tired parents hardly ever know what the children watch. It is an easy way for the tired parents to solve a baby-sitting problem.

In Sweden we hardly have any meals together any more. Parents eat where they work and the children are supposed to eat at school. But how many children eat when, say, boiled fish is served?

The evening meal is maybe a cup of tea in front of TV. The mother is too tired to cook and during the weekends the house must be cleaned and the laundry done too. A rather odd problem was brought up by the school nurses. After longer holidays children returned to school hungry and the nurses found out that the children had hardly eaten a warm meal during the holiday. School doctors pointed out that very often children came late in the afternoon and complained about headache or stomach-ache. It turned out that they were just afraid to go home to an empty flat or house. Some of them didn't even close the front door until the parents came home.

Of course all these problems would not be solved overnight if every family could have a parent at home. But as it is a disaster for the families and children today we have to do something. If families are to function effectively there has to be a mother at home. How that is going to be solved economically is for the Government to find out. At present the situation is crazy. If I look after children outside my home it is called work, but raising my own at home is called a 'hobby'.

So let's start from there and give housewives a chance to stay at home as long as the children need, not as long as the politicians want. Give a woman help when and if she wants to return to work when the children are grown up. Give every child an equal right. Don't act as in Sweden where 30% of the children get 70% of economic support i.e. those in the day-care centres.

Today Sweden's children are born and taken to the day-care centres to be educated the right way: the grown-ups work to be able to pay taxes for the centres and the old ones are put away and they should just have the decency to die as soon as possible!

Let me quote Mother Teresa's opinion about Sweden. She got the Nobel prize for peace some years ago and was interviewed in all our papers. She said she felt sorry for the kind of poverty she found.

It was a different poverty from her slum in Calcutta. We suffer from lack of love and respect for one another, and this poverty was unknown in her slum.

Well, this is a dark picture of a wonderful country. But it is important for you to know about it.

# Feminism, the Family and the Future

## *Valerie Riches*

Those who know of Katarina Runske's stark account of Sweden, *A Society Without a Family*, will be shocked by the comparative ease by which the institution of the family can be destroyed in a civilised country in a comparatively short space of time. We should heed her warning because there exists already the means by which the same situation can be achieved on an international scale: I refer to the legally binding United Nations Convention on the Elimination of All Forms of Discrimination Against Women, which came into force in 1981 and has already been ratified by 100 countries throughout the world, including Britain.

However, before examining this radical feminist charter, we need to look at some of the seminal writers and ramifications of radical feminism, and their effect on women themselves, men, children and the family. For the sake of convenience I will use the word 'feminist' during this paper, whilst realising the wide variety of views embraced in the feminist movement, from the benign to the radical.

Feminism as a political force came into being in the 19th century as the suffragette movement, whose original goals for civic reform and the legitimate right to vote paved the way for equal pay for equal work, vocational opportunity and openness within the professions. The suffragettes were, by and large, high-minded family women who were interested in eradicating injustices against women, not female supremacy. As a result of their contribution, we can rejoice to see a greater sensitivity in many men, particularly in the nurturing of their children in partnership with their wives. It is encouraging to see increased confidence in young women as they launch out to develop their natural gifts.

However, over the last thirty years the pressure for radical feminist policies has been pervasive and determined. As a result, the legitimate fight for the removal of legal discrimination against women, and a society offering equal opportunities based on individual free choice has been overtaken and superseded by feminist political extremism.

It was Simone de Beauvoir's monumental and erudite study of women, *The Second Sex*, published in the early fifties which provided the intellectual time-bomb for the women's liberation movement which exploded in the 1970s. She was the first passionate spokesman for the feminist cause since the suffragette movement.

Betty Friedan's book *The Feminine Mystique*, published in 1963, known by its critics as 'The Feminine Mistake', managed to convince women that no woman of any intelligence could possibly limit herself to the tedium and inanity of housewifery without going mad. She compared the life of a housewife with a prisoner in a Nazi concentration camp; of emptiness, nothingness, forced to adopt childlike behaviour, controlled by the needs of others. Henceforth the 'needs of others' were to be turned into self-centred pursuits, and women were persuaded by writers like Germaine Greer to be sexually liberated and to express their sexual inclinations and anti-male sentiments. They did so, in words that would make a sailor blush.

## Vengeance and Hate

Many of those women who were persuaded by Friedan's arguments came from broken homes and marriages. They turned their vengeance and frustration on their husbands. The growth of lesbianism within the feminist movement has been noted by Betty Steele in her book *The Feminist Takeover*, and others who bear witness to the fact that husband-hating soon became man-hating in general. For some feminists only relationships with other women are tolerable, fulfilling and acceptable within the sisterhood. Gloria Steinem, who dismisses men as expendable, told a class of young women: 'We are becoming the men we once wanted to marry.' How sad for a woman to say that.

Vengeance and aggression have become characteristic of radical feminism, providing the fuel for demands for more power, and more control. These women have contributed to the emasculation of men emotionally, sociologically and legally. As the feminist newspaper HERizons put it: 'Women must achieve equality with men. But who wants equality with animals. I don't wish to be his equal. I'm already better than he is....'

Men have become the scapegoats for the emotional and psychological problems of some women. Men, like women, are no angels. But, without any opportunity to defend themselves, they have been charged and condemned as the enemy and certainly as the competitor. Often rejected as provider and protector they are unable to speak against the trends for fear of being described as male chauvinist pigs. We cannot be surprised if some turn to their own gender, in their need for acceptance and intimacy.

## 'Destroy the Family'

Some radical feminists call for the destruction of the family. As one of them said once in 1973: 'We want to destroy Judeo–Christian civilisation. To destroy it, we must destroy the family. In order to destroy the family, we must attack it at its weakest point, the unborn child. That is why we are in favour of abortion.' How many feminists go along with this extremism is hard to say. But virtually all feminists see the family and child rearing as a great source of oppression. One such, Roxanne Dunbar, has written: 'How will the family unit be destroyed?... The alleviation of the duty of full-time care in private situations will free many women to make decisions they could not before. Women will be free to leave their husbands and become economically independent, either through a job or welfare.'

To enable women to be released from the 'female trap' of motherhood, feminists press for widespread and all-encompassing child care facilities; we, the taxpayer, being expected to subsidize their liberation. The British government, to its shame, has already started this process by providing third-party child care tax relief, and in so doing is assisting feminists to destroy the family.

Governments have been persuaded to enact abortion laws to allow women the 'right' to choose to destroy their unborn children, whilst with reverse discrimination, men have had their paternal responsibilities removed in respect of their unborn children.

The feminist movement is helping to tear the family apart: there are fractured families, mangled marriages; neglected children and adolescents searching for love and meaning in life; women suffering from post-abortion syndrome; women desperately trying to have babies before their biological time-clock strikes midnight; we have rapidly declining birth rates in the Western World signalling the suicide of nations. There is a deep well of human unhappiness, confusion, violence and suicide everywhere, so much of it avoidable. I sincerely believe that only women can bring about peace. Their role is central and has forever belonged to them. Women set the rhythm of life. They have the biological ability and psychological propensities that enable the human race to sustain itself.

## United Nations Convention on Women

Against all the evidence, and common sense, differences between the roles and status of women have been squarely attributed to environmental and social influences. The belief that women naturally differ from men has been rejected. It is argued that the scarcity of women in roles traditionally reserved for men has been due to masculine repression and lack of feminine opportunity rather than innate feminine characteristics.

Thus the linchpin of contemporary feminist argument is that, apart from a few insignificant biological differences in shape, men and women are basically the same. Any differences in aims, interests and achievements are due to pre-conditioning in society. We dress girls in pink and boys in blue. We teach boys to be tough, and girls to be gentle. Hence boys tend to be leaders in society, while women are left with inferior pursuits. The answer is quite simple, they say. All we have to do is to redirect the sexes towards traditionally opposite pursuits. Only when the sex roles are merged will women have equal rights with men in every way.

Under the terms of the United Nations Convention on the Elimination of All Forms of Discrimination Against Women, the feminists' crazy world view of 'human rights' is to be achieved. This *legally binding* radical feminist charter aims to ensure that men and women become interchangeable in every area of human activity—political, economic, social, cultural, civil or any other field.

The Convention's approach to the family is radical. It calls for 'a change in the traditional role of men as well as of women in society and in the family'.

Governments are to undertake all appropriate measures, including legislation, to modify or abolish existing laws, regulations, customs and practices which constitute discrimination against women.

The Convention is highly discriminatory against woman's traditional roles as mother and home-maker. In fact it ignores them. It regards women as mere instruments of the workforce. It calls, not for equal opportunity of choice, but for 'maximum participation of women on equal terms with men in all fields'.

This means that women should constitute half the workforce in every trade and profession, no matter how dirty, heavy or unsuitable the work. Governments will be required to take 'temporary special measures' to achieve this—that is, the introduction of quotas, such as pertain in the USA, where the federal courts have imposed gender quotas on police departments.

The Convention has nothing to say about women who may not want to work, or may not wish to return to work after the birth of a child. The specific calls for health and social security benefits all relate to women who are members of the labour force.

In Russia, the unisex workforce Utopia envisaged by the United Nations has actually been achieved. However, the status of women has not been improved. A leading Russian dissident and feminist, Natalya Malachovskaya, has said that emancipation means much harder exploitation than before. In Russia women are overworked, underpaid and exploited. They are forced to do hard labour and lift heavy burdens... She says: 'In Russia we are all slaves, but a woman is the slave of a slave.'

None of the 'rights' called for in the Convention have anything to do with marriage or rights relating to children. Motherhood, once the glory of womanhood, is couched in negative terms throughout the Convention by the use of such phrases as 'the function of reproduction', 'the role of women in procreation', and 'maternity as a social function'. What does this mean? Are children born to parents, or are they the property of the State?

Motherhood must not be allowed to interfere with careers; jobs must be kept open and governments are required to provide 'a network of childcare facilities' to enable women to get back to work as soon as possible after childbirth.

Being a mother may be no easy task, but at least women are endowed with the right equipment. Whatever the feminists say, most women want to be mothers. Yet just when nature has prepared them to enjoy their natural, superior skills, the UN Convention infers that motherhood is an obsolete and socially repressive role.

It is interesting to note the bleak comment made by the 'chairperson' of the British Equal Opportunities Commission: 'American women climbed the career ladder fast, but when they got to the boardroom, they looked around and saw all the men had pictures of their families on their desks—but *they* didn't have families.'

No differences between men and women may be recognised and governments are obliged to 'modify the social and cultural patterns of conduct of men and women with a view to achieving the elimination of... stereotyped roles for men and women'.

The Convention flies in the face of a large body of scientific research which demonstrates that the differences between men and women are biological not social. The recent book *Brain Sex* by Dr Anne Moir and David Jessel supplies ample evidence of this. The differences stem from chemical reactions in the womb which cause male and female to develop in different ways.

In the male brain the functions are more precisely located, particularly the visuo-spatial skills which are located in the right hemisphere. It is these skills which enable men to read maps, compose music and handle abstract intellectual concepts better than women. The best woman chess player comes about 2,000 on the mixed list. Women, on the other hand, have their verbal skills more precisely located in the left hemisphere of the brain. Girls learn to handle language faster than boys, and they continue to excel in situations requiring human sympathy and understanding. Women are not inferior to men. They just happen to excel at different things. Men can read maps but women can read characters. Which are more important, maps or people?

It is unrealistic to deny any longer the existence of male and female brain differences. Feminists lay themselves open to ridicule when they deny scientific evidence because it is politically inconvenient, or when they induce women, who would otherwise have been contented wives and mothers, to think of themselves as inferior because they have not pursued careers outside the home.

What does the Convention mean by stereotyped roles? As Dr Glenn Wilson says in his book *The Great Sex Divide*:

> If... masculine and feminine stereotypes were arrived at by some accidental social decision, then the same 'accident' has occurred in virtually every... society, animal and human, that has ever been known; a coincidence rather too remarkable to be taken seriously.

Programmes of reverse discrimination which have sprung up in the USA and Britain are likely to be damaging as well as fruitless. The psychiatrist, Dr Anthony Stevens, says in his book *Archetype*:

> Contemporary confusions over gender roles, and the sexual aberrations and social insecurity to which these confusions give rise, provide a vivid illustration of the misery that can be caused when biological reality is perverted in the cause of political dogmas. That women should be forced by delusory theories to compete with men, on masculine terms and on masculine territory, is a madness generated by a culture whose members have become alienated from their archetypal roots.

Yet, against all the weighty scientific and psychiatric evidence available, the Convention demands the elimination of any stereotyped concept of the roles of men and women at all levels and in all forms of education by the revision of textbooks and school programmes and the adaptation of teaching methods.

Here we are taken into the realm of mind control. We must convince our children that their perception of the obvious physical and psychological differences between boys and girls have been a terrible mistake. This is brainwashing quite literally. Elementary observation of human physiology reveals that men are sinewy and firm; women soft and flexible. Yet our Equal Opportunities Commission produced a chilling handbook, *An Equal Start*, for those working in nurseries and day-care centres. Little ones must not imbibe a sense of their own identity and worth about their gender. Banned are such expressions as 'Can I have two strong boys to help carry this table?' or 'Here's a picture the girls will like. It's a wedding'. In Tasmania, the local education authority sent a team of anti-sexist librarians into a school to purge its library of over 500 'sexist' books, including *Snow White*, *Born Free* and, of course, the Bible.

The United Nations Convention may be regarded by the feminists as a triumph of women's rights. But I believe that history books will one day describe it as a monumental aberration, to create 'a world of uncommon nonsense', as G.K. Chesterton put it.

The Japanese philosopher, Michito Hasegawa, has said of the Convention:

> The cultures of individual nations and ethnic groups merit mutual respect not

arbitrary modification by outside forces. So much damage has been inflicted upon the people of the world by the white man's belief that its culture alone is universal, with the consequence of imposition of its religion, languages, customs and values on other cultures... An attitude without consideration of differing cultural systems is the epitome of colonialism.

## A World of 'Uncommon Nonsense'

Chesterton's world of 'uncommon nonsense' was to be seen in the programme of the Calendar of Summit Events for the First World Summit of Women which took place in Montreal in June 1990. This chilled the heart and mind. Growing more radical with age, feminists are fighting on all fronts demanding power in civilisation, in politics, religion, the media, in reproduction, sexuality, education and in language.

This programme has been used as the base for the cover of a recently published book, *Feminism v. Mankind*. This contains ten chapters by women from different parts of the world who, in their concern for the peaceful and just development of society, challenge the excesses of radical feminism. But is there still time to stop the spread of the 'uncommon nonsense' and prevent societies following the Swedish situation? Historically, as we know, many women have achieved great works and social reforms without sacrificing husband, children and the extended family.

Quite clearly feminist excesses can only be corrected by accepting the differences between men and women. As Dr Alice von Hildebrand has said:

> Their combined message would not only provide us with a design for restoring the delicate balance between both the physical and the spiritual ecology of the world but might very well have more far-reaching consequences for global harmony and co-operation generally.

Fortunately, there is always hope. As a French wit put it: 'The battle of the sexes will never be won because there is too much fraternising with the enemy.' It is women themselves who must resist the call to join the men to gain power in the world. We should cherish our right to be different. We have the answer to that lament: 'Why can't a woman be more like a man?' It is time we exploded the myth that men and women are virtually interchangeable, all things being equal. All things are not equal.

Women must now strive to accord proper social status to motherhood and the family. The very fact that marriage is for humans the norm throughout the world, when as we know men are more disposed against the institution, has represented a truly remarkable triumph of the female brain and heart.

There are far more important things in life than power in the world. When we women, whether married or single, celebrate the admirable complementarity of the sexes, Woman's mystery and glory will be recognised again, and men and women can move forward together into the post-feminist era to harmonious family life.

# Pressure on the Family

## Rob Parsons

There's no doubt the family is under pressure, but in one sense the family was built for pressure; the family is centrally important to society in the areas of procreation, nurturance, emotional gratification, primary socialisation, stabilisation of adult motivation and social continuity. I want to mention three special pressures which modern society brings.

Firstly, the pressure of the 'me' generation. It's a message that has been preached at us for three decades 'You, as an individual, are the most important person. You have a right to personal happiness, personal freedom, personal fulfillment at all costs!'

That's the message of the 'me' generation in a nutshell. It says to us, 'Take what you want and take it now, this is your right.'

I remember the phrase, 'For the sake of the kids'—'we're staying together for the sake of the kids.' I see too much pain in these areas to believe that this is always the answer, but I want to say that 'For the sake of the kids' is a good reason. It fights tooth and claw with the message of the 'me' generation, but it's still a good reason.

Recently I went to a fair, and there to my delight was an old style coconut shy. I was determined to show my kids some skill in this area.

I threw everything at that coconut including those three wooden balls I'd purchased, and eventually it fell. And the family can fall, when you bombard any unit of relationships and tell its members year after year that its feelings as individuals are paramount, you will cause it to fall because relationships are at least fifty per cent commitment against the odds.

And so we are fighting the pressure of a 'me' generation.

But that leaves other pressures waiting in the wings. When Dr James Dobson was asked to mention the things more than any other that militate against family life, he didn't even hesitate. He said, 'Fatigue and time pressure, the sheer pressure of daily life.'

For example, a man comes home from work, his wife is waiting for him, she may have just come home from work herself, but has got a meal together. He's about to rush out to another meeting, together they have this precious hour around the table with their family. She has long ceased to try and talk to him at this time because he is always so distant, but the kids haven't given up, 'Daddy, I came second in spelling today,' then the boy chimes in, 'Daddy, Simon hit me.' The father grunts but is completely preoccupied, until the telephone rings and a little voice says, 'Dad it's for you'—and then that man comes alive and he's dispensing his counsel, his wisdom, his strategy, and a little boy and a little girl are watching him, and they're not stamping or kicking or screaming, it would be better if they were, but the message they're getting loud and clear is 'this matters to him, this brings him alive.' I've been that man and I understand that pressure and it can rip the heart out of a family.

We simply do not have time for each other today. We watch TV together, take the kids to piano, ballet, kung fu and the chess club, we do aerobics or darts, or play skittles or bingo, or bridge, but we do not have *time* for each other.

Pressure like that breaks homes.

It is my belief that there are couples married for twenty plus years who have not had twenty minutes in those twenty years, actually talking to each other, letting each other know how they feel, their hopes, their hurts.

And that time pressure wreaks havoc in the lives of our children. We live in a society where so many of our kids are starved of time.

I hold out no more hope of us changing the sheer pressure of society's life in the short term than I do of sorting out the 'me' generation. But the good news is we don't have to change it to make a difference, only expose it and make families realize what is going on. We need to tell parents all across the country that the door of childhood closes so quickly and so finally.

I've spent the last ten years lecturing to business people. And in recent years I've inserted just a few minutes on the importance of home life and how quickly those incredible opportunities pass. Time and time again when I have done that, it's that they've wanted to talk about in the Coffee Break. It rings a chord in us.

I want to read a folk song to you:

> My child arrived just the other day,
> he came to the world in the usual way—
> But there were planes to catch and bills to pay,
> he learned to walk while I was away
> and he was talkin' for I knew it and as he grew he'd say,
>
> I'm gonna be like you, Dad
> You know I'm gonna be like you.
>
> And the cat's in the cradle and the silver spoon,
> Little boy blue and the man in the moon.
> When you com'in home Dad?
> I don't know when,
> but we'll get together then—
> you know we'll have a good time then.
>
> My son turned ten just the other day
> he said, Thanks for the ball, Dad, com'on let's play.
> I said not today, I got a lot to do.
> He said that's okay,
> and he walked away but his smile never dimmed,
> it said I'm going to be like him, yeah
> you know I'm going to be like him
>
> And the cat's in the cradle and the silver spoon,
> Little boy blue and the man in the moon.
> when you com'in home Dad?
> I don't know when,

but we'll get together then—
you know we'll have a good time then.

Well he came home from college just the other day,
so much like a man I just had to say—
Son, I'm proud of you, can you sit for awhile?
He shook his head and said with a smile,
what I'd really like Dad is to borrow the car keys
see you later, can I have them please?

When you com'in home son?
I don't know when
but we'll get together then—
you know we'll have a good time then.

I've long since retired and my son's moved away,
I called him up just the other day.
I said I'd like to see you if you don't mind,
He said, I'd love to Dad—if I can find the time—

You see my new job's a hassle and the kids have the flu
but it's sure nice talkin' to you, Dad.
It's been nice talkin' to you.

And as I hung up the phone, it occurred to me—
He'd grown up just like me; my boy was just like me

And the cat's in the cradle and the silver spoon,
Little boy blue and the man in the moon.
When you com'in home Son?
I don't know when,
But we'll get together then, Dad,
We're gonna have a good time then.

I can almost hear the criticism: this is sheer emotion. Don't you believe it! When I read those words to a business audience the other day, a director of a management company asked me for a copy. The other day I met him and he said, 'I've read that to top executives of major companies, who've attended my course on business management. At the end of the day it was that that they wanted to talk about.'

I want us to let that message loose all over this country, because I don't believe we can change the status quo immediately, but we can enable people to see what's going on.

The third and what I consider is the greatest pressure is that of isolation. It falls into two categories.

Firstly there's a physical isolation. So often today the family is isolated from its roots and the wider extended family. It is true that the concept that in previous generations the house was filled with all kinds of relatives is a myth. The Family Policy Studies Centre has shown that for the four centuries previous to this one, the average home size was about five to six people. The difference is that in previous generations, extended family lived near—mother, father, aunties, grandparents.

A study conducted at Bristol University by Bernard Ineichen looked into social isolation in Yate, a new town near to Bristol in the 1970s. They found a high degree of anxiety in two areas:

Firstly, coping with child rearing without the backup experience from the new mother's mother. And secondly, there was an incredible anxiety in these isolated families in dealing with the trauma of death in the family. My heart goes out to parents coping with a cot death or perhaps teenage suicide, without the physical mutual support over an extended period of the extended family.

When I was a child I lived in one of a long row of terraced houses. We didn't have inside toilets, bathroom or hot water. People would say with pride, 'at least we can shut our own front door'. It became a catch phrase of dignity. But in many of our modern homes that have every amenity, shutting the front door condemns those families to a living hell of isolation.

But the second element of isolation is not physical, but psychological—many families going through incredible trauma and believing it's only them.

For the past two years, my wife Dianne and I have toured the country with a seminar called 'Marriage Under Pressure'. Almost 12,000 people have attended. Our main theme has been openness, honesty and an admission that we too have had hard times, times when we have not felt 'in love', when we have not communicated, when we have found it hard to resolve conflict, when our sex life was not all it might have been. Do you know what I've seen when I've looked out at hundreds of faces at those seminars—sheer relief, that says, this is not just us. One lady came to me recently in tears at the end of such a day and said, 'I now believe there is hope for me.'

These are pressurized situations and all the more so because almost every one of those people in isolation will tonight close the door of their home and say in their hearts, 'this is only us, this is our problem.' And those pressures will mount and eventually those people will take their place in the line of statistics of broken homes and damaged lives. The great challenge for us today is to reach them before that, reach them way before crisis counselling, reach them in order to break that isolation.

We must each take off the cardboard replica fronts so many of us have worn and bend to help others through the hard times as fellow sufferers. You know there is enormous power in weakness. Sometimes as carers our lives seem to be so 'together' in every way we actually put people off. If some of us can get from somewhere the courage to share a little of our own failure and weakness, we may actually set others free as well.

I would love to say that in spite of it all the family is a great survivor that it will pull through, but who knows?

But I know this, that it's worth fighting for against the pressures—the 'me' generation, and the culture that robs us of even time to love and builds walls of isolation around tragedies. The family is worth fighting for, even against the odds!

# 'Personal View' from Young Parents

## Paul and Helen Danon

*Paul:* We have four children. I am an only child from a family which was a good family, and I thank my parents for that. They don't believe in God but gave me nevertheless a good and happy upbringing, a real love for family. So it was something I always wanted to do right from the beginning. In due course I fell in love with Helen and wanted to marry her. But one of the things that surprised me later on, when we had children—when we had our first child particularly—was that I fell in love with him as well, which I didn't exactly expect! I just thought that we would have him, and he would be in the family, and he would be ours, and it would be cute, and so on. But I actually fell in love with him, and I have fallen in love with my other children since. It is something that I would like to impart to people who are not yet married and not yet had children, that you do actually fall in love with them. That is my experience anyway.

I work in a computer company, a white-collar type of job. It is the kind of job where it takes place outside the home as so many jobs do these days. People have mentioned what work and overtime can do to you, and what it means to be out of the house in the evenings and at weekends when you are doing overtime. But what about being out of the house all day? A few hundred years ago and in a more traditional society where that persists, the family was an economic unit and people worked together. The children saw their parents doing something meaningful. I don't think my children see me doing anything meaningful, because I am out all the time. They don't even see me with a bag of money at the end of the day because it all goes straight into the bank.

Then there is also this pressure for overtime. It seems that there can be an attitude amongst employers that part of their job is to confine people, confine them away from home to be in the Company and to be good 'Company-men'. I have experienced, and so have my friends, pressure in being expected to do overtime. This means overtime which in my sort of job, a white-collar sort of job (nothing very senior, but a service industry), is not paid for. It is just expected, and it is something that I personally—and as far as I've got any control of it—feel I should fight. But you need courage because you might be within your legal rights, but you don't necessarily get on in the firm or even stay where you are in the firm for very long by asserting your legal rights. I wonder also whether employers don't have a responsibility, especially those who believe in God. Employers: when you apply pressure to your people to stay late for the company or for the cause, isn't that undue pressure? Is that proper?

Could you afford to take on extra labour to do the extra thing? Because in the end, with the crisis project, the client doesn't end up paying any more, and the company doesn't pay any more, especially in the kind of service industry I am in. The people who pay for the 'running late on the such and such project' are the family. The children and the others at home—they are the ones actually paying for a short run on some project in the service industry. It doesn't seem fair, and it is a constant battle not to be brow-beaten and subtly threatened into staying late and getting in early for the sake of the firm, for the sake of being a good corporate guy.

*Helen:* I am at home and often on the frustrating receiving end of that when it does happen. Not that it happens every day. But I see in the children's eyes, the way they react, when I have to explain that Daddy's going to be late again. We do try to have a routine of family meals. Perhaps we're exceptional in that we do have the children home at lunch time as well. I consider this a great blessing and a gift. We instigated it because the lunch-time provisions for them at school was a rather mundane hour and a half of playground play that didn't seem to be disciplined at all. So we decided that we would have them home at lunch time. That is a break for them and it is a break for me. Yes, it ties me to the house, because I know I have got to be there by 12.00 with some food on the table, but it is also a privilege to have them home in the middle of the day. It means that I get the 'first go' at what they have been doing in the morning. So we have a debriefing session for the morning, and then we have a six o'clock supper, when Paul is there, most of the time, and where they can share with Daddy the things they have been doing. Again, that time is precious. A man can be on another planet, and we all try and bring him down to earth with spelling tests and sports days and football matches and piano lessons, and whatever else they have been doing! Family meal times are an anchor point for all of us: husband and wife as well as children. It is so easy just to sit there and munch away and then get up and go off and do your own thing, but actually to put leading questions, open-ended questions, so all the children can share the conversation—that's really worthwhile. We try to include all, even down to the two year old: we talk about the rabbit, or something he has been doing during the day.

Role models, we feel, are very important. Yes, we are traditionalist, people will call us old-fashioned. We do dress our girls in dresses, we do let them grow their hair long; they do play with dolls. But it hasn't been a pushing into that role. They have accepted it naturally, although it has come with some forethought on our part. Our sons aren't great mechanics or computer wizards (least of all the two year old!), but it seems to us more natural that they will go in those ways. The children are all very caring, and in fact John Paul, our nine year old, is exceptionally so. I never thought that he would be such a caring older brother to a two-year old with a seven year age-gap. Again, the world would say that children that far apart aren't going to have any relationship at all. But from the minute that Edmund, the little one, was born, that older brother has looked after him, cared for him, even rescued him in very many situations. On one occasion Edmund actually wandered out of the house and we lost him. John Paul helped the policeman find him and identify him and carry him back to the police station.

We hear a lot about fostering independent people, independent children, to fight for what they want themselves. But do we really live as a society on independence? Surely not. We should be dependent on each other to make a social structure, to make a family work. In a family, the joy is the dependency on each other. Home is a place where we can sit back, let our hair down, kick our shoes off and whatever, and be ourselves. It is a place of relaxation and not just a centre for recreation facilities. It's somewhere where you are a family together.

*Paul:* Some things we don't do the way we would wish, because I am absent from meals for instance. But family prayer times do seem to work, for some reason or other, and must be a grace from God. Our family prayer time is now quite regular. Of course, it can get very routine. We find ourselves saying the same prayers night after night, but at least we do it. It gives us a focus for the day.

What about voluntary work? I'm not getting at people who do this. But my feeling is that we should be wary. I have been doing it off and on, and I don't think I have much to show for it. Bits here and there, they add up to nothing except time maybe taken from the family. All those meetings and maybe nothing to show for it.

*Helen:* What about allowing boys to be boys and girls to be girls? I can see that in our school we have a lot of crusading against what is considered 'sex stereotyping' within simple things like the reading scheme, which obviously occupy the child's learning period at the ages of five and six. The 'Janet and John' and the 'Peter and Jane' old pictures really are disappearing. Now the pictures show figures all dressed in dungarees and with ear-length hair, so it is very difficult to see who is who: just two figures, say rowing a boat. I do protest about that, but I am seen as something of a nutcase if I go into school to see the Headmaster. I feel sometimes that he can see me coming and think, 'Oh no, what is she going to go on about this time!' But I feel I have to do it, although it hurts sometimes. The thing that worries me is that I see parents who are putting their children into school and who seem to think, 'Right, that's it, I've done my bit for the first five years' (or even less, if the children have been to nursery school), and 'Now it's the turn of the school'. They don't question anything that the school does. I feel very strongly that as parents, even in State schools (in independent schools, I suppose, you expect it, because you are paying even more for it), we do need to keep contact with the teachers and the Head, to keep our children on the right tracks. Ours is a dear little school and the teachers' efforts are laudable. But we are not just handing our children over as clay to be moulded in the way the schools want.

*Paul:* What about physical discipline? Well, we've used it and it works, and on many occasions I have wished we used it more. Rather than getting all cross and wound up ourselves and exhibited bad temper to the children, the physical discipline could have brought the matter to a head. It would have made it quite clear straight away that what they were doing was wrong and they should stop. It is remarkable how quickly it is over—the child forgets about it and so do you.

*Helen:* In our family life, we have been supported greatly by people around us, Christians for whom we care very much and who care for us. I would like to pay tribute to them here and now, and to our own parents, who have given us so much to go on in the past. But to live within a Christian environment, where there are people around the block, who you know you can call in any emergency is a huge help. When little Edmund disappeared it was a case in point: everyone was out on the street in about five minutes. Those people care for us, we care for them, we have the same sort of values and we can rely on them, and know that they are trying to bring up their children the same way. That sort of support has gone for most people. Many families are these isolated nuclear units. I see it in my work with the Natural Child Birth Trust. In a sense a group like that is providing the support that the community can't in many ways, when people have babies and launch into parenthood.

So, the support of like-minded people is just so important to families. I pray that that in our family it will continue into the future as we become older parents, and give support too through the teenage years as well.

*Paul:* The media came asking questions because they heard that we were going to take part in the Family Congress. One of their questions was 'What if one of your boys turns out to be a practising homosexual, or one of the girls gets pregnant before she's married, what do you do then? Will you have failed?' That was a pretty devastating question, but what came to me then was a thought that I hadn't had before. It was this: we pass on to our children an example, and sometimes our example is bad, and that's when we need their forgiveness. Not grovelling, but as person to person. But, in the end, the most important thing, no, the most important *Person*—we need to convey to our children is going to help them deal with situations when we won't be there any more. It is the Lord God. It is Him that we have to convey, with His help. In that way, we are somehow able to subdue some of our anxieties, and put it more into His hands. If we can convey some element of the good Lord to our children, then when it is too late for further input from us, when they have to go away from home and begin their own lives, then they will have the most precious gift of all: the gift of faith in God.

# 3. POPULATION, FAMILY AND FERTILITY

## Overpopulation: Facing the Facts

### Prof Julian L. Simon

Public hysteria about population growth has broken out again. The message you get from reading the newspapers and magazines is that the conditions of life have been getting *worse*, and that population growth is responsible. And these ideas have consequences.

But in 1990 there is an important new element not present twenty years ago. The theories of the population doomsayers have now been discredited by a solid body of scientific research.

Twenty years ago doomsaying statements about population growth had not yet been disproven. The doomsayers could base their assertions upon their raw intuitions coupled with primitive Malthusian reasoning, without fear of being contradicted by solid evidence.

By ten years ago, science had already disproven the anti-population ideas. But the new ideas were still an unusual minority position, and it was not unreasonable for one to be sceptical. The research results which had already begun to accumulate could still be ignored as 'controversial' by the World Bank, AID, UNFPA, and other U.S. and international agencies.

But in 1986, the National Research Council and the National Academy of Sciences published a book on population growth and economic development prepared by a prestigious scholarly group. This 'official' report reversed almost completely the frightening conclusions of the previous 1971 NAS report. 'The scarcity of exhaustible resources is at most a minor constraint on economic growth', it now said. It found benefits of additional people as well as costs.

Even the World Bank reported in 1984 that the world's natural resource situation provides no reason to limit population growth.

By 1990, anyone who asserts that population growth damages the economy must either turn a blind eye to the scientific evidence, or be blatantly dishonest intellectually.

I shall today try to show you that if we raise our gaze from the frightening articles in the newspaper about today and yesterday, we can see that life has been getting *better* over the last centuries and decades, here in Great Britain and the United States as well as in the rest of the world, in most of the important material aspects of our lives. And there is no persuasive reason to believe that these trends will not continue indefinitely.

The reason that life has been getting better is that people's efforts *make* it so. And more people mean faster progress of civilization.

Before moving on to data, I wish to state a qualification that tends to get overlooked: I do not say that all is well everywhere, and I do not predict that all will be rosy in the future. Children are hungry and sick; people live out lives of physical or intellectual poverty, and lack of opportunity; war or some new pollution may finish us off. What I *am* saying is that for most relevant economic matters I have checked, the aggregate *trends* are improving rather than deteriorating.

Also, I don't say that a better future happens automatically or without effort. It will happen because women and men will struggle with problems with muscle and mind, and will probably overcome, as people have overcome in the past—if the social and economic system gives them the opportunity to do so.

Let's quickly review a few data on how human life has been doing. Let us begin with the all-important issue, life itself.

The most important and amazing demographic fact—the greatest human achievement in history, in my view—is the 'recent' decrease in the world's death rate. It took thousands of years to increase life expectancy at birth—the number of years that people could expect to live at the time they were born—from just over 20 years to the high '20's. Then in just the last *two centuries*, the length of life you could expect for your baby or yourself in the advanced countries jumped from less than 30 years to perhaps 75 years. What greater event has humanity witnessed?

Then starting well after World War II, the length of life you could expect in the poor countries has leapt upwards by perhaps fifteen or even twenty years since the 1950s, caused by advances in agriculture, sanitation, and medicine.

Is this not an outstanding triumph for humankind? It is this *decrease in the death rate* that is the cause of there being a larger world population nowadays than in former times.

Let's put it differently. In the 19th century the planet Earth could sustain only one billion people. Ten thousand years ago, only 4 million could keep themselves alive. Now, 5 billion people are living longer and more healthily than ever before, on average. The increase in the world's population represents our victory over death.

One would expect lovers of humanity to jump with joy at this triumph of human mind and organization over the raw forces of nature. Instead, many lament that there are so many people alive to enjoy the gift of life. And it is this worry—a misplaced concern, as we shall see—that leads them to approve the inhumane programs of coercion and denial of personal liberty in one of the most precious choices a family can make—the number of children that it wishes to bear and raise.

Throughout history, adequacy of supplies of natural resources has always been a source of concern that has led to calls for population control. Yet the data clearly show that natural resource scarcity—as measured by the economically-meaningful indicator of cost or price—has been decreasing rather than increasing in the long run for all raw materials, with only temporary exceptions from time to time. Take, for example, copper, which is representative of all the metals.

This trend of falling prices of copper has been going on for a very long time. In the 18th century B.C.E. in Babylonia under Hammurabi—almost 4000 years ago—the price of copper was about 1200 times its price in the U.S. now relative to wages.

Regarding oil, the price rise in the 1970's did not stem from an increase in the cost of world supply. The cost per barrel in the Persian Gulf still is perhaps 15-25 cents. Concerning energy in general, there is no reason to believe that the supply of energy is finite, or that the price of energy will not continue its long-run decrease.

Food is an especially important resource. The evidence is particularly strong for food that we are on a benign trend despite rising population. The long-run price of food relative to wages, and even relative to consumer products, is down, due to increased productivity.

Famine deaths due to insufficient food supply have decreased even in absolute terms, let alone relative to population, in the past century, a matter which pertains particularly to the poor countries. Per person food consumption is up over the last 30 years. And there are no data showing that the bottom of the income scale is faring worse, or even has failed to share in the general improvement, as the average has improved.

Africa's food production per person is down, but by 1990 few any longer claim that Africa's suffering has anything to do with a shortage of land or water or sun. Hunger in Africa clearly stems from civil wars and collectivization of agriculture, which periodic droughts have made more murderous.

There is only one important resource which has shown a trend of increasing scarcity rather than increasing abundance. That resource is the most important of all—human beings. Yes, there are more people on earth now than ever before. But if we measure the scarcity of people the same way that we measure the scarcity of other economic goods—by how much we must pay to obtain their services—we see that wages and salaries have been going up all over the world, in poor countries as well as in rich countries. The amount that you must pay to obtain the services of a driver or a cook has risen in India, just as the price of a driver or cook—or economist—has risen in the United States over the decades. This increase in the price of peoples' services is a clear indication that people are becoming more scarce even though there are more of us.

About pollution now: How many people think that our air and water have been getting more polluted in recent years? Though the data I have available apply mainly to the United States, much the same picture describes Western Europe. The evidence with respect to air indicates that pollutants have been declining. With respect to water, the proportion of monitoring sites in the U.S. with water of good drinkability has increased.

Every forecast of the doomsayers has been wrong. Metals, foods, and other natural resources have become more available rather than more scarce throughout the centuries. The U.S. famine deaths they forecast we would see on our television never occurred. The Great Lakes are not dead; instead they offer better sport fishing than ever. We have not had to worry about 'What will we do when the pumps run dry?' The main pollutants, especially the particulates which have killed people for years, have lessened in our cities. But nothing has reduced the doomsayers' credibility with the press or their command over the funding resources of the federal government.

Let's dramatize these sets of changes with a single anecdote. The trend toward a better life can be seen in most of our own families if we look. For example, I have mild asthma. Recently I slept in a home where there was a dog, and in the middle of the night I woke with a bad cough and shortness of breath. When I realized that it was caused by the dog dander, I took out my twelve dollar pocket inhaler, good for 3000 puffs, and took one puff. Within ten minutes my lungs were clear. A small miracle. Forty years ago I would have been sleepless and miserable all night, and I would have had to give up the squash-playing that I love so much because exercise causes my worst asthma in the absence of an inhaler.... Or diabetes. If your child had diabetes a hundred years ago, you had to watch helplessly as the child went blind and died early. Now injections, or even pills, can give the child almost as long and healthy a life as other children.... Or glasses. Centuries ago you had to give up reading when your eyes got dim as you got to be 40 or 50. Now you can buy magnifying glasses at the drugstore for nine dollars. And you can even wear contact lenses for eye problems and keep your vanity intact. Is there not some condition in *your* family that in earlier times would have been a lingering misery or a tragedy, that nowadays our increasing knowledge has rendered easily bearable?

To sum up the statistical history, there now are more people on earth than ever before, and also better material conditions of life than ever before. A reasonable first-order hypothesis, then, is that a larger population leads to a better life rather than to a poorer life. These data by themselves are far from conclusive, of course, but they certainly suggest that the scientific burden of proof is upon anyone who suggests the contrary view that more people have a negative effect in the long run.

Sound scientific practice seeks a theory that fits the broad range of data. The Malthusian theory of increasing scarcity, based on supposedly-fixed resources, which is the theory that the doomsayers rely upon, runs exactly contrary to these data and to the long sweep of history. And therefore it makes sense to prefer another theory. And the theory that fits the facts very well is this:

More people, and increased income, cause problems in the short run. This presents opportunity and prompts the search for solutions. In a free society, solutions are eventually found. And in the long run the new developments leave us better off than if the problems had not arisen.

Yes, more consumers mean less of the fixed available stock of goods to be divided among more people. And more workers labouring with the same fixed current stock of capital mean that there will be less output per worker. The latter effect, known as 'the law of diminishing returns', is the essence of Malthus's theory as he first set it out.

But if the resources with which people work are *not* fixed over the period being analyzed, then the Malthusian logic of diminishing returns does not apply. And the plain fact is that, given some time to adjust to shortages, the resource base does not remain fixed. People create more resources of all kinds.

That is, when we take a long-run view, the picture is different, and considerably more complex, than the simple short-run view of more people implying lower average income. In the very long run, more people almost surely imply more available resources and a higher income for everyone.

I suggest you test this proposition as follows: Do you think that our standard of living would be as high as it is now if the population had never grown from about four million human beings perhaps ten thousand years ago? I don't think we'd now have electric light or gas heat or autos or penicillin or travel to the moon or our present life expectancy of over seventy years at birth in rich countries, in comparison to the life expectancy of 20 to 25 years at birth in earlier eras, if population had not grown to its present numbers.

There have been perhaps a dozen competent statistical studies, starting in 1967 with an analysis by Nobel prizewinner Simon Kuznets covering the few countries for which data are available over the past century, and also analyses by Kuznets and Richard Easterlin of the data covering many countries since World War II. Incidentally, it was those statistical studies that converted me in about 1968 from working in favour of population control to the point of view that I hold today. I certainly did not come to my current view for any political or religious or ideological reason.

The basic method is to gather data on each country's rate of population growth and its rate of economic growth, and then to examine whether—looking at all the data in the sample together—the countries with high population growth rates have economic growth rates lower than average, and countries with low population growth rates have economic growth rates higher than average. All the studies agree in concluding that this is not so; there is no correlation between economic growth and population growth in the intermediate run.

Of course one can adduce cases of countries that seemingly are exceptions to the pattern. It is the genius of statistical inference, however, to enable us to draw valid generalizations from samples that contain such wide variations in behaviour. The exceptions can be useful in alerting us to possible avenues for further analysis, but as long as they are only exceptions, they do not prove that the generalization is not meaningful or useful.

The research-wise person may wonder whether population density is a more meaningful variable than population growth. And indeed, such studies have been done. And again, the statistical evidence directly contradicts the common-sense conventional wisdom. If you make a chart with population density on the horizontal axis and either the income level or the rate of change of income on the vertical axis, you will see that higher density is associated with better rather than poorer economic results.

Check for yourself: Fly over Hong Kong—just a few decades ago a place seemingly without prospects because of insoluble resource problems—and you will marvel at the astounding collection of modern high-rise apartments and office buildings. Take a ride on its excellent smooth-flowing highways for an hour or two, and you will realize that a very dense concentration of human beings does not prevent comfortable existence and exciting economic expansion—as long as the economic system gives individuals the freedom to exercise their talents and to take advantage of opportunities. And the experience of Singapore demonstrates that Hong Kong is not unique. Two such examples do not prove the case, of course. But these dramatic illustrations are backed by the evidence from the aggregate sample of countries, and hence do not mislead us.

Hong Kong is a special thrill for me because I first saw it in 1955 when I went ashore from a U.S. Navy destroyer. At the time I felt great pity for the thousands who slept every night on the sidewalks or on small boats. It then seemed clear to me, as it must have to almost every observer, that it would be impossible for Hong Kong to surmount its problems—huge masses of impoverished people without jobs, total lack of exploitable natural resources, more refugees pouring across the border each day. But upon returning in 1983, I saw bustling crowds of healthy, vital people full of hope and energy. No cause for pity now.

Consider this example of the process by which people wind up with increasing availability rather than decreasing availability of resources. England was full of alarm in the 1600's at an impending shortage of energy due to the deforestation of the country for firewood. People feared a scarcity of fuel for both heating and for the iron industry. This impending scarcity led to the development of coal.

Then in the mid-1800's the English came to worry about an impending coal crisis. The great English economist, Jevons, calculated that a shortage of coal would bring England's industry to a standstill by 1900; he carefully assessed that oil could never make a decisive difference. Triggered by the impending scarcity of coal (and of whale oil, whose story comes next) ingenious profit-minded people developed oil into a more desirable fuel than coal ever was. And in 1989 we find England exporting both coal and oil.

Another element in the story: Because of increased demand due to population growth and increased income, the price of whale oil for lamps jumped in the 1840's, and the U.S. Civil War pushed it even higher, leading to a whale oil 'crisis'. This provided incentive for enterprising people to discover and produce substitutes. First came oil from rapeseed, olives, linseed, and camphene oil from pine trees. Then inventors learned how to get coal oil from coal, a flourishing industry in 1859. About then, other ingenious persons produced kerosene from the rock oil that seeped to the surface, a product so desirable that its price then rose from $.75 a gallon to $2.00. This stimulated enterprises to increase the supply of oil, and finally Edwin L. Drake brought in his famous well in Titusville, Pennsylvania. Learning how to refine the oil took a while. But in a few years there were hundreds of small refiners in the U.S., and soon the bottom fell out of the whale oil market, the price falling from $2.50 or more at its peak around 1866 to well below a dollar.

Here we should note that it was not the English government that developed coal or oil, because governments are not effective developers of new technology. Rather, it was individual entrepreneurs who sensed the need, saw opportunity, used all kinds of available information and ideas, made lots of false starts which were very costly to many of those individuals but not to others, and eventually arrived at coal as a viable fuel—because there were enough independent individuals investigating the matter for at least some of them to arrive at sound ideas and methods. And this happened in the context of a competitive enterprise system that worked to produce what was needed by the public. And the entire process of impending shortage and new solution left us better off than if the shortage problem had never arisen.

The most important benefit of population size and growth is the increase it brings to the stock of useful knowledge. Minds matter economically as much as, or more than, hands or mouths. Progress is limited largely by the availability of trained workers.

Here we must address another crucial element in the economics of population growth—the extent to which the political-social-economic system provides personal freedom from government coercion. Skilled persons require an appropriate social and economic framework that provides incentives for working hard and taking risks, enabling their talents to flower and come to fruition. The key elements of such a framework are economic liberty, respect for property, and fair and sensible rules of the market that are enforced equally for all.

In earlier years, there could be an honest difference of opinion about which kind of economic system—free enterprise or centrally planned—would be the more effective. By 1990, however, there is *irrefutable evidence* that an enterprise system works better than does a planned economy. And under conditions of freedom, population growth poses less of a problem in the short run, and brings many more benefits in the long run, than under conditions of government control.

And at the heart of a free, market-directed economic system, according to Friedrich Hayek, the greatest living expositor of such a system, are two general institutions: private property, and the family. They are both necessary for economic development. An unfree, centrally-directed socialist system will necessarily prevent the free existence of these two institutions. It is no wonder that the churches' traditional teachings come into conflict with Communist regimes.

To illustrate, compare China with Singapore. China has a coercive population policy, including forced abortions, because its leaders think its economic development requires population control.

Contrast Singapore. Despite its very high population density, that tiny city-country now suffers from a labour shortage, and imports workers. Singapore even offers incentives for middle-class families to *have more children*, in contrast to its previous across-the-board population-control policy.

China's problem is not too many children, but rather a defective political-economic system. With free markets China might soon experience the same sort of labour shortage as Singapore—which is vastly more densely settled, and has zero natural resources. (And this does not mean a 'free' system such as China is talking about now; it is quite unlikely that a truly free market can coexist with a totalitarian political system, because a free economy is too great a political threat).

So to sum up: In the short run, all resources are limited. An example of such a finite resource is the amount of attention that you will devote to what I have to say today. The longer run, however, is a different story. The standard of living has risen along with the size of the world's population since the beginning of recorded time. There is no convincing economic reason why these trends toward a better life should not continue indefinitely.

The key theoretical idea is this: The growth of population and of income create actual and expected shortages, and hence lead to price run-ups. A price increase represents an opportunity that attracts profit-minded entrepreneurs to seek new ways to satisfy the shortages. Some fail, at cost to themselves. A few succeed, and the final result is that we end up *better off* than if the original shortage problems had never arisen. That is, we need our problems, though this does not imply that we should purposely *create* additional problems for ourselves.

I hope that you will now agree that the long-run outlook is for a more abundant material life rather than for increased scarcity, in the U. S. and in the world as a whole. Of course such progress does not come about automatically. And my message certainly is not of complacency. In this I agree with the doomsayers—that our world needs the best efforts of all humanity to improve our lot. I part company with them in that they expect us to come to a bad end despite the efforts we make, whereas I expect a continuation of successful efforts. And I believe that their message is self-fulfilling, because if you expect your efforts to fail because of inexorable natural limits, then you are likely to feel resigned, and therefore literally to resign. But if you recognize the possibility—in fact the probability—of success, you can tap large reservoirs of energy and enthusiasm. Adding more people causes problems, but people are also the means to solve these problems. The main fuel to speed the world's progress is our stock of knowledge, and the brake is our lack of imagination. The ultimate resource is people—skilled, spirited, and hopeful people—who will exert their wills and imaginations for their own benefit as well as in a spirit of faith and social concern, and so inevitably they will benefit not only themselves but the poor and the rest of us as well.

# Population, People, and Environment

## *Prof Jacqueline R. Kasun*

I am very glad that there is an environmental movement in the world today. The movement is very credible—in fact, politically formidable, although the environmental problems which gave it birth are still far from solved.

However, seeing that the public was genuinely and widely alarmed about the destruction of nature, people and groups have joined the environmental movement with the intention of using it for their own purposes that have little to do with defending nature. Foremost are those who say that in order to rescue the environment we must reduce the number of people. This was not the position of the environmental movement in its beginning, but now, all too often, it is.

Those special interest groups who have always wanted to control other people's reproductive lives have hitched their wagons to the environmental star.

By 1981 the major environmental organizations in the United States had joined with the principal population control groups—the Population Crisis Committee, the Population Reference Bureau, Zero Population Growth, the Population Action Council, regional Planned Parenthood groups—to call upon Congress for a national plan to stop the growth of population.

The reason it has been so easy to promote the belief that 'overpopulation' is the main cause of environmental degradation is that it seems so plausible. I believed it myself, and wrote about it in one of my books some years ago. But is it true?

One of the first things to shake my faith in this belief was Barry Commoner's demonstration that increases in pollution were not proportional to population gowth but to changes in technology. Commoner showed, for example, that the percent increase in pollution due to synthetic pesticides was seven times as great as the percent increase in population between 1947 and 1970 in the United States, while the percent increase in pollution due to nitrogen oxides in motor fuel was sixteen times as great, and the percent increase in pollution due to detergent phosphorus was forty-six times as great as the increase in population. The problem was not that there were too many people but that society was shifting very rapidly to new and highly polluting technologies. This meant that even a drastic reduction in population could not by itself reduce pollution very much. To reduce pollution we would need to attack the polluting technologies directly.

Common sense was a second element in my developing agnosticism. What good, I asked myself, had population control achieved or could it achieve in any of the most polluted places on earth? Could the Chernobyl nuclear accident be attributed in any way to the lack of birth control? Clearly, it was human behaviour, not human numbers, that caused that catastrophe. And it is behaviour, not numbers, which must be the focus of any effective effort to improve the environment.

A third reason for my agnosticism was my growing realization that mankind has always lived in crowded conditions. From the beginning of human history we have crowded together in cities not because of lack of space on the planet but in order to work together, to buy and sell, to exchange goods and services. Our cities and towns have always thronged with people and traffic—horses, donkeys, and camels in ages past, motor vehicles today. Ancient Athens, Rome, Carthage, Beijing, Alexandria were great and crowded cities. Accodingly, Plato, Aristotle, and Confucius, as well as several fathers of the early Christian church worried about 'excessive' population growth.

None of these earlier city-dwelling philosophers could soar over the earth and see that outside of their immediate view there were almost no people at all. And so it is with us. The earth is still mostly empty. Simon has shown that less than 3 percent of the land area in the United States is used for urban settlements and transportation. The biologist Francis P. Felice has shown that all the people in the world could be put into the state of Texas, giving each person the space available in the typical American home. Farmers use less than half of the world's arable land and only a minute part of the water available for irrigation. About thirty per cent of the earth's land area is still covered with forest. Nevertheless, although we have all the room in the world, as the saying goes, we crowd together, but this is not a sign of 'overpopulation'.

Finally, a very serious problem for me is the tendency among some self-proclaimed spokesmen for the environment to slip away from strict truth. Some are making exaggerated claims in order to dramatize and call attention to what they believe is a good cause. Some believe that private owners cannot be trusted to take good care of the environment. Some are seeking money or power, or both, for themselves. Fortunes are being made from the billions of dollars that are being spent ostensibly to improve the environment. Some groups are hoping to frighten people into accepting restrictions on childbearing which they would otherwise not permit.

To illustrate my point, there are many frightening stories about deforestation in Brazil. Population control groups say that this is an ecological catastrophe and that overpopulation is the cause. Brazil covers an area that is 35 times the size of the United Kingdom (121 times the size of Ireland) and has less than one-twelfth as many people per square mile as the United Kingdom (about a third as many people per square mile as Ireland); two-thirds of Brazil—an area 23 times the size of the United Kingdom (81 times the size of Ireland)—is covered with forest.

It is probably true that an area the size of Switzerland was logged in Brazil in 1989. But Switzerland would fit into the forested area of Brazil 138 times; that is, Brazil cut a fraction of 1 percent of its forested area in 1989. This was probably less than the volume of timber growth that was occurring. Moreover, during the 1970's Brazil planted over 250,000 hectares of forest per year.

The Food and Agricultural Organization estimated that world forests covered 4 billion hectares in 1950; again in its 1988 Yearbook the estimate was 4 billion hectares. In 1980 it estimated that there were 2 billion hectares in temperate areas and 2 billion in tropical areas. I counted the areas given for tropical countries in the 1988 Yearbook and found 2 billion hectares, as before.

Hysteria over Brazil and overpopulation only deflects our attention from the real problem and engages our support for activities that will not solve that real problem.

According to Werner Fornos of the Population Institute, 'runaway population growth' is the reason 'earth's forests are disappearing, its top-soils eroding, deserts expanding, its species vanishing, and its ozone layer thinning.' Global climate change is probably the most terrifying ecological threat.

The known facts about climate, however, are less than illuminating. Experts agree and measurements clearly indicate that the carbon dioxide content of the air has increased since the last century from 280 parts per million by volume to 335 parts per million by volume, perhaps as high as 350 ppmV. Some scientists predict that this will cause global warming because of the reduction in the outgoing radiation from earth to space. On the other hand, it is also generally acknowledged that the radiation from the carbon dioxide will cool the stratosphere. There are many unknown factors in the carbon-cycle, not the least of which are the effects of the oceans which cover more than 70 percent of the surface of the earth.

In this 'cascade of uncertainty', as it has been called by two investigators, it is possible to arrive at almost any conclusion, depending on the assumptions one programs into the computer model. The U.S. Environmental Protection Agency resolutely plunged through this sea of unknowns in a recent report to Congress; it simply *assumed* that the earth's temperature will increase by 5 to 9 degress F, an amount which is two to three times higher than the estimates by most other groups. The lesson of this story is that if you want to forecast a catastrophe, just go ahead and do it and forget about reasoning or evidence.

Is there any evidence of global warming in the actual measurements of earth's temperature? James Hansen of the U.S. National Aeronautics and Space Administration says that the globe has warmed by one-half of a degree to seven-tenths of a degree centigrade over the past century.(35) However, a group of scientists at the National Oceanic and Atmospheric Administration studied temperature and rainfall records at 6000 stations in the United States for the past century. They found a great deal of year-to-year variability but no trend upward or downward.(36) Scientists at Massachusetts Institute of Technology have studied records of ocean temperatures which have been collected since the mid-19th century. They report finding 'no appreciable difference between 1856 and 1986.' Whom then should we believe and what should we do?

In view of the uncertainties and disagreements, probably the best counsel is that of Professor H.E. Landsberg, former president of the American Geophysical Union, who, along with other scientists, recommends that we continue measurements and observations until we know more about the situation, and, in the meantime, plant more trees. If this were done intensively in urban areas, it would counteract the buildup of carbon dioxide from the burning of fossil fuels because trees transform carbon dioxide into oxygen.

The alleged depletion of ozone is also fraught with uncertainty. The phenomenon of declining ozone in the stratosphere over Antartica begins in August or September and disappears by November, apparently in relation to the intensity of the sun's rays reaching the area at that season. It has been monitored only during the past decade. The models which have been created to try to explain the occurrence do not account for half the ozone occurring in the stratosphere. This means that we are very far from being able to explain the phenomenon. We don't know whether man-made chlorofluorocarbons or natural sources of chlorine, such as volcanoes in the region, are the cause. We don't know whether the ban on chlorofluorocarbons (CFC's) enacted in 1987 will reduce the so-called 'hole'—so-called because it is believed to be confined to Antartica. CFC's are used in refrigeration equipment; a ban on them will be especially burdensome to the developing countries which are beginning to use refrigeration.

The danger in the loss of ozone is that greater amounts of solar ultraviolet radiation could reach the earth, causing higher rates of skin cancer. However, measurements in the United States between 1974 and 1985 show an actual *decrease* in ultraviolet radiation, the exact opposite of what should be expected if ozone is being depleted. This decrease may be related to the production of *excess* ozone which is a genuine problem in urban areas such as Los Angeles.

(It has been suggested that one reason the ozone hole has become such a popular cause is that the existing patents on chlorofluorocarbons are expiring and their manufacturers now hope to establish new patent monopolies on the substitutes which they are creating. They could do this more easily if the old CFC's were banned.)

The cause of urban air pollution is not human 'overpopulation' but overpopulation of motor vehicles, encouraged by governments that were eager to stimulate the motor vehicle industry. The human population of the United Kingdom grew by about 1 million persons between 1970 and 1987. But the motor vehicle population grew by 11.5 million during that same period. There are now 244 motor vehicles per square mile in the U.K.

I would like to emphasize the importance of prices in improving the environment. When people are allowed to use the air and rivers, lakes, and oceans as 'free' dumping grounds for every kind of waste, as has happened in many countries, especially the industrialized countries, these resources become polluted. Free access, or subsidized access, to any good, whether it is a highway or a fishing ground or a herd of buffalo or a forest, invites overuse and abuse.

Aristotle noticed that people take the best care of their own land and homes and animals because they reap the benefits of their own good work and pay the costs of their own mistakes. Government planners, on the other hand, pass the costs of their mistakes to the public. It is therefore not at all surprising that modern governmental planning for progress is the source of so many environmental as well as economic disasters. The planners have a handy alibi for their failures in alleged 'overpopulation'. But 'overpopulation' is in no way responsible. The problem is misuse of resources and this is the fault of government. When government ignores the full costs of its own projects or allows private citizens to ignore the full costs of their activities, those costs do not disappear but in fact become much larger than they otherwise would be. When no one owns the trees, as in some parts of Africa, no one plants trees but everyone who can find one pulls it up for firewood.

Similarly, when governments do not allow citizens to receive the full benefits of their work, people produce less. Tragic examples of this abound in those countries where governments have required farmers to sell their crops at less than cost; the result has been widespread starvation.

Modern governments, eager to manage everything, are now responding to the perceived environmental threat by spending massive amounts of the taxpayers' money on it. The government money serves as an incentive to invent environmental crises and do all the wrong things about them.

People do respond to economic incentives. This is why we need not fear 'overpopulation'. It has become increasingly costly to raise children and therefore the birth rate has fallen (to a lower level than may be optimal in some countries). But modern governments, committed to the pursuit of 'progress', have encouraged activities which are less benign than raising children and which have placed stress on the environment. In Eastern Europe there is dawning a new appreciation for allowing full-cost-benefit pricing to guide economic activity. If and when this new dawn reaches the rest of the world, there will be new hope for mankind and the environment.

# Contraception: a Scientific Scrutiny

## Dr Niklaus Waldis

The modern methods of contraception are:

1. Ovulation inhibitors, usually called oral contraceptives, OCs or 'the pill'
2. The inter-uterine device, or IUD, also called 'the coil'
3. Male or female sterilisation
4. The sheath, or condom
5. Spermicides

The big breakthrough in family planning came with the ovulation inhibitors in the late fifties/early sixties. They were invented by Pincus, tested in Costa Rica and Haiti, and then put on the market.

The IUD made of ceramics already existed at the beginning of this century, but it was dropped due to bad experiences. In our age of new synthetic materials it has made a comeback.

Sterilisation has also been long known. The large scale breakthrough came with the new surgical technique of laparoscopy, which made laparotomy unnecessary.

The condom was long despised, and superceded by the other methods. It regained a very dubious form of respectability only because of the spread of AIDS.

There is no doubt that we owe the revolution in contraception to the ovulation inhibitors.

## 1 *Ovulation inhibitors*

Mechanisms — inhibition of ovulation
— cervical mucus
— tubal factor
— inhibition of nidation

At this point let me briefly explain conception, and the development of the new human being during the first few days of its life.

From the vagina, the sperm pass through the cervix. The cervical glands produce mucus both as a barrier and a nutrient for the sperm. The sperm continue their way up the uterus (womb) into the fallopian tubes. Here, they meet the egg. This comes out of the ovary during ovulation. After conception, the new human being develops and is progressively moved down to the uterus via the tubes. This takes a few days. There, the embryo is implanted in the endometrium for further nutrition and growth. This is what we call nidation or implantation.

The pill was originally meant to inhibit ovulation by suppressing the ovaries with high doses of female hormones. Due to adverse side effects, the hormone content of the pills had to be reduced. Nevertheless, it could be proved that ovulation occurred in an average of 7% of cycles. Ovulation always produces a chance of conception and pregnancy. The actual pregnancy rate was less than the 7% predicted, therefore other factors which might have interfered had to be sought.

Some said that thickening of the cervical mucus creates a barrier against the ascending sperm, but this barrier isn't that effective. Two other mechanisms turned out to be more important: the tubal factor and the inhibition of nidation. The hormonal change caused by the pill affects the movements of the tubes. The transport of the embryo is thus slowed down. By the time it reaches the uterus, the embryo is too old and can no longer survive. It literally dries out, failing to achieve the life-saving implantation which would provide the necessary nutrition for further development. This is an early abortive mechanism.

The pill also changes the endometrium in such a way that, even if the embryo reaches the womb in time, nidation cannot take place because the endometrium is insufficiently developed, and the embryo dies—another early abortive mechanism.

Now we can understand a statement made in the USA in 1985 at the National Abortion Federation Congress: 'Make no mistake, the pill and IUD are abortive'.

## *Side-effects of the pill*

There is much controversy about the side-effects of ovulation inhibitors. These side-effects were all known at the end of the sixties, but it took twenty years before they became generally known to the public. I list the most important side-effects which are generally recognised as being caused by oral contraceptives (OCs).

*(a) Cardiovascular side-effects.* In Britain in 1977, the Royal College of General Practitioners published a retrospective study in the 'Lancet', followed in 1981 by a prospective study, each over a time span representing two hundred thousand woman-years. According to these studies, takers and ex-takers of OCs suffered a death rate from cardio- and cerebro-vascular side-effects 40% above the average, especially from heart attacks and brain haemorrhages, whether they had taken the pill for a long or for a short time. The risk to the woman increased with age, particularly for those over 35, and was multiplied by smoking. Further studies confirmed this: the risk of brain haemorrhage for smokers was 5.7 times greater than for non-smokers, for OC takers 6.5 times greater than for non-takers, and for those who both smoked and took OCs, this risk was 22 times greater.

There is a clear risk of thrombo-embolisms associated with use of the pill. Even the 17–24 age group was affected. The incidence of side-effects remained the same after oestrogen doses were reduced. The risk of thrombo-embolism was particularly high with some of the newest micropills containing 'gestoden'.

The risk was so high that the West German Health Ministry felt obliged to issue a preliminary warning pointing out the risk of veinous thrombosis from the pill. It is worth noting the defensive efforts of the pill manufacturers, who made futile attempts to whitewash it, but the West German Health Ministry would certainly not have issued a public warning without good reason.

*(b) Promotion of infection.* Some studies showed a reduced risk of pelvic inflammatory disease (PID) with the pill. However, more recent studies between 1987 and 1989 proved the opposite: women who take the pill suffer a 70% higher rate of chlamydial and gonococcal infections than those who do not take it.

OCs encourage chlamydial infections in the true pelvis. These are more difficult to recognise, diagnose and treat than other infections, e.g. gonococcal infections. These female genital infections lead to more extra-uterine pregnancies, to sterility and to premature deliveries; and the newborn child can be infected during delivery, with chlamydia, resulting in potentially fatal pulmonary infection.

A recent American theory suggests a possible link between the spread of AIDS and ovulation inhibitors, even independently of sexual behaviour. It proposes that, as OCs are steroid hormones similar to cortisone, they weaken the immune system and help the spread not only of chlamydia infections but also of AIDS. Investigations are being made to determine if even viruses can mutate into the dangerous HIV forms, e.g. because of changes in the vaginal environment brought about by ovulation inhibitors.

*(c) Cancer risk.* The occurrence of cervical cancer increases with the strength of the pill and the length of use. It should also be noted that smoking 20 or more cigarettes a day increases the risk of contracting cervical cancer 3–4 times. Increasing quantities of alcohol were responsible for pre-cancerous changes.

Apart from that, we know today that the earlier the first sexual activity, the less hygienic the first partner, and the more often partners are changed, the sooner cervical cancer is likely to develop.

This sexual behaviour is, of course, closely associated with modern contraception.

High-dosed combination preparations afford protection against cancer of the womb. Sequenced, and all other preparations, increase the risk of cancer of the endometrium. Therefore 'Oracon' was the only sequenced preparation to be taken off the market. As the high-dosed preparations are hardly ever used today, due to their cardiovascular side-effects, this protective effect is reduced or even completely absent.

The use of OCs protects against ovarian cancer, according to the length of use. Since these results stem from old studies with high-dosed pills, it is possible that the protective effect is lessened as the dose is reduced. This has still to be investigated.

The risk of contracting breast cancer increases with the length of OC use. This has been confirmed in a study carried out by the Imperial Cancer Research Fund's epidemiology unit in Oxford, and published last year in the 'Lancet'. Progestagen-only pills may have a protective effect.

Professor Joyeux, a French cancer specialist, also sees a significant connection between OCs and breast cancer. Because the carcinoma involved only appears after many years, numerous studies which discount such a connection are unreliable, as they were made over too short a time span. At present, there is an explosive increase in breast cancer. However, in Europe this is not discussed, in contrast to the USA, where OC-use is falling extremely rapidly.

In China, there has been a return to natural methods because sterilisation and OCs were too expensive, and due to a proven increase of breast cancer.

Taking the pill for more than 4 years increases the risk of skin and liver cancer.

*(d) Psychological and sexual side-effects.* As psychological disorders the pill may cause depressive moods varying to full blown depression.

Especially with the newer oral contraceptives, a large proportion of women suffer from a reduced libido, to the point of total loss. This can be traced back both to the hormonal effect and to the separation of sexuality and procreation made possible for the first time by the pill.

It is known that simply the possibility of becoming pregnant significantly raises the libido. If, however, a method of family planning is used which deliberately excludes the possibility of reproduction, nature subconsciously switches off with time, resulting in loss of libido. It is interesting to note that, given time, even a total loss of libido can be reversed after discontinuation of the pill. This has frequently been demonstrated by a change to natural family planning.

*(e) Various side-effects.* Oral contraceptives also cause benign tumors of the cervix, ovary, breast and liver. They produce gastrointestinal changes and eye disorders.

Anomalies of babies occur more often, if the mother becomes pregnant whilst using the pill or within 6 months after discontinuation. This could be proved with histological examinations of spontaneous abortions. Maybe the effect of those babies who had chromosomal breaks and survived, will appear only in the next generations.

## Contradictions in the literature

If we look through all the publications concerning the pill, we find much controversy. It is not rare that a study is contradicted by a following one. Considering the matter logically, something doesn't add up. The truth cannot include both points of view, so at the very least, doubts must arise.

The lawyers say 'in dubio pro reo'. This applies as well to medicine, but here the doubts should plead for the patients. A doctor must stand by his hippocratic oath 'primum non nocere', above all never to harm the patient.

Never before has such a potent drug with so many unknown qualities been administered to healthy people for no medical reason. Never before, after the discovery of so many serious side-effects, has a drug been kept on the market as long as the pill. Never before was there a drug which brought the pharmaceutical industry so much money. In the USA, the pill has been described as the biggest money-maker in pharmaceutics.

## 2 The intra-uterine device (IUD)

The coil is primarily an early abortive device. Implantation of the embryo is prevented by a reactive inflammation of the endometrium. Even the copper content of the modern coil makes no difference to this in principle.

As side-effects, infections are important here too. They frequently lead to tubal occlusion, sterility and a great risk of tubal or ovarian pregnancies. Fitting an IUD to a nulliparous woman thus constitutes malpractice in terms of conventional gynaecology. Perforation of the wall of the womb can also occur, with the risk of injury e.g. to the intestines. Bleeding and pain are further side-effects.

For these reasons, around 2,500 lawsuits are pending in the USA with damages claims into the $ billions. This is why the coil was removed from the American market in early 1987. According to some sources of information, this was done by the industry itself even before the Food and Drug Administration had announced a ban. This clever move was intended to enable production of the coil to continue with the aim of exporting it. Further exports would have been very adversely affected by the FDA's verdict.

## 3 Sterilisation

Male or female sterilisation is a surgically irreversible method of birth control. For men the surgical risk is very low. For females there are several risks, about the same as for any abdominal surgery under general anaesthetic, but with an increased risk rate if sterilisation follows delivery or abortion. As sterilisation is not an essential operation, these risks are definitely too high. They should be near zero as for any other type of elective surgery.

The subsequent effects are extrauterine pregnancies due to failure of sterilisation. Extrauterine pregnancies of any origin are held responsible for around 10% of deaths of mothers in childbirth. Other effects are increased tampon shock syndrome and period disorders resulting in more hysterectomies.

In men sterilisation may lead to kidney damages.

Sterilisation causes sexual and psychiatric disorders in both males and females. Questioned about it, many of those who have undergone sterilisation loudly proclaim their satisfaction, but on the other hand report unwelcome circumstances afterwards, which they nevertheless dissociate completely from the operation. This ambivalence gnaws at their subconscious and causes even greater difficulties.

The risk of developing these problems is particularly high for persons who are sterilised in association with delivery, caesarian section or abortion, who are sterilised for medical, psychiatric or eugenic reasons, as it is for those who already have disturbed personalities prior to the operation or who have problems in relationships and poor contraceptive motivation.

This shows that sterilisation, in other words the definitive loss of fertility, is an act which cuts deeply. In 1978 about 5% of women regretted their sterilisation. According to medical literature, this had already risen to 10–15% by 1986. Last year on German TV they said it was 80%. This tendency is self-explanatory.

## 4 Sheath or condom

The condom is a means of birth control with only preventive and no abortive action. Criticised due to its very high failure rate, it has now suddenly regained popularity as protections against AIDS. Given time, you will contract AIDS from an infected partner even if you always use condoms. The reason is straightforward:

Investigations showed that intact quality-proved condoms have microscopic holes. These holes are wide enough to allow 30–50 AIDS viruses to pass through. Now you can imagine how safe it is to use condoms. It also shows the irresponsibility in the information on protection against AIDS.

## 5 Spermicides

These too, are very unreliable as a means of birth control. There is, however, a new aspect: all spermicides containing the substance 'Nonoxinol-9' not only disrupt some functions of the sperm, but also cause chromosome changes, so that abnormalities of the embryos can result. Nevertheless deformities have not yet been proved. The attitude of some producers is that the resulting abnormal embryos would in any case usually be lost in early abortions. Thus here too is an early abortive mechanism, which was previously unrecognised.

## Summary and consequences of contraception for society

These then, are the risks to the individual. What are the side-effects of artificial contraception for society as a whole?

1. Modern 'anti-conception' enabled excessive sexual permissiveness through the separation of sex and reproduction. Sex became the number one consumer-good and increasingly took place outside the community of marriage. Among young people, the age at which the first sexual experience took place fell drastically.
2. Destruction of the moral foundations of the Western world, particularly the Christian countries, by the sexual revolution and legalised abortion. The latter is currently the most widely-used method of family planning. (According to the WHO, about 50 million abortions a year.) In particular, this destroys the morals of the young.
3. A massive population 'implosion' in the industrialised nations.
4. Devastating medical side-effects, above all from the pill and the coil, resulting in further burdens on overloaded health services and budgets.
5. An increase in sexually transmitted diseases (STDs) due to sexual permissiveness. The consequences of this are increasing tubal pregnancies and tubal sterility. This provides material for artificial reproduction techniques such as IVF and thus reproduction separated from sex. So a vicious circle is set up.
6. The spread of Aids as the worst form of sexual transmitted disease, through the changes in sexual habits. OCs are possibly directly involved in the spread by encouraging the mutations of viruses into

more malignant forms, facilitating infection and promoting the onset of illness through 'steroid-like' weakening of the immune system.
7. Abortion could not be stemmed by contraception. Artificial family planning was promoted with the slogan 'prevention is better than abortion', supported by certain moral theologians. As abortion was and will continue to be necessary to safeguard against failures of contraception, it comes as no surprise to discover that the very same lobbies promoted both contraception and abortion. The latter has increased most in those countries with the highest acceptance rate of anti-conception. Thus the slogan 'prevention is better than abortion' is shown to be inaccurate.
8. The search for new, more perfect methods of family planning, as modern contraception is unsatisfactory due to the side-effects and failure rates. These are now available in the form of RU 486 (progesterone antagonist) and Epostane (progesterone syntheses blocker) combined with prostaglandins, which enable medicinal abortion into the later stages of pregnancy, replacing most of the surgical abortions. There is also the Antibaby-Vaccine (anti-HCG-vaccine) soon to come into use, likewise a method of early abortion.

If we consider the whole matter soberly and logically, we have to admit that the price we pay for modern artificial contraception is very high. Is this a price we should have to pay?

The way out of this situation cannot lie in the development of further, more effective, safer contraceptives—even if these really were preventive and not abortive in their mechanism—but in the cessation of sexual permissiveness. A new understanding of sexuality must be established. Quote the usually liberal-minded publishers of the '*Obstetrical and Gynaecological Survey*': 'Multiple partners—promiscuity, if you will—does not make for good monogamous marriage. Broken homes make "orphans of our children"..... We need to preach the gospel of premarital abstinence. As women's primary physicians, we have the responsibility for at least trying to educate them.'

Modern, especially young, people must be refamiliarised with the creative sense and purpose of sex. We must learn anew to grasp the full import of the words 'made in His image'. The only course which will do justice to the complete human being in a dignified manner is, in my opinion, Natural Family Planning (NFP).

# Parents and Children: Education in Human Relationships

## *Mercedes Arzu Wilson*

From 1983–1987, Family of the Americas developed and field tested a family-centred educational programme in human sexuality which promotes chastity and respect for life. It is offered in four sessions:
- The Family as a Centre of Love and Life
- Discovering Self-Worth and Establishing Communication
- The Normal Growth and Development of Human Sexuality
- Respect for Human Fertility: The Wonder of Life.

The programme was developed to strengthen the family as the first and best source of education in human sexuality for children, and this goal was accomplished because it:
- involves parents and their children in an educational process based on traditional family values;
- develops and strengthens communication among family members;
- helps parents identify and communicate their values to their children;
- builds and reinforces the confidence of parents in helping their children through the difficult times of puberty and decision-making;
- provides information about child and adolescent development, and
- presents the latest research about the anatomy and physiology of human fertility, and respect for life from the moment of conception.

The main objective of our programme is to counteract the many sex education programmes that are placing our youth in serious danger not only of totally destroying their innocence early in life, but also encouraging them to experiment prematurely in sexual activity.

## The importance of the family

Early family life and how it is interpreted by the child contributes a great deal to the formation of attitudes, values and behaviours which are likely to endure into and throughout adult life. It is true that the family is not the only molding force in a child's life; schools, friends and institutions of higher learning also influence attitudes and values. However, nothing has greater impact on a child's life than his family experience. When children receive proper training in the home, they will develop the ability to recognize the truth when they hear it or reject falsehood and propaganda when they encounter it in the outside world.

Parents must communicate to their young children that life does have meaning and that everyone has a unique purpose and mission in life.

The child will carry the influence of this early training with him wherever he goes, and it will continue to influence his behaviour whether he realizes it or not.

While changes within our society have resulted in many variations of the traditional family structure, the basic needs of children have not changed. Children continue to have two basic needs which are important to their becoming healthy human beings:

- the need for unconditional love and affection
- the need to know that they are unique and irreplaceable.

While our present society is able to accommodate many variations of family life, it is important to continue promoting and striving for the ideal family structure in which children are cared for by both a mother and a father in an unbroken marriage bond.

In today's modern society, we sometimes hear parents relishing the time when their children will be out of the house or out of college so that their burden of responsibilty can be over. Parents must never lose sight of the fact that their children are their responsibility forever. They must never insinuate that their children are a burden because children are extremely sensitive. Instead, parents should let their children know that no matter what moral or physical crisis they might encounter, they will always stand by them. When children have this kind of assurance, they are more likely to come to the parents first with their problems.

Children who are cherished and valued by their parents will feel the same desire to care for the frail and aging parents instead of putting them in an institution where they are likely to receive impersonal care and feel unwanted and forgotten by family and friends. The elderly also need a purpose in life, to have someone to live for and someone who cares. Experience shows that caring for elderly members in the home brings great benefits to the family. For example, children learn to be loving, caring, and considerate as a result of doing things for others in the home. This adds greatly to the child's feelings of self-worth.

And so the circle of love and life continues—parents bring children into the world with love and these same children see the aging parents out of this world with love. This is how love and life have been perpetuated by families down through the centuries.

And now we enter the subject of sex education. Parents are the primary educators of their children in all matters, including human sexuality.

Parents are the real 'experts' when it comes to education in human sexuality, for a number of reasons:

1. Parents love their children and have their best interests at heart.

2. Parents know their children and their needs better than anyone else.
3. Parents convey attitudes and values about life and sexuality as they interact with their children each day; in fact, children learn primarily from this 'modelling' by the parents.
4. Parents are the guardians of their vulnerable children and need to protect them from sexually explicit information which tends to break down the innocence and natural modesty of children.
5. Parents are available to their children for support, questions, etc.
6. Parents have much wisdom to share which comes from the faithful living out of their commitment as husband and wife and parents.

## Dangers confronting the family

Many family experts are telling us that the basic structure of our society, the family, is under assault in a way unprecedented in history. Many social scientists see the breakup of the family as potentially more destructive than the atomic bomb.

The idea that each person should pursue material gratification and pleasure as one of life's goals is constantly propagated in the mass media. Prof. Viktor Frankl says:

> 'The problem of our time is that people are caught by a pervasive feeling of meaninglessness accompanied by a feeling of emptiness. Our industrial society is out to satisfy all needs and our consumer society is even out to create needs in order to satisfy them. But the most human of all needs, the need to see meaning in one's life, remains unsatisfied. People may have enough to live by, but more often than not they do not have anything to live for. This is most perceptible in the younger generation... and consists of depression, aggression and addiction. There is ample empirical evidence to the effect that suicide proneness, violent behaviour and drug dependency are, in fact, due to a loss of meaning.'

On the other hand, teens who have been taught to love and respect themselves and others, who have received loving discipline from their parents, and who have observed and been inspired by the generosity and gentleness of their parents, will have a realistic optimism toward the future.

It is a known fact that human beings cannot live without love. If this love is not provided in generous amounts by the parents, children will usually seek it in the first person who gives them any kind of attention and this could lead to serious problems.

Unfortunately, many teens do not have a positive attitude toward the future because they have not experienced the happiness that comes from unconditional love within the family.

Even within intact families there is often an absence of values and goals to guide the decisions and activities of the family. In many cases, both parents are working and working increasingly longer hours. These families have accomplished having a TV set in the living room, kitchen, and bedroom. Everyone of driving age in the family has a car and family members travel to vacation spots all around the globe. Many of these families appear to have lost sight of what truly has lasting value in their lives and the lives of their children—things such as acts of mercy and kindness for others less fortunate. Sharing what one has with others can bring a rich meaning to life, produce emotional and spiritual growth and become a family's greatest and richest contribution to the future of the family, community, and nation.

Conversely, the parents' relationship can be a major stumbling block in the rearing of children. Ill will between parents can often cause one parent to deliberately oppose the other, especially on issues relating to discipline. For example, one parent may attempt to compensate for unfairness or harshness toward the child on the part of the other parent; the compensating parent may put up with misbehaviour, shower the child with gifts or become permissive when the child asks to do something he is not ordinarily allowed to do. When parents get into this kind of power struggle, the children may use it as an opportunity to manipulate both parents to get what they want. The child learns which parent is willing to be the 'pushover' and will consistently go to this parent with requests. Deep down the parent knows this permissiveness is damaging to the child and destructive of family and marriage.

Children who experience strong and loving parental leadership within the family feel secure. Children respect and trust parents who are not afraid to be strong leaders. Children need and want their parents to be in charge.

Values are taught by word and example. What one is makes more of an impression than what one says. Parents who are good models not only verbally communicate their values to their children, but also live out these values in their daily lives so that the children see their parents are people of integrity.

Throughout life, children observe their parents and gradually parents begin to see the results of the upbringing in the home. What parents provide for their children during these formative years will ultimately determine the course of their children's lives and what they will become.

Friends must be chosen who have similar values; otherwise, the adolescent will face strong pressure to conform.

## *Discovering self-worth and establishing communication*

Every person is born with self-worth, an inherent value and dignity, which cannot be earned or taken away. Children, whose parents are able to help them discover their true dignity as persons, are likely to grow into healthy adults who are capable of loving and being loved.

Even in families hurting from a broken marriage, the committed love of one or both parents can work against this happening with the children. While separated or divorced couples may not be able to live with each other, they can maintain a committed relationship with the children, which will enhance their own self-worth as well as that of their children.

Even the courage eventually to leave the family and become independent comes from healthy relationships within the family; healthy family living produces individuals who feel secure in their own worth and ability to be able to establish a life for themselves while maintaining a healthy bonding with their family of origin.

Love is the best preventive measure parents can use to insulate their children. If children receive love in the home, they are less likely to go out and seek it elsewhere. And they are less likely to make harmful decisions which would bring shame to their family because they cannot bear the thought of hurting those with whom they have loving and caring relationships.

Parents must be sensitive to the child's need to feel loved even when he has failed. Discipline should be loving and directed to the correction of the problem rather than the destruction of the spirit of hopefulness within the heart of the child.

Parental obligation will, at times, require that parents put aside their plans in order to be available to help their children. This commitment cannot be compromised because of the convenience or difficulty of a particular situation. Parents must be willing to do whatever is necessary to help their children, even when it is not easy or convenient.

Yet... **love is an attitude of fulfillment rather than sacrifice** because when we love another person nothing we do is too much; loving others brings out the best in us and makes us realize that the pleasure of giving surpasses that of receiving. This is illustrated by the fact that, as children mature, they derive much more pleasure from the giving than receiving.

This brings up the issue of 'spoiling children' by giving them all they ask for or want. The child's need is for love not things. Sometimes parents feel guilty because they have not spent enough time with their children and they try to compensate with material gifts. This is not done for the child but to make the parents feel better. Especially when families are materially wealthy, parents will have to discipline themselves by not giving too much to the child. Children learn gratitude and appreciation best when they must plan and wait for something they want rather than have it given them without any effort on their part.

The problems of small children tend to carry over into adult life and are often expressed in problems and infidelity in marriage. Adults who were spoiled as children were never required to be thoughtful, considerate and responsible.

The ability to look beyond oneself, to give to others without expecting anything in return, are hallmarks of the person who really understands what love is.

Affection is the easy part of love that comes naturally to most parents. It's easy to forget children's continuous need for affection as they grow older, especially as they approach the teen years when there is a natural tendency to distance themselves from parents and family. Likewise, parents need and want expressions of affection from their children/adolescents. After all, parents are people too and people never outgrow the need for affection.

Sometimes parents are quick to discipline and slow to give recognition for good behaviour. On one hand, parents want their children to behave and act maturely but, on the other hand, they tend to forget that good behaviour is learned and needs reinforcement.

Discipline is an expression of love and an education in justice.

Adolescents often go through periods when they want more freedom without an increase in responsibility. Granting a request for greater freedom should be based on the willingness and ability to accept the increase in responsibility.

When a parent acts irresponsibly and grants this privilege before the teenager is prepared, it is a disservice to the community as well as to the teen. If the teenager were to have an accident under these circumstances and sustain a permanent disability, he may well blame his parents for allowing him a privilege before he was mature enough to handle it.

## Communication and the art of listening

Because family values are often in conflict with the values of our society, parents have to take a stronger stand for their own values and make sure they communicate these to their children through example as well as verbally. Nowadays, some consider it 'normal' and healthy for young people to become sexually intimate before marriage. And it is discouraging to note the number of parents who have bought into this philosophy. Parents must emphasize to them that normal and healthy adolescent relationships do not include sexual intimacy.

A promiscuous relationship is an inappropriate and unhealthy substitute for other kinds of communication because:

1. When sexual intimacy comes before marriage, the relationship loses its potential for true intimacy and becomes purely physical.
2. The couple bypass the important steps of getting to know each other. They get locked into using sexual intimacy as a substitute for authentic communication.
3. Once people become involved physically, it is twice as hard to go back to the gradual sharing of thoughts and interests that form solid relationships.

## The struggle of the family

The most essential requirement for honest communication between individuals is trust and confidence. This is no less true when it involves communication between parents and their children. Through this daily contact and interaction, children will come to value their parents not only as leaders and teachers, but as their most trusted friends.

## The normal growth and development of children and adolescents

For a young person, the proper understanding of sexuality is not something that occurs because a parent has explained human sexuality well in a one-time discussion. Chastity formation is part of a youngster's identity formation and begins long before the teenage years.

Words of advice and gifts of your best wisdom will be listened to carefully. Sometimes puberty-aged youngsters appear to be scoffing and not listening, but this is often a smokescreen to hide their true feelings and interest. Do not be dismayed by it; just impart what you want them to know. Impart it as lovingly and carefully as you can, and if you do it clumsily, don't worry.

Children of all ages seek to please their parents. If they feel it is impossible to win their parents' esteem, love and respect, they will try to get it elsewhere because no one can live without love.

In spite of all this, however, we know that rejection of parental values can occur even when parents have done their best. There are strong forces in the environment which may seduce children into experimenting sexually or with drugs. However, when parents have been consistently and unconditionally loving during the early years, children almost always return to parental values after a time of maturing.

Girls would be shocked to hear boys often admit to the fact that they many times use promiscuous girls as mere objects of pleasure and then discard them and would never consider any of them to be the mother of their children. It seems that girls are willing to give a little bit of sex for a lot of love, and boys are only willing to give a little bit of love for a lot of sex, until they become more mature and serious about looking for a future wife.

It is particularly important that we help young women understand how society has manipulated them into believing that they must compete with men instead of giving themselves wholeheartedly to the unique contribution of the feminine influence which our world needs so badly.

There are many sexually immature young men and women in society because they have not learned self-control. Somehow, we have assumed that sexual maturity involves the ability to lift the barriers of sexual discipline rather than the ability to be in control of our actions. This discipline should be taught from early childhood as a preparation for the future. The need for self-discipline in sexuality is no different from the need for that trait in every other aspect of our daily lives.

It would be a strange society indeed if the government said cigarettes are wrong, alcohol is wrong, drugs are wrong, lying, stealing, and all forms of violence are wrong, but in sex you can do no wrong.

It is the job of parents and educators to assure young people that they are capable of leading ordered and responsible sexual lives. We all have a responsibility to our own bodies, to the welfare of those we love and are responsible for, and to society at large, including the generations to come.

But what can parents do if they suspect that their older teen is sexually involved? Turn against him/her or grudgingly accept the situation in order not to lose their own son or daughter? This is not an unusual situation in today's permissive society which condones this kind of widespread behaviour.

Parents are sometimes reluctant to voice their strong disapproval and therefore give tacit approval to the situation. A parent may even feel compassion for young people who are sexually active because they think it is impossible to control sexual impulses at this age or not follow suit when everyone is doing it. Parents who were able to contain their sexual desires before marriage should not allow themselves to be deceived into believing that this generation of young children cannot accomplish the same goal. However, if parents do not practice self-control themselves, they will not believe that teens can control themselves either. Confused and misguided, parents encourage promiscuity when they provide prophylactics and the Pill for their adolescents, thinking this will solve the problem of an unwanted pregnancy, instead of realizing that this promotes adolescent immaturity and the possibility of further difficulties in their later years.

Tell your son or daughter that there is a higher incidence of divorce among couples who have lived together before marriage and a greater prevalence of cervical cancer among women who were promiscuous during the teen years.

Women at high risk for developing cervical cancer are those who are sexually active before age 20, those who have sexual intercourse with three or more partners before age 25 or who have intercourse with someone who has had three partners. This information may be enough to encourage young people to abandon this lifestyle and recommit themselves to chastity. Another practical point is the fact that a large portion of those who find their way to top positions in the more honourable corporations and professions have done so with the support of intact families.

Raising teenage children will certainly challenge your growth level, identity and abilities as a parent. As a matter of fact, it may challenge almost everything about you. But faithfulness and dedication to your children will be important parts of your own growth as a person. It may not be easy, but God does give special help to parents. You are co-creators with Him, and He too has a vested interest in them.

# Natural Family Planning: the Scientific Background

## Dr Eric Odeblad

When I was a medical student in the early 1940s, we learned that the cervix is a canal, the sperm goes in, 9 months later the baby comes out, and we also learned that there could be cancer in the cervix. However, science has progressed and I have had the opportunity to contribute a little in this field and so I will try to explain about the physiology of the cervix, how it acts and what mucus is and its role in natural family planning.

When I started my research on cervical mucus in the beginning of the 1950s, all people believed that the mucus plug as a whole changed during the cycle. But this turned out later on not to be so. It turned out that the cervix actually has the capability of producing 3 different mucus types.

There is very fluid mucus allowing the sperm to swim. There is intermediate viscosity mucus which has the capacity to attract sperm cells which are not normal. So only the high quality sperm cells are allowed to progress beyond the uterine cavity and to fertilise the egg cell. Then there is very high viscosity mucus. Before the fertile phase and after the fertile phase, this mucus forms a plug which does not allow any sperm cells at all to penetrate into the cervical canal.

The cervix is a much more complicated organ than we usually believe and for me the cervix is an ingeniously created organ which has a very important function in fertility to regulate the sperm entrance and the sperm selection in the cervix, and that this last function is very, very important for the health of mankind.

Diseases of various kinds in the cervix can disturb the reproductive functions of a woman. When the mucus symptom begins, there is an increased secretion, first of the intermediate mucus and then of the very fluid type. These two mucus types together form what we call the fertile type mucus.

Let us then examine how the crypts in the cervix are arranged. The crypts are the units secreting various types of mucus. The cervix is made up of about 400 to 500 crypts. Some of them produce the fluid mucus allowing the sperm to be transmitted; some of them produce the intermediate mucus allowing the low quality sperm to be removed from the swimming sperm collection. There is also a crypt producing the high-viscosity mucus.

So the cervix is made up of secretory units called the *crypts*. Some diseases can affect some of the crypts but not all. While each crypt contains thousands of cells, there are thousands of small cells, each cell secreting mucus. All these secretions must be co-ordinated; they must occur synchronously, to have a good function of the cervix, and this synchronism is regulated by the hormones. The nervous system also plays a role here. There are nerves coming into the cervix which can modify and change a secretion. But the main regulation of this function is just the hormones.

In my research I was able to go into this crypt, insert into single crypts a very, very small glass capillary, and remove mucus from one secretory unit, and I could measure the viscosity of the mucus coming from one isolated secretory unit. After examining a large number of samples we saw clearly the presence of these 3 mucus types. In there were imprisoned sperm cells. Nearly all of them were in the low viscosity mucus. This was definite scientific evidence that the cervix secretes 3 mucus types and that low viscosity mucus is the sperm conducting mucus, which we call the S mucus, (S for sperm transmission). The intermediate viscosity sperm mucus (called L) locks in the low quality sperm cells. And the G mucus, forms a grid through which the sperm cells cannot pass and it forms a mucus plug in the cervix during the infertile phases of the cycle.

There is a correlation between the fertile periods and the various types of mucus, and the charting of the woman's mucus symptom. We have made hundreds of records like this.

The stretchiness of the mucus varies during the cycle, and the cervix functions a little differently in different age groups. In younger women there is a longer period of fertile mucus; a young woman is fertile during more days in the cycle than the elder woman is.

We must recognise how complicated the function of the cervical mucus really is. In the S mucus, (sperm conducted mucus) there are molecular aggregates which are hanging down and vibrating in the mucus, and these vibrations help the sperm cells to swim upwards. So there is actually a co-operation between husband and wife in fertilisation in a way I think we have not known before. In a microscopic scale there is a co-operation between the woman's mucus and the husband's semen to achieve the best possible conditions for fertilising the egg cell.

It gives an illustration of what research has done, and can do, and will do in the future, to understand natural family planning. There still remains many fields of research which will help us in the future to improve the natural family planning methods and make these methods available in the future for more and more women with diseases of various kinds and in all parts of the world.

# Natural Family Planning—the Experience of a Teacher

## Mrs Veronica Pierson

I learned about Natural Family Planning from Doctors John and Evelyn Billings, an Australian-born couple from Melbourne. Dr John is an eminent neurologist and Dr Lyn a pediatrician and endocrionologist.

Dr John Billings was first approached by a marriage guidance counsellor in the 50's and asked if he would try to research a natural means of controlling fertility which was acceptable to people generally. The reason he was asked was that it was known that he and his wife Lyn (Evelyn) had (and still have) a particularly good marriage relationship. He started to do some research but soon discovered that the symptom upon which the method was to be based was the most important parameter of fertility and something only the woman could experience, namely the cervical mucus secretion. He therefore asked his wife Lyn to help him, and along with a hundred couples and scientists from various parts of the world they perfected the Ovulation Method some thirty years ago. The method is now used in 122 countries and by more than 50 million couples, and the World Health Organisation puts it at 99% effective when correctly learnt and used by a motivated couple. Though scientifically based it is very simple. Dr Evelyn Billing's book 'The Billings Method of Family Planning' was recently featured in the Bestsellers Window of Foyle's Bookshop.

This natural method takes advantage of the biological fact that women are infertile more often than fertile throughout their reproductive years.

Through the Billings Method, a woman learns to recognise the fertile phase within her menstrual cycle. The phase is that time when conception may occur, and is accompanied by the secretion of a particular type of mucus from the cervical crypts in the uterus. The mucus developes several days prior to ovulation (release of the egg from the ovary), therby giving early awareness of impending fertility. This mucus is necessary for sperm survival and transport.

Prior to learning the method, some women have thought that the mucus was an abnormality, perhaps an infection, and have sought treatment for it.

The practice of the Ovulation Method provides an extremely effective way of birth regulation. Scientific studies indicate that with proper instruction and motivation, this method in actual practice is 98% effective while being far safer than the most popular artificial or chemical methods.

Family planning should not be simply a means of preventing birth but must involve the whole person and our ability to respond to one another. The family is its own individual society and society is built on the family. The very way in which a couple relate to one another regarding their sexuality will be absorbed by any children they already have and will affect the future behavioural pattern they will have regarding their sexuality when they grow up and there will be nothing at that stage that the parents can do about it except watch and pray.

Sadly we see one in three marriages breaking down and a high percentage of infertile couples. It is normal for one in ten couples to be infertile but when I started teaching N.F.P. in 1979 it was one in eight. Now the official figure is one in six but I believe it to be nearer to one in three or four couples who are sterile. Perhaps we should ask ourselves why? Sexually transmitted diseases are more rampant than any other form of disease. There are, for example, 18 kinds of genital wart viruses. Something in the order of 13 of them lead to cancer of the cervix. We are told that the condom will help to prevent sexually transmitted diseases. Its lowest failure rate if 5% but the real failure rate of the condom is more like between 15 and 25 per cent and that is only, on average, on 25% of a woman's cycle. There is hardly a day goes by that I don't receive a call from someone saying 'The condom split or burst, what do I do?'

My Natural Family Planning Centre in Vauxhall in South West London is in the telephone directory amongst Family Planning Clinics and most people do not know the difference between Natural Family Planning and artificial means of birth control. It was Professor Jerome Lejeune who told me that for every year that a woman takes the birth control pill her cervix ages two years. It is sad for women who put their career first and come off the Pill in their thirties only to find difficulty conceiving.

My work has involved not only teaching more than a thousand people, mainly couples, but also giving a variety of group and public talks. In the school year of '88–'89 I gave 27 lectures in a London school to sixth form groups. Initially it was meant to be four talks but they kept inviting me back.

In the 1920s two doctors worked out that ovulation occurred about two weeks before menstruation and that the woman was fertile for a few days before ovulation and a few days afterwards. If she took a series of calculations over six months she could say that she was, for example, infertile from day 1, to day 10, and then fertile from day 10, to day 18, and then infertile for the rest of the cycle. The trouble came when there was a one off very short cycle or a one off much longer cycle. It is however, worth noting that this Calendar Rhythm Method was as effective in its time as the condom.

The Temperature Method was the second of the natural methods to be developed and came into being in the 1950's. It requires the woman to take her temperature first thing every morning and keep a simple graph. This graph will show that the temperature rises slightly (point one or point two centigrade) after ovulation has occurred and tells the woman that she is infertile from the fourth day after the rise until the next mentrual period occurs. If the woman is pregnant the temperature will stay up until the baby is born.

The Ovulation Method (the Billings Method) was the third natural method to be developed. As I have explained, the Ovulation Method relies on the fact that at some time between menstruations, a woman has a white or colourless vaginal discharge of mucus. This mucus symptom is not an abnormality but an indication of good health and tells a woman that it is now the time when an act of intercourse may cause pregnancy. The woman is potentially fertile while the mucus symptom is there plus three days afterwards which is the time allowed for ovulation to take place and allows for the life of the ovum (egg). The woman has to do nothing that she would not normally do except to pay attention and keep a simple record at the end of each day. The Method can be used during all variations of a woman's fertile life, from puberty through to the menopause, during regular and irregular cycling, after childbirth and in the pre-menopause years. It will be reliable. It is best taught as a couple Method where couples are concerned. Most couples require an introductory talk and 2/3 short follow-ups at about monthly intervals. In special circumstances they may need more follow-up tuition e.g. post Pill or during breastfeeding, and we usually see them at fortnightly intervals earlier on. It is inexpensive and helpful in the achievement as well as in the avoidance of pregnancy. It is immediately reversible and does not distort. The most usual comment which men make is: 'Why didn't I grow up with this knowledge? My whole approach to women would have been different if I had'.

It has to be said that the Billings method of N.F.P. cannot be combined with any artificial means of birth control.

In 1985 when the Doctors Billings were doing a U.K. tour they asked me if I would try to open a London Centre. In 1987 they opened that centre which is still very small. Before the opening, I went to buy some carpeting in a small shop. The manager came out to serve me and asked me where I wanted the carpet for. I explained it was for a charity. He asked me what sort of charity. I told him that it was a Natural Family Planning Teaching Centre of the Billings Ovulation Method. He replied 'Oh really!' When I was engaged to be married someone taught me about this but began by saying 'Now I am going to tell you something and you are going to go away and laugh like anything'. Then he went on: 'I did exactly that, but do you know he was right about natural family planning!'

# NFP—A More Human Alternative

## *Dr Zhang de Wei*

### Introduction

The Ovulation Method (OM) of Natural Family Planning is one of the popular fertility regulating methods used in developed and developing countries all over the world. On the base of our preliminary clinical observation which was carried out from October 1987 to May 1988 in Shanghai, China, we organized 6 sub-centres, 5 in urban and 1 in rural, to recruit more volunteers to use OM for contraception. During the past 2 years from June 1988 to May 1990, 688 reproductive-aged couples have been recruited, taught, instructed and observed. Most of them kept using the method for more than 12 months. The result was satisfactory and the observation survey was analyzed.

### Material and method

*Subjects*. Among the 688 reproductive-aged couples recruited to use OM for contraception, were 53 couples continued from the preliminary study in Shanghai. The occupation, education level, age and menstrual patterns of the 688 users are shown in Tables 1-4.

Before using OM 640 of the couples had used various contraceptive methods which they felt unsatisfactory in varying degrees. Among them 73 couples had

Table 1. Distribution of Occupation

| Occupation | Worker | Farmer | Technician | Staff member | Medical staff | Total |
|---|---|---|---|---|---|---|
| NO. | 208 | 40 | 71 | 238 | 131 | 688 |
|  | (30.23%) | (5.81%) | (10.32%) | (34.59%) | (19.04%) | (100%) |
| % | 36.05% | | | 63.95% | | 100% |

Table 2. Distribution of Education Level

| Education level | Primary school | Middle school | High school & College | Total |
|---|---|---|---|---|
| NO. | 276 | 300 | 112 | 688 |
| % | 40.12% | 43.60% | 16.28% | 100% |

Table 3. Distribution of Age (24–48 yrs)

| Age (yrs) | 20–29 | 30–39 | 40–49 | Total |
|---|---|---|---|---|
| NO. | 80 | 487 | 121 | 688 |
| % | 11.63% | 70.78% | 17.59% | 100% |

Table 4. Types of Menstrual Pattern

| Types | NO. | % |
|---|---|---|
| Normal Cycle | 560(81.40%) | 81.40% |
| Short Cycle | 55( 7.99%) | |
| Long Cycle | 44( 6.40%) | |
| Irregular Cycle | 13( 1.89%) | 18.60% |
| Breastfeeding | 6( 0.87%) | |
| Premenopause | 10( 1.45%) | |
| Total | 688(100%) | 100% |

Table 5. Contraceptive methods used before using OM

| Contraceptive method | NO. | % |
|---|---|---|
| Condom | 256 | 37.21% |
| Safety period | 168 | 24.42% |
| IUDs | 126 | 18.31% |
| Oral conctraceptives | 44 | 6.40% |
| Spermacides | 40 | 5.81% |
| Extravaginal ejaculation | 26 | 3.78% |
| No method | 28 | 4.07% |
| Total | 688 | 100% |

Table 6. Findings of gynaecological examination

| Findings | | NO. | % |
|---|---|---|---|
| Normal | | 511 | 74.27% |
| Vaginitis | | 18 | |
| Cervicitis | I | 133 | |
| | II | 15 | 25.73% |
| | III | 3 | |
| Uterine Myoma or Ovarian Cyst | | 8 | |
| Total | | 688 | 100.00% |

changed to several other artificial methods, but had found no method satisfactory either (Table 5).

Some of the users suffered from chronic cervicitis, vaginitis or other gynecological diseases (Table 6).

*Instruction and follow-up.* The 688 users were taught, instructed and followed-up by more than 40 NFP teachers who were trained twice by the NFP Teaching

92  Families for Tomorrow

Training Courses during 1987-1988. These were sponsored by Family of the Americas Foundation cooperating with Shanghai Municipal Family Planning Commission.

Users recorded the daily change of their own cervical mucus every night and followed the 'Early Rules' and 'Peak Day Rules' of the Ovulation Method to avoid pregnancy.

Usually a whole follow-up course lasted 3 months. In the case of a few couples who could not understand OM completely within 3 months, the course was prolonged appropriately.

## Results

A total of 10,175 Woman Months (WM) were observed. Among the 688 couples 605 were using OM for more than 12 WM, while 83 discontinued before 12 WM due to various causes (Table 7): occurrence of unplanned pregnancies 37, unwillingness due to inconvenience 22, and some other causes such as divorce, partner went abroad etc. 24.

The time (WM) unplanned pregnancies occurred was shown as Table 8.

Table 7. The Amount of Woman Month observed

| Woman Months observed | <12 | 12-18 | >18 | Total |
|---|---|---|---|---|
| NO. of Users | 83 | 468 | 137 | 688 |
| Total Woman Months | 530 | 6,760 | 2,885 | 10,175 |

Table 8. The Woman Month unplanned pregnancies occured

| The WM | 1 | 2 | 3 | 4 | 5 | 6 | 7 | 8 | 9 | 10 | 11 | 12 | Total |
|---|---|---|---|---|---|---|---|---|---|---|---|---|---|
| NO. of pregnancy | 0 | 1 | 3 | 5 | 1 | 3 | 7 | 8 | 5 | 0 | 4 | 0 | 37 |

*The pregnancy rate.* A total of 37 pregnancies occurred, giving a pregnancy rate of 4.36/100 Woman Year (WY). It is important to distinguish between pregnancies which result from user-failure and method-failure. In our study the rate of method-failure (i.e. couples do abstain on the proscribed fertile days) was 1.18 pregnancies/100 Woman Year (10 users). The majority of pregnancies resulted from user-failure: the rate of pregnancy resulting from 'conscious departure from the Rules due to an inability to maintain abstinence' was 0.71 pregnancies/100 Woman Year (6 users). In addition, 2.12 pregnancies/100 Woman Year occurred (18 users) because of inaccurate application of the method, i.e. the subjects did not fully understand the method or its application (4 users) or the couples had experienced difficulty in following the rules because of continuous mucus discharge (4 users), illness (2 users) or other circumstances such as an overseas trip, too busy etc. (8 users) that made it difficult for the subjects to observe or chart the mucus; and 0.35 pregnancies/100 Woman Year (3 users) could not be satisfactorily classified (Table 9).

Table 9. Pregnancy rate and its causes

| Causes | No. of pregnancy | % Woman Year |
|---|---|---|
| Method-failure | 10 | 1.18 |
| User-failure | | |
| 1. Conscious Departure from the Rules | 6 | 0.71 |
| 2. Not fully understand the method | 4(0.47%) | |
| 3. Difficulty in following the rules because of: | | |
| 3.1 Continuous mucus discharge | 4(0.47%) | |
| 3.2 Illness | 2(0.24%) | |
| 3.3 Other circumstances | 8(0.94%) | |
| 4. Could not be satisfactorily classified | 3 | 0.35 |
| Total | 37 | 4.36 |

*The effective rate of Ovulation Method.* According to the pregnancy rate due to method-failure analyzed above the effective rate of the Ovulation Method for contraception used in our study was 98.82/100 Woman Year.

*The continuation rate of Ovulation Method for contraception.* The probability of discontinuation from the study for all reasons was 9.79/100 Woman Year (83 couples). If we exclude 24 couples who discontinued OM due to non-method causes, then the continuation rate was 93.04/100 Woman Year.

*The teaching time needed for fully understanding OM.* Most of 688 couples (93.31%) can understand the Ovulation Method for contraception within 3 months by teaching and instruction. Only a few (6.10%) needed longer time (Table 10).

Table 10. Teaching time needed for fully understanding OM

| Woman Month | Got pregnant before understanding | 1 | 2 | 3 | 4 | 5 | 6 | Total |
|---|---|---|---|---|---|---|---|---|
| No. of Users | 4 | 205 | 305 | 132 | 26 | 14 | 2 | 688 |
| % | 0.58% | | 93.32% | | | 6.10% | | 100% |

## Discussion

- This observation was set on the base of our preliminary study. Our teachers of the Ovulation Method had some experience, so that the results were more satisfactory than before. It further confirmed that OM is an effective contraceptive method.
- Some people in our country think that OM of NFP can only be accepted by the intelligentsia, but in our study more than $\frac{1}{3}$ of users were ordinary workers and farmers (36.05%) and more than $\frac{1}{3}$ of

users only received primary school education (40.12%). This suggested OM can be also accepted by non-intelligentsia.
- The menstrual patterns of 18.60% users were abnormal cycles and 25.73% users suffered from infection of reproductive organs or other gynacological diseases—all of them can use OM. Thus it also showed that OM for contraception can be used under various conditions.
- The principle of instruction and follow-up of this study was carried out following the teaching pattern proposed by Family of the Americas Foundation. Our NFP teachers and users felt this system is easy to teach and learn, so we think this is appropriate to be performed in China.

## *Summary*

The Ovulation Method of Natural Family Planning is a safe, effective, simple and natural contraceptive method. In order to ensure its effective rate, teaching, instruction and follow-up are most important.

We recommend it is taught step by step under the guidance of the Family Planning Commission at all levels in our country.

*References*
Gray, R.H., Kambic, R.T. (1988) *Epidemiological studies of natural family planning*, Human Reprod., 3(5):693.
Xu, J.X., et al. (1990) *A preliminary report on application of Billings natural family planning for fertility regulation used in China*, Reproduction & Contraception 10(2):53.
Wilson, M.A. (1980) *The Ovulation Method of Birth Regulation*, New York, Van Nostrand Reinhold.
Wilson, M.A. (1986) *Love and Fertility*, USA, BBE.
Billings, E., Westmore, A. (1988) *The Billings Method*, New ed. Australia, Anne O'Donovan Pty Ltd.
World Health Organization (1987) *A prospective multicenter trial of the Ovulation Method of natural family planning*, V. Psychosexual aspects, Fertility & Steril. 47(5):765.
Labbok, M.H. et al. (1988) *Factors related to Ovulation Method Efficacy in three Programs: Bangladesh, Kenya and Korea*, Contraception 37(6):577.

# Cultural Shocks and Social Calamities

## *Dr Kongolo Mulumba*

This last decade of the 20th century seems to mark for all parts of the world a time for reorientation, and of revision. With a more subtle cutting up of the globe into industrio-economic areas, and a less violent opposition between dominant political ideologies, one can affirm without risk of contradiction that progress is certainly happening. Contacts and exchanges between nations multiply and certain great questions *ipso facto* become world-wide. Among these burning questions are the menace weighing on the environment, drug traffiking and the circulation of international capital.

Almost the whole of Africa could be described as 'developing countries', characterized by:

— serious debts
— weak industry
— rapid population growth
— great economic inbalance.

Seeking rapid development, policies and programmes of every kind have been put forward across the continent. The most important and well-known are the population programmes, and also those aimed at re-establishing major economic balance, commonly called 'programmes of structural adjustment'.

We need to examine the implications of these programmes on the lives of individuals and communities in Africa.

First, let us examine the motives of the governments and international organisations for these programmes.

## I Population programmes and structural adjustment programmes: content and justification

### (A) *Population programmes*

The African backwardness in the domain of industry is, as taught by most of the textbooks on economics, the cause of a weak national per capita gross product and an underdeveloped economic growth. Seen from this point of view, any gains in the economic field are always annihilated by an ever-growing number of human beings.

The population programmes are aimed at slowing up the population growth through policies of voluntary Family Planning led by governments. This great objective is translated into educational and health programmes directed specifically at African women with the only aim of helping them to have fewer pregnancies. In Zaire, primary and secondary school curricula will soon comprise an element of education on population questions. The UNFPA (Population Fund of the United Nations) feels that it is necessary to make young people aware of the problem so that as adults, they will act responsibly with respect to procreation. The UNFPA foresees the intensification of the sale of contraceptives by travelling salesmen with the idea of making their use more commonplace and acceptable everywhere.

Through television we can see certain political themes that capture people's attention more than others and dominate the news. For the moment, the fashionable topic is the environment. In order to justify policies of family planning this new subject is exploited. The UNFPA, in the person of its executive director—a woman—says that it is urgent for women of Third World countries to give birth to fewer children in order to preserve the environment. Their numerous offspring, they say, are endangering the future of the world by destroying forests. Less forests means more carbon dioxide in the air and Mme Sadik feels it is vital that there should be less human beings on the earth.

UNFPA strives also to show African women that there are other possibilities of status besides motherhood. The education of girls is thus a favourite hobby horse.

## (B) *Structural adjustment programmes*

As far as structural adjustment programmes are concerned, they are set up in order to encourage African countries (and elsewhere) who are in debt, to face the financial and economic crisis in which they are plunged by having recourse to the advice and the adjustment loans of the World Monetary Fund and the World Bank. These organisations provide for countries who ask for help in controlling national expenditure so as to free from national budgets enough resources to balance public finances and ensure the payment of the debt. The gross total of this debt is owed to commercial banks of industrial countries. It is crippled by floating interest rates which protect these banks from risk but make the people concerned carry a very heavy burden.

Working with the American dollar as a term of reference, African countries have had to undergo the counter-effects of devaluation and this has also increased the volume of their debt.

Ill-conceived and badly-managed production structures have also aggravated the economic and financial difficulties of the continent. Civil wars, political regimes of corrupt and spend-thrift dictators and bad climatic conditions have also done terrible things to the social and financial apparatus of the continent.

The structural adjustment programmes therefore aim at helping the countries face their obligations with regard to their debts. The measures taken at the level of each country are essentially concerned with monetary policy, balance of payments, public finances, lax policy and cost-of-living control.

It is therefore like a doctor who has only one medicine in his bag which the World Monetary Fund and the World Bank have invariably preached all over the world:

— devaluation of money
— reduction of public spending
— increasing taxes
— moderating of salaries
— liberalisation of exchange and prices
— raising the internal interest rates
— a draconian calendar for the repayment schedule to the debtors.

The fact that more than one country has had to re-structure the payments several times is witness to the very mitigated success of this policy. Between 1976 and 1982, Zaire has had recourse to four 'restructuring' of payments. Between 1983 and 1986, measures were taken to reduce government spending, especially the spending on social services.

These measures, as we will see later on, have had deplorable consequences on the health and economic security of families.

## II The African viewpoint—cultural shocks

### (A) Background

The Population programmes have been applied to an Africa where a child is the most precious thing anyone can possess. The confrontation between food resources and population is a view which appears cynical to an African.

Only very recently, it was not done at all to count people before serving food to them. As a matter of principle, one serves what one has and it is up to the people eating to know how to share, to make sure that each one gets something. In African culture, it is ridiculous to refuse to feed anyone who asks for food. The idea behind this attitude is reciprocity. If one day *you* are hungry, you could ask *him* for food. The price is therefore the possible future service rather than the value of the goods itself. Thus to ask a person to suppress (by contraception or abortion) their own child, is to ask them to deny what they are. 'They are asking for my insides', said a woman to whom a doctor had advised contraception.

To reduce the question solely to the economic aspect does not fit in with the African mentality. Procreation in Africa is not derived only from the aspiration for descendants or for personal satisfaction but very often and most of the time, from a collective and social need. There are therefore social rules which come into play, as for example:

*(1) Gifts and repayments of dowries.* All over Africa, it is always the boy's family who gives a dowry to the girl's family on marriage. This dowry is a token of the alliance which is made between the two clans. It sanctions the marriage and guarantees its stability and gives the right of the fatherhood of the children to the husband. It is therefore very important for a family which wants to ensure its future to see to it that all their sons get married and pay what is necessary for it. All the members of the extended family help with this.

The children being now a part of the clan, the parents whose daughter marries are obliged to give all the goods they receive to their son or to a nephew who will in turn use them to pay for the dowry when he gets married. With time, moral obligations are created which weave a complex social web derived from this unceasing movement of dowries. Thus people have more children so that once they have married off their daughters, they can in their turn help a member of the family to take a wife. The game of gifts and repayments of dowries can extend over three or four generations. The children inherit the obligations and rights of their parents, which make the mechanism even more complicated. It is an honour to help the son of someone who has helped you and to acquit oneself honourably of his obligations as a future son-in-law. This element is today a determining factor in the marriage of young girls.

*(2) The stakes of fertility.* Procreation is still the best means of having descendants (we are not yet into test-tube babies). If the dowry guarantees the stability of the marriage, the child is its cement. A marriage where procreation takes place has more chances of maintaining itself than where there are no children. The child is therefore a seal between the two clans from which spouses come. Therefore, fertility and especially feminine fertility become the stake between two groups: clans where many cases of sterility have been noted are not recommended to young people as groups where one can choose a future wife. The role of the child as a link between families is such that even after divorce, relations between the two clans are pursued independently of the former spouses. The principal reason is the psychological needs of the child for whom they try to avoid having to choose between the family of the mother and that of the father. The husband's brothers and the wife's sisters can meet and discuss the future of the children if the two spouses are no longer capable of talking about them calmly.

*(3) The child as a link in the chain of social communication*
— Between the spouses especially in case of conflicts
— Between spouses and their respective in-laws.

All the horrid things one would like to say about one's mother-in-law, one says about one's daughter, especially if she is herself a mother-in-law and preferably when she is present! In the case of discontent, the wife can always pretend she is talking to her daughter who needs educating.

*(4) Valuing women as mothers.* A woman who voluntarily or involuntarily has no children is considered infirm. She is widely pitied. 'Every union of a man with a woman is similar to that of God with the Earth. Woman however, is predestined by God to continue His creation: man's role is only that of a helper. Life is a potency deposited by God in the depths of every woman or nearly every one' (Barbier 1985).

*(5) Belief in reincarnation.* According to this belief children are ancestors who were long since dead and who have returned to live in the family.
  To refuse to procreate therefore means to twist God's designs and to prevent those who want to return from being born. It is therefore to go against God's plans. This mentality is reinforced by the fact that people consider that nobody has paid anything in order to be born. Since one hasn't paid anything oneself, one should necessarily let others come to this earth in the same way.

*(6) Attitude to life.* In Zaire, in the province of Shaba, one of the attributes of God is 'Vidie nurine Bumi', which means 'Master of Life'. In this region, as well as in the rest of the continent, the belief is that only this Being is able to give to man the breath of life. I too think that this is right. He is also called Shakapanga, which means Creator, because 'we are all products of his field and of his flock'.

Man therefore does not give life without the intervention of the Creator. If human beings are born, it is because they were in God's plan, because not one of us is unknown to Him.

*(7) Meaning of blood.* Blood is a fundamental element in African tradition (Barbier 1985). To share the same blood is part of the culture and of the sense of belonging which in turn rules mechanisms of solidarity. 'Blood is the gift of self, image of sacrifice and suffering. Blood symbolises woman, the giver of life. Transmitted by her, it expresses pride and shame, virtues and vices' (idem).

To die without transmitting one's blood is a cause of desolation for an African. If there is a cause for which people are ready to undergo the worst sacrifices in Africa, it is children. That is why to incite people to make use of contraception, for purely economic or financial reasons, is to fail to understand the cultural background of Africa.

In any case, Africa has not yet any other alternative. She has to count on her children until she can make her own way.

## *(B) The Form*

*(1) Inadequate programmes.* The contraception programmes often organise training sessions or radio and television programmes. Produced with the participation of doctors and nursing staff, these programmes frequently use quite crude language which is not sympathetic with African traditions. African languages are in fact full of euphemisms which are used in place of words which are considered as too strong. eg. A woman will say 'I am placed high up' instead of saying 'I am pregnant' (Luba euphemism).

By wanting to be emancipated these people often only succeed in doing psychological violence to their audience.

*(2) Curtailed education.* The above-mentioned courses on sexual education are merely disordered and untimely revelations for children. Contraception used to be taught in the past in initiation sessions directed by old people.

It contained a whole variety of forms of communication and conjugal life according to the days of sexual encounters. The elements which prevailed here were mutual respect and discipline. After a long period of abstinence the spouses would give each other presents and share a meal with a few intimate friends.

However, this cultural and even romantic aspect is sacrificed by new teaching which only aims at one thing: the immediate pursuit of sexual pleasure which would encourage the use of contraceptives.

*(3) Ill-chosen targets and abuse of confidence.* By directing their programmes towards women and children, governments and directors of population programmes try to influence the weakest and most vulnerable people. The wife does not have the last word in determining the number of children she has. The primary or secondary school child who has been given ideas about sex and contraception will be duly tempted to experiment with these things.

School is a place for positive education. By sending their children to school, parents hope that they will be well taught and that this instruction will complete the education which they themselves have begun to give them at home. The distillation of ideas and concepts hostile to the local philosophy which schools promote is therefore alien to their mission of education and guidance.

Here it is useful to ask whether UNESCO which supports these programmes is not moving away from its essential goal, which is the protection of cultures.

## III Effects of the programmes

### (A) Population programmes

The population programmes contribute to accelerate the deterioration of morals.

They also contributed to the destruction of clan solidarity by reducing the whole demographic question to the number of children being born. A strictly economic and financial philosophy which underlies the policy encourages Africans to abandon the spirit of mutual aid and assistance. Anyone who already reduces the size of his own family is not ready to help the extended family.

Most Africans who have been in touch with the ideas and actions of family planning remind us that the services often employ people who are little inclined to consider individual problems and treat people as irresponsible beings.

This attitude shocks them because aid, of whatever nature, must respect the individual. This lack of consideration is an indication of the whole philosophy of these policies, dictated by hypothetical considerations alien to the Continent. Africa does not need speculation. It wants to resolve its problems and above all to preserve its culture.

A woman is respected for her maternity. And, in my opinion, this is not more dishonourable than a diploma or a high-flying job.

### (B) The structural adjustment programmes

The structural adjustment programmes have not had the effects that were hoped for. Rather, they have provoked, through the inductive method, the reduction of social budgets. In Zaire, measures taken on the advice of the World Monetary Fund aimed at reducing internal consumption in order to redirect a part of the national riches towards production, led to the freezing of salaries without similar price controls. 'The corrolary of this phenomena was the rapid degradation of buying power for the people' (UNICEF 1990). Family life was profoundly affected by this. Thousands of people saw their fate rapidly change. Indeed, in order to face the fall in income, families sold some of their property and forced the children, especially girls, to abandon their studies in order to obtain a paying job. Budgets for public health lost 25% of their value compared to the period before the intervention of the International Monetary Fund.

The freezing of salaries advocated by the IMF had the effect of diminishing the volume of internal financial transactions, of slowing up internal cash flow and as a side result that of also slowing up the whole internal economy itself.

As for the liberalisation of prices, it leaves shopkeepers and especially importers, the freedom to fix their own prices.

Since these have to be continually aligned with foreign currencies, the rise in prices is almost permanent.

These two programmes exercise concerted pressure on populations. One advocates the reduction of the number of human beings, but taking into account the numerous goods and services which the members of the family give each other without any financial benefit, for the moment Africa cannot offer itself this luxury. The programme of structural readjustment contributes to the destruction of the social state by causing extreme irrational hardship for the sake of false economic equilibrium.

Finally, the crisis of the present debt is a crisis of liquid assets. Having 40% of the world's hydroelectric potential, the greatest diamond and chrome reserves, 50% of gold and 90% of cobalt deposits, Africa is far from being the planet's poorest continent. It is important for her to preserve its cultural and demographic riches in order to fully exploit its natural resources.

The positions taken up by the International Monetary Fund and of the mass media in the West cause enormous harm to the Continent, presenting a negative and false image. The action of IMF and of the population programmes would contibute to the progress of the Continent if it took more care of the people themselves than of theoretical economic solutions.

## *Conclusion*

In this period when innumerable calamities befall the Continent it is vital that policies take into account the aspirations of the majority who are trying to escape from political and economic burdens.

There is no *timing* for development and Africa is not backward by any time scale. It is no use trying to change its nature by denying it its most fundamental cultural characteristics.

This time of world reorganisation is beneficial for all regions of the world, including Africa. My hope is that Africa may seize her chance and find her own way, for her destiny is in her own hands.

More than all the economic help available she needs sincere friends who are concerned with the problems of the masses and not with human reduction programmes.

We will not reduce poverty by killing the poor. 'Poverty won't disappear when there are no more poor people left' but through the concerted action of nations respecting human dignity.

# 4: SCIENCE, CONSCIENCE AND THE FAMILY
## The New Medicine

### *Nigel M. de S. Cameron*

What is going on in medicine today? We all know about the amazing advances in technique, and some of the problems they present. We also know that many of the values of the old medicine—the medical tradition—are being revised; indeed, they are being thrown out. The discipline of 'medical ethics' or 'bioethics' spells out the problems, and is developing so fast that every few months a new journal is founded to discuss it. In the journal which I edit, *Ethics and Medicine*, we try and develop a Christian perspective on these subjects.

'Medical ethics' has become an arena in which the struggle is on for fundamental human values. Nowhere else in the modern world is the conflict clearer, between all that is best in Christian civilisation and all that is most threatening in the post-Christian barbarism of the secular society. For many years this society has been living off the moral capital of the Christian faith, and so-called humanism hung onto Christian values while claiming it could dispense with Christian religion. But if you go on spending capital you finally run out. As Dr Carl F.H. Henry has memorably put it, the humanitarianism is going out of humanism. Its increasingly raw naturalism is reviving the pagan values of the pre-Christian cultures.

But what *was* the old medicine? What *is* the new medicine? And what can we do about it? I'm going to ask those questions in turn.

## 1. *The old medicine*

Hippocrates was a great clinician, and that is part of the reason for his influence in medical values. But the Hippocratic Oath which he or his followers put together has proved one of the most important documents of western civilisation.

First, value and technique go hand in hand. The doctor's skills and the doctor's ethics are inseparable. In the oath this is underlined by the fact that the person who swears it agrees not to tell any of the tricks of the trade to someone who hasn't. In other words, medical skills are only for Hippocratic doctors. No-one else can be trusted with them.

Secondly, these values are grounded in God. The importance of human life lies beyond itself. The Hippocratic Oath is an *oath*. Hippocrates wasn't a Christian, and Jews and Muslims as well as others have taken his medicine as their model. But his values only really make sense if you believe the reason human life matters is to be found in something beyond it.

Everything else follows, especially the sanctity of human life. In Ancient Greece abortion was common, and doctors were often asked to help their patients die. Hippocrates said No, and he welded technique and values into a medicine which has stood the test of more than 2,000 years. Margaret Mead, the famous anthropologist, has called the Oath 'one of the turning-points in the history of man'. In Hippocratism, for the first time, we have 'a complete separation between killing and curing', two acts which in primitive societies will always tend to be in the hands of the one person, the sorcerer, the witch-doctor.

This radically fresh approach to medicine proved a force of great power. It began as a minority medicine, and cannot have been popular in a primitive society in which there was liberal abortion, suicide and euthanasia. Yet finally it triumphed, and it is no wonder that the young church seized this humane medical enterprise and adopted it as a model for Christian medicine.

## 2. *What is the New Medicine?*

'Society always is attempting to make the physician into a killer—to kill the defective child at birth, to leave the sleeping pills beside the bed of the cancer patient.' (Margaret Mead). As the tide of faith has ebbed this Christian Hippocratism has been disowned and ignored. There are new values in this post-Christian society, and chief among them is the idea that there really are no ultimate values at all. You can pick and choose. You can do what you like—except that you must never tell me what *I* should do; that is the great prohibition of the liberal society.

So medicine has been cut free from its Hippocratic moorings, and the old ideas that value and technique go together, and that behind the value of human life there lies the life of God—these foundation-stones of the humane medical tradition are treated with scorn.

The most obvious characteristic of the New Medicine is its rejection of the principle of the sanctity of human life—that the taking of life can never be an option in clinical management, for whatever cause. In place of this principle is 'respect for life', which sadly means no more than that we shall value human life as much as we choose to value it. *How much* we choose to value it, in particular circumstances, depends on other things.

Liberal abortion is the plainest example of this New Medicine.

And abortion has of course led to the killing of handicapped babies, who have been called fetuses *ex utero*.

Alongside this, the pressure for euthanasia is mounting; in Holland it has overflowed into practice as thousands of people are deliberately killed every year.

The fragmenting of medical values is leading to *a model of medicine which is merely contractual*. In the old medicine, the doctor was a professional who went around trying to heal sick people. In the new, he is a contractor; you bring him in to do what you want him to do. You tell him, you pay him (directly or indirectly), and he does it, like a builder or a plumber or a gardener.

Maybe you want to be healed. Maybe you want to end it all.

Maybe you want him to care for your pregnancy. Maybe to dispose of your unwanted unborn baby.

Maybe you want him to help granny to get better. Maybe you want him to get rid of her.

People call the old medicine 'paternalised', because it carried the notion that 'doctor knows best'. There are bad things about paternalism, and patients do have a right to know what is going on and to consent to it. Yet in Hippocratic medicine the doctor's options are limited, must be limited. He is freed—and so are you—from the temptation to forget that life is sacred. The system of values is built into medicine. The doctor isn't a contractor, paid to do whatever you want him to do; he's a professional, paid to do what he is trained to do and nothing else—to heal, and not to destroy.

There are other ways of looking at this contrast. There is the question of *suffering*. People talk a lot today about the doctor's mission to 'relieve suffering'. When I first read the Hippocratic Oath the most astonishing thing I found was that it did not refer to the relief of suffering at all. Of course doctors relieve suffering, but there are limits to their power—moral limits as there are practical limits. I believe Hippocrates in his great wisdom decided to make sure that none of his doctors would think that suffering has to be relieved *at all costs*.

Yet of course that is how the taking of life—in abortion and all the rest—is defended. It's a balancing act, the doctors say, between the sanctity of life and the relief of suffering. Sometimes one is on top, sometimes the other. But the sanctity of life is a supreme value. It cannot be qualified or it evaporates. Everything else must be subordinate.

That is what Hippocrates said, and it was his genius which gave rise to our medical tradition. Little by little it is now being overwhelmed.

Another key idea is that of *power*. When the doctor becomes a contractor he becomes the agent of his employer, and he exercises power on behalf of his employer over his patient. This is more obvious in a system of private health care, but the principle is the same in the National Health Service and other social health care systems. In Hippocratic medicine the doctor still gets paid—has always been paid to do his job—but he comes carrying his values in his medical bag. He comes to serve, and he knows and everyone knows that is is going to do the Hippocratic thing and nothing else. Yet now he is the agent of his patient, or the family, or an insurance company, or the state, and there are other considerations determining his decisions than the interests of the patient. In this situation of supreme vulnerability for the patient, medicine has become an instrument of power. If you believe that to be extravagant, look at what can happen to a handicapped baby.

We must not be misled by the the idea that what we are seeing is progress, though that is what we are told. It is actually the very opposite, it is regress, for the new medicine—with its view of the doctor as a contractor rather than a professional, with its belief that there are more important things than human life, with its separation of value and technique, and its model of medicine as power rather than service—the new medicine is a sophisticated, technological throw-back to the primitive world of pre-Christian and pre-Hippocratic values.

Make no mistake: this is a new barbarism, cradled in a new pagan culture which is fast displacing the Christian inheritance of the west. And, increasingly, this is becoming obvious from the candid arguments which its most enthusiastic advocates are daring to present. A recent article in a leading medical journal presented an eloquent case for euthanasia, and high among its arguments was the practice of primitive tribes in killing or abandoning their unwanted babies and old people.

## 3. What can we do?

It is all too easy for us to see abortion, or euthanasia, as an isolated issue. In our commitment to the protection of life we must not, dare not, lose sight of the wider picture. In these developments all we have seen is post-Hippocratism flexing its muscles. The brave new world of medicine has hardly begun to dawn. The profession today is still deeply influenced by Hippocratic and Christian values. The resurgence of pre-Hippocratic barbarism has hardly begun, but begun it has, and we do not know where it will stop.

The struggle is for the soul of medicine, yet it is also for the soul of our civilisation. All of the humane values of our society are under threat. In the shift from medicine as service to medicine as power we have an inkling of the way in which power will be exercised in the world of the future. As humanism takes leave of its Christian roots the future looks bleak. Yet even as we grasp that bleak vision we have taken the first step toward preventing its coming about. Next, we must convince our friends and our neighbours, our churches, and all who share with us the vision of a humane society, of the gravity of these changes.

Secondly, *we must understand something more about Hippocratism*—because the Hippocratic creed was forged by the doctors of ancient Greece as the creed of a minority. It was a manifesto, the reforming manifesto of a band of daring doctors who lived in an age of liberal abortion, and of euthanasia, and who said No. Our medicine will be an alternative medicine, and its clinical secrets will be open only to those who first accept its ethical values. This was dissident medicine more than twenty centuries ago, and it must be the model for dissident medicine today. The Hippocratic Oath was written and sworn as a protest against the old barbarism, and if we would resist this barbarism revived we must own it anew as the bulwark of human medicine in a day of moral crisis.

# Biological Research: Opening Pandora's Box?

## *Suzanne Rini*

When I was in England in 1978 I rented a little cottage down in Lyme Regis, because it is a very idyllic little place by the Channel, full of history and very close to nature. One of my fondest memories of that time is going out into the garden at night and looking at the stars; they seemed so much closer and more precise to one's vision than they do in the United States, at least where I live, which is in a very urban area. During my stay, I was invited to a party with some of the local people. One of the men there was rather symbolically living in the local coffin-maker's house! But he had manufactured and marketed a new idea: a very large piece of paper that could be plugged in and fixed to a ceiling, and it had on it all the constellations, so that one could enjoy the stars inside. I immediately took a terrible dislike to this man, because of what he was doing, this manufacturing of glow stars. And I wrote a short story called 'Stark Raving Mad', because I saw in that effort a kind of creatorial complex, a kind of effort to reduce nature to just some kind of gimmick for sale; and I also saw in it the splitting apart of human unity. With glow stars, every person by himself can lie in bed and look up and enjoy 'the Firmanent', which of course is artificial. In the real world, the world of Western civilisation and probably universally of all civilisation, men go out one by one, joined by others, until a collective civilisation is formed, to watch the stars....

I believe that our technological fetish, our creatorial complex, has led to that being reflected in new biotechnological techniques, that are indeed a kind of new primitivism and a new barbarism. They describe, in fact, the extent to which we have become separated from Nature, separated from God and separated from each other. It is the privacy doctrine run wild.

In 1986 a journalist friend in New York, mentioned to me the fact of non-therapeutic foetal experimentation. Quite frankly, I thought it was some kind of propaganda from the pro-life movement. I simply could not accept that anyone would experiment on a live baby, abortion notwithstanding. I wasn't even taking into account the abortion law. I didn't care about it. I saw the idea of experiments on embryos as a lie, and I had terrific doubts. But this friend was very credible, so I decided to look into it myself, and found out through contacts I made and materials that I was able to collect, that it was indeed true.

First, I was appalled by the experiments themselves. They had a sort of barbaric stupidity and insensitivity. One was the 'Dutch Famine' experiment, in which they took pregnant women who were going to abort, and delayed the abortion for two weeks to a month. Researchers then put them on a malnutrition diet that mimicked the condition for something called the Dutch Famine. Now of course if you starve a woman and only give her a caloric intake of three hundred calories a day, the marks of it are going to be on the baby that she bears. That was their whole design. In my mind it was a stupid, barbaric and cruel project, that was about as close to gathering medical data as taking a temperature is to high science.

Now some of the other experiments were also extremely barbaric. Some of the American researchers from the United States went to Finland and there they delivered live babies. Of course they called them aborted, but that is a lie. What they did was to deliver by hysterotomy about seven or eight babies, who were in the premature range, around seven to eight months, and they extripated, that is they cut off their heads, and they profused them with all kinds of nutrients in order to get data about the brain.

Another researcher, from Hungary, who worked with a non-national collaborator, is reporting the results of an experiment that he does. He takes live aborted babies at about five to six months gestation, through a prostaglandins delivery, & he cuts out the beating hearts and profuses them in a tank with caffeine to decide what is the amount of stress on the human heart that is provided with caffeine.

One can see from these particular experiments the total lack of sensitivity that the researcher is able to gather in order to do the work. When the National Institute of Health in the United States held a conference in 1973 on foetal experimentation, and whether it should go forward, one of the arguments against such experimentation was that it would barbarise and desensitise, not only the researcher, but also the wider community. But of course it has gone on. It has burgeoned and grown, and it has given all of us many new techniques that we have not had before and which many people do not know were founded on non-therapeutic foetal experimentation. For instance, amniocentesis was founded in the United States. This can be aimed at aborting a baby that is found to have some kind of chromosonal anomaly or genetically inherited disease, of which there are now about thirteen hundred that can be trapped in the womb. All the work-up for amniocentesis, also for phytoscophy, that can pick up anomalies like haemophilia and sickle anaemia, was carried out on foetuses to be aborted. Needles were tested on them, and the way to enter into the amnion or into the skull for the blood testing, was all tested on these babies. The interesting part is that many of the babies died from the experiment rather than from the abortion for which they were scheduled. Amniocentesis and phytoscophy are exactly linked to negative eugenics, so we see that abortion sponsored the killing of more infants.

This is a social Darwinist dream, to be able to get rid of the handicapped.

Of course I found the experiments horrific, but I found the mentality behind the experiments to be, in a sense, even worse. This mentality was very often supplied by the medical ethics community, and in the United States this amounts to a very tightly knit cabal. Most of the more moral, more absolutist ethicists do not get asked to the symposia. It is mostly one type of crowd that seems to be the engine powering the new biotechnologies and giving the permission and the rationale for them.

One researcher from France, Professor Jean Bernard, did supply a maxim that I think shows the mentality behind the various biotechnologies that we already have, and surely the ones that we are going to be getting. He said 'the means are necessarily unethical and ethically necessary.' This is very interesting because it is so brash, with twists of words. It is really just simple utilitarianism. Some of the other manifestos I found also very shocking. A very prominent ethicist in the United States came before the 1973 Commission. The issue before the Commission was whether or not babies that were still alive—either in utero or post-abortion—would be allowed to be experimented upon. This is part of her testimony: 'The group of cells cannot feel the anguish or pain connected with death, nor can it fear death. Its experiencing of life has not yet begun, it is not yet conscious of the interruption of life, nor of the loss of anything that it has come to value in life, nor is it tied by bonds of affection to others. If the abortion is desired by both parents, no grief will be caused, such as that which accompanies the death of a child. Almost no human care and emotion and resources have been invested in it, nor is such an abortion in consequence brutalising for the person voluntarily performing it or a threat to society, because there is no semblance of human form, no conscious life or capability to live independently, no knowledge of death, no sense of pain. Words such as "harm" or "deprive" cannot be meaningfully used in the context of abortion and foetal research.'

It amazed me that someone in the twentieth century in the United States, which claims to be a democratic country, could stand up and testify in those terms. Here we have the 'privacy' doctrine. The parents don't want the baby, but what about the rest of us? Are we unable to grieve any more for a member of the human community? We are being told by this testimony that the baby is meaningless to the rest of us. It is only of concern to the persons who are choosing the abortion of the child.

So with this, of course anything can go. The researchers came forward and they washed their hands of the issue by saying, 'We are not the ones who put abortion into the law. We had nothing to do with that, and we are only trying to work for the amelioration of all kinds of difficult medical situations in which people can find themselves.' And so we see that the ground work had been made through the abortion. Abortion may not be the only focus for organisations interested in the family, but is certainly the bench-mark, the phenomenal occurrence, that has opened the door to so many things: we cannot ignore it.

One of the interesting aspects of the new biotechnologies is that they claim that much of what they do is therapeutic. You cannot just dismiss this. Look at the area of transplants. The aborted foetus delivered by prostaglandins is routinely harvested now for pancreatic cells which can ameliorate juvenile diabetes. This is a terrible disease: young adults usually will go blind, and may have to have limbs amputated. This is a very, very difficult argument for most people to skirt or negate. I have seen groups of patients with Parkinsons Disease who are up for the transplantations of foetal neurons arguing amongst themselves whether or not they should do this. I talked to a woman at a pro-life convention who said, 'Intellectually and morally I can't accept it, but if it were my child, I would do it.' This has all set us with very difficult choices. Only the Christian who has absolutely perfected his or her will, can resist this. It is a question I think that should haunt all of us. Intellectually it is possible to be against anything. When it comes down to one's own situation, then sometimes we are drawn in to what we object to morally.

Transplants raised the spectre, with abortion on the books as a legal choice in most countries now, of a woman and man conceiving a child in order to have a certain organ harvested for another member of the family. And because we have the privacy doctrine, I find it very hard to believe that that will be able to be avoided. At the moment there are some legal strictures against it, but it can really just depend on finding a doctor willing to do it. And here again, some ethicists have prepared the ground for allowing these aborted babies to be used for this ominous type of harvest.

Here is the testimony of another ethicist on the subject. This tackles the case of conceiving and having an abortion in order to get a kidney. The first thing is to dispose of the fact that the baby is a person. She discusses the status criteria of what she calls 'problematic entities' and watch where she places the foetus. On problematic entities, her list of these includes foetuses, non-human animals, alien life forms, intelligent machines. She tells us that 'it will not do to make genetic humanity, that is mere genetic affiliation with the human species, either a necessary or a sufficient condition for the possession of full moral rights. My candidate for a species neutral criterion for this possession of full moral rights, is what I call personhood. A person has the actual capacity for consciousness, complex and sophisticated perception, rationality, self-awareness and self-motivated behaviour. Foetuses, one might say, as yet have no will, they do not desire life or anything else.' Then she goes on to say, 'Foetuses, especially those as old as five or six months, elicit our sympathy and tempt us to endow them with moral rights. Not only because they are potential people, but because they look disconcertingly like people. Their physical features are recognisably human.' She assures us that 'this sympathy is misplaced. Unless there is a good deal more conscious activity in the foetal mind, then we have reason to suspect in such cases a proper respect for the right to life requires that it not be respected where it does not exist.'

So if you have mentalities like that advocating foetal experimentation, then why should we be surprised that we are now getting euthanasia? And not just euthanasia. The biotechnology now exists that has brought us 'cryogenics'. Someone has a brain tumour and there is no cure for it, so freeze him until a cure can be found. In the freezer lockers that we have in the United States in California, there are two rates. One rate is for the head alone, the other rate is for the entire body to be frozen. So we have a kind of consumerism. I contend that cryogenics, and artificial wombs, and some of the other things that we are beginning to see, are aimed at opening up new markets. Just as lawyers in the United States opened up the market of personal injury cases from accidents, so now the medical profession is opening up new markets in transplantation, in cryogenics, in artificial wombs, in artificial insemination.

Doctor Bernard Nathanson has stated that in New York the homosexual community is now lobbying the medical profession to insert fertilised eggs into the abdomen of the homosexual man, so that he can bear a child. Lesbians in the United States are taking advantage of artificial insemination and of surrogacy. They very often will call upon a male friend to impregnate them and then they go on to have the baby.

The other thing that is happening is that a doctor will actually kill one person in order to cure another. That is the new proposition for the neuron transfers. What this involves is the live abortion of a foetus that is not wanted around, they are saying, possibly five to six months of gestation. They are not sure about this and are thinking possibly about upping it to eight or nine months, because abortion in the United States is legal up to the full term. They need to persuade a woman that she can help someone with Parkinsons disease or Alzheimer's, if she delays the abortion for a little bit longer in case the nine month or eight month neurons prove to be more efficacious in this technology. What this operation entails is the live abortion of the baby through hysterotomy, that is a miniature caesarean section. (Thus it is really a birth, it is not really an abortion. But the baby is unwanted, so somehow it gets called an abortion.) Surgically it is a very painful procedure. The cornea is entered, or the skull, in order to get the neurons, and the researchers in the United States who are asking to go ahead with this have proposed to ameliorate the pain of the surgery with anaesthesia. Heretofore, you have not been allowed to anaesthetise a baby that was going to undergo experimentation, nor were you allowed to do anything particularly painful, although that is rather a bit of window-dressing when you come down to it. But with this new request, new questions are raised. Anaesthesia usually means that you are saving the patient pain and then he is going to come out of it and live, and that the surgery is for his or her own sake. But in this situation, this baby is being anaesthetised, the neurons will be taken, and the baby after the anaesthesia wears off, will not live, it will simply be left to die on the table.

At the same time that this surgery is being painted as a compassionate possible amelioration of Parkinson's disease, which claims ninety thousand new victims a year. We are also talking about the saving of spinal cord injury patients, of which there are upwards of one million new patients a year, and possibly prospectively they think even for Alzheimer's disease. So you are talking about an enormous amount of primary aborted babies that would undergo the surgery.

So here we have doctors killing one person in order to save another. The whole image of the primitive 'shaman' comes alive in this technology. He kills you and he cures you, and he has no point of view.

One of the doctors in the United States who was on the forward team for the neuron transplants, has a caveat. If any journalist wants to interview him, he will not allow any questions on ethics—none. He is doing the most controversial thing in the world, but you can't ask him one question on ethics, or he will not speak to you. And journalists. instead of walking away from him, go in and abide by his rule: no questions on ethics. At the same time, he has an ethicist from one of the universities in the United States, writing article after article in the ethical and in the medical journals promoting what he wants to do. And this is the role that the ethicist is now playing in many of these technologies. This doctor, I think, is symbolic of a new breed. I believe that the ethical debate will end. I think we are in the preliminary stages of these technologies. For instance, we don't have hybridisation of human beings. We do have them of animals, but we don't have them yet of human beings. Nor do we have genetic engineering. It is not yet on its feet enough to breed superior or inferior for certain kinds of industries. But I think with this doctor setting a trend and saying that he will not talk about ethics, eventually, maybe in five, ten or more years, (maybe even quicker than that, because things are moving very, very quickly) that the ethical arguments will simply become obsolete. People will simply choose these certain medical techniques. They will think that they are good.

That brings me to a question that I have been asked a couple of times when I have been giving lectures. On one occasion a very serious man, who is himself a research doctor, said, 'What shall we do?' We are scientists, we want to look at these things. We have curiosity, we want to know.' Someone else said, 'What you are talking about in not allowing these things to go forward, is that you are talking about censoring thought itself.' You have to be very careful with this, because when you see the brashness and the insensitivity of the people who are promoting certain ideas and techniques, they are not sensitive to your arguments. This is a form of warfare. You have to be a little bit combative. Most people are unaware that many of the technologies, especially those involved in foetal transplantation and foetal experimentation of many kinds, have been criticised as bad science. For instance, with transplants, even with the neuron transplants, there is another way to go about it. They can grow cells in laboratories, and not use baby after baby after baby. In every one of their papers, in every one of their ground-breaking suggestions, they always use the same phrase: they want to use babies from abortion because it's cheap and because they're available. What the public doesn't know is that there are other ways to go about the research that would be ethical. For instance, with drug-testing, when the Commission met in 1973, people from the Marine Laboratory in New York said, 'You don't have to use foetuses and embryos to tell you which drugs are lethal. We have been testing drugs on sea urchins eggs for years, and we could have told you about thalidomide, had we been asked to test that drug.' This is a very important point. And when we move over into hybridisation, into cryogenics, into artificial wombs, we are talking about technologies pure and simple. There is really not much medicine involved here.

In 1988, I had a conversation with a world famous mathematician, for whom I was doing some research work, and he mentioned to me that already the physicists who were planning to help with the installation of factories in outer space, were talking about the possibility of breeding certain genetic types, possibly dwarfs and of some mental retardation, to work there. They would be suitable because of the dullness of the operation and also because of their height, with the law of gravity as it operates in outer space. And he was talking about it in the most factual terms. Now who is going to own these people? When someone is unfrozen in a society a hundred years from now, what will their situation be? Will that society be hostile to them? Will they claim them? Will they treat them? Are we actually going in the direction of human slavery? We must get back to basics—to a more profound understanding of humanity, and of human suffering. We need to recognise the message that the Cross has for mankind. And that is a task for the theologians. I hope they take it up!

# Seven Wishes for Life

## *Professor Jérôme Lejeune*

These days, human intelligence is submerged by two contrary waves. One is the marvellous wave of understanding.

The other wave is an ominous one, the wave of obscuratism: the more we know about genetics, about mechanims of life, the less we know about human nature and about what is a human! British scientists are in the forefront for the good wave of understanding, but the British law makers are in the forefront of the disaster in the obscurantism wave.

Living matter does not exist. Matter cannot live, it cannot even be reproduced. When you reproduce a statue, what is reproduced is not the matter of the statue, because the replica is made of something else than the original. What is reproduced is the information imprinted in the matter by the genius of the sculpture. All genetics is about discovering what produces the animation of matter: because matter can be animated. We are animated matter. In life there is a message and if this message is human, then this life is a human life. Matter, if animated by a human nature, will be able to build a body in which a spirit will manifest itself inside the flesh. That is Genetics. That is the definition of a human being.

But now, if spirit really does animate matter (which is the core of our science of Genetics) we have to wonder whether the gifts of the Spirit could not help us to understand what is life.

There are seven gifts of the Spirit.

## *Wisdom*

Medicine can be defined by many systems of diagnosis, of prognosis, of treatment, but it has one function which can be summarised in one phrase—'*hatred of the disease and love of the disabled*'. If we change those terms of reference, if we begin to fight on the same side as the disease, eliminating the patient in order to eradicate the disease, we have an abortion of medicine. For example, in a circus, when there is an accident, you ask the veterinarian to kill the horse, but you ask the surgeon to rescue the rider. If the surgeon deliberately kills the patient, medicine has been changed for veterinarian technique. I hope, in this country, you will have the wisdom to differentiate between the one who uses biology as applied to animals, and the one who applies biology to mankind.

## Understanding

To respect every man, to try to care for him without asking him all his qualities, we need to know that every human being is to be respected just because he belongs to our species and that everyone is unique and irreplaceable.

That every human being is unique has been known for hundreds of years and statistically demonstrated at least fifty years ago. The number of combinations of genes is so great that we were sure that everyone had a specific constellation for himself. But that was a calculation. Now we can see it. Two years ago, it became general use, after the discovery made in this country by Jeffries four years ago. He manipulated DNA and was able to extract a very small probe of DNA, which recognises very specific segments of this very long message. When you extract the DNA from cells, you split it with specific enzymes which makes it migrate in an electric field, and you use the probe made by Jeffries. The result looks similar to the bar code that you find on any object in a supermarket, these various lines of different width, separated by different spaces, that a special optic device will read, feeding the information into the computer. Immediately the computer will tell you the name of the product, the quantity resting in the stock, and the price of the pack. The Jeffries technique tells us just the same thing. At one glance, we will see that those bands are only found in this particular human being. But if you study the genetic bar code of the father and mother of a child you will find that of each small line characteristic of that baby, half of them come from the father and the other half from the mother. This combination is unique, as it was unique in the father, as it was unique in the mother. Now we know that, we can say every human being is unique and we can even have a computer able to read it, like in the supermarket. In fact our Jeffries bands are a kind of identity card, which cannot be falsified and that you carry with you all your life, and demonstrate that you are this very person begot by these two persons. But there is something the computer will never read: the price of this person: because human life is priceless. This was understood when you could not buy a human being. Now, unfortunately, some scientists make an enormous mistake, and they suppose that human life is priceless because it has no value.

## Counsel

Nearly two thousand four hundred years ago, the founder of medicine, Hippocrates, made all his disciples swear, 'I shall not give a poisonous drug to anyone, even if required to do so, and I will not suggest such a thing, and I will not give any abortive drug to a pregnant woman'. In the same phrase, he said no to euthanasia, no to abortion. And for two thousand four hundred years, all the masters of medicine have given that oath. Now there are voices pretending that we have made progress. We can detect very early in pregnancy some pathological conditions that are directly deleterious for the baby. We can even detect minute difficulties, even dispositions that will appear very late in life. We can, for example, detect the gene of Huntington's disease, a very severe nervous disease which occurs after forty years of perfectly normal life. We can also detect Alzheimer's disease, a terrible dementia which in some cases is genetically transmitted.

Now, is it wise, prudent, is it good counsel, to propose to kill the patient because the disease has been detected early in their life, during the time that they were still inside the womb? I don't think so. Disease is a heavy price that every generation has to pay. It is a heavy price for the patients suffering, for the family in enduring and for the society in helping both the patient and the family. But this cost is the exact price that civilisation has to pay to remain humane.

## *Fortitude*

During the last three years, no advances in medicine have resulted from experimentation on humans. Achievement in controlling all the diseases which had been quoted three years before as requiring experimentation on human embryos, (Down's Syndrome, Haemophilia, Muscular Dystrophy and Mucoviscidosis) were obtained by science without *one embryo having been at risk by scientists*! Nevertheless, Britain's Parliament voted that a human being which is not yet fourteen days old is not a British citizen, is not even a member of our species! It is, for me, unbelievable that in a country of such a long legal tradition, such an enormous mistake can be made. If it was true that, after fecondation, a human being is not yet alive, there would never be a human being. 'If what they say is true, there is something rotten in the kingdom of Nowhere'.

## *Knowledge*

Nearly a year ago I was a witness in a Tennessee court; seven embryos had been frozen but now the parents were leaving each other. It was in Maryville; the name of the lady was Mary, and at that time she wanted to rescue her seven hopes who were frozen. The judge had to decide whether they were an item which could be liquidated, or whether they were human beings who should be protected. He decided that they were not things, because since slavery has been abolished there is not a third category between things and human beings. He decided that they must be given into custody and stated that custody should be given to the parent who wanted the lives of the children, and not to the one who wanted them to be frozen for ever. It was a judgement of Solomon.

Time and temperature are the definition of the flux of the reality. If we lower the temperature, we slow down the movements of the molecules, which is a measure of the time elapsing, and we freeze the time. We don't freeze the life of the embryo; it is the time which is stopped. If temperature comes back, life will manifest itself again.

## *Piety*

Piety is a reverence for those who have begotten you. Two years ago Sorani discovered in Britain that the father and mother do not exactly transmit the some message to the baby. The man underlines some sequence of the DNA on some given points. The woman does the same, but not at the same points. Nobody had believed this before Sorani's discovery, nobody had predicted it. If an egg is produced with the normal content of chromosomes, but all of them coming from mother, with no DNA marked from the father, this egg is not a human being. It cannot develop itself into a baby. It will just make various tissues, various specialisations of cells. It will make spare-pieces, skin, teeth, nails, hairs, but will not build a person. We call it a dermoid cyst or a teratoma, a kind of tumour.

Similarly, if there is only the marking of DNA from the father, it would not be a human being either. It will produce cysts, which look like little plastic bags, (hydatiformis mole) it can even degenerate into a cancer (chorio-epithelioma). So we know, by the demonstration of this special imprinting of the DNA by each sex, that we need to have one father and one mother to build a human being. One reads in the newspapers, that one can manipulate eggs in order to beget between women: to place the nucleus of a girl friend and include it inside the egg of a woman, so that the woman will become pregnant from her lesbian partner girl. That hypothesis is not propounded out. As we know from the discovery of Sorani that nature will not allow this to succeed; it would just make a teratoma, a kind of cancer, nothing else. The same for the 'gay nightmare' of producing a child by two different males: taking out the legitimate nucleus of an egg and putting inside two different sperms from two different men, and implanting it in some uterus to be rented. It would not work. This is an entirely 'has been' idea, it would not be possible, it is forbidden by nature. Similarly, a clone taken from a cell of a grown-up, will not be made. Even if you extract the nucleus of a cell and put it in an egg, it would not become a human being, because it does not have this special imprinting which is only made during the maturation of the male and feminine sexual cells.

'*Honour thy father and thy mother*' is really a commandment from God, because nature obeys it. You cannot have only two fathers and you cannot have two mothers; '*Honour thy father and thy mother in order for your life to be long on this earth*', because, if you do not have the genetic imprinting from your father and your mother, you will not be conceived at all!

## Fear

'Abandon hope, all those who come here', is not the kind of fear that I wish you will have, but rather a fear of abandoning the reverence for the Creator, of losing the respect for his creature. Technology is not bad. Even interventions upon the human genome are not to be banned *a priori*, as long as it is made in the interest of that very person in which it is made.

Every day we are getting more powerful, but not wiser, and so we get more dangerous. One of the dangers, for example, is the abortion pill, the RU486. It is the first anti-human pesticide. It uses two different drugs. It is a binary ammunition of chemical warfare. One, poison, the anti-progesteron, paralyses the system which allows the baby to be nourished by the mother, and the other, a prostaglandine, expels the baby. This binary ammunition should be forbidden in the world. Mr Bush and Mr Gorbachev have agreed to destroy the stockpile of chemical warfare that they had in their countries. If these deadly abortion pills are used, if produced industrially, they will unleash a kind of chemical warfare hitherto unknown to man.

'Timete Dominum et Nihil Aliud'; 'Have fear of the Lord and of nothing else'. That is the true liberty of the Spirit. And we need it absolutely, because in the years to come, Science with Conscience will be necessary to avoid the ruin of man.

# Post Abortion Syndrome: Trauma & Cure

## *Dr Susan Stanford*

There is hardly a place in the world today, particularly in the Western press, where when we hear the word 'abortion', whether whispered or screamed, it does not immediately evoke an emotional response within us. We have the media doing a tremendous job polarising those 'radical pro-life' groups or 'radical anti-abortionists' trying to inflict their Christian values on us middle-of-the-road folks. But it brings up feeling in almost everyone. And sadly it doesn't bring up feeling, or too often it doesn't, of 'how can we help that woman who is in that crisis pregnancy?' What we read in the press is always that people's rights are being denied if abortion is restricted. But I always say, as many of you have heard I am sure before, from others, 'what about the effect on the woman and her long-term peace of mind?'

The topic of abortion in America has become a highly written about, a highly documented topic. Interestingly enough, and to their credit, the *Los Angeles Times*, a highly reputed, though very liberal paper, has just been conducting a series of 'looking at itself', and by 'itself' it means all the press, and the way they report abortion. What we see is that they are admitting that there has been a bias. Sadly, psychologists like myself, and people like yourself, too frequently focus on the aftermath of abortion; we see women who are struggling, who are suffering post-abortion syndrome, because the press has told them, 'Honey, what's the matter? You shouldn't be worrying about that. Just put it behind you, just get over it. Let go of it.' But those of us who know the truth know that it is not that simple. Most of those women who abort know deep inside themselves that they have aborted *life*. They can deny it: 'It was just tissue, just cells. I'll get over it. I won't think about it. I'll get busy with my life.' She needs to numb herself to the grief, because all abortion is loss, the loss of human life, and we cannot deny such loss and grief. She may, through her denial, repress those feelings, but, they live inside her like a tumour, like a cancerous tumour that has a pus, contaminating the rest of her life. She becomes numb to other feelings, she feels deadened in some of her relationships, she has recurring nightmares about babies or baby kinds of things, she has intrusive recollections about the abortion; she tries to push them away, but they continue to come back, she may find herself struggling with forgiveness, getting irrationally mad, not being able to forgive somebody, when in fact the real root is the lack of forgiveness to herself, or the forgiveness that she has needed to ask from God. She need not even understand that she needs to grieve. This overall lack of truth in the papers about women suffering has unfortunately kept them in the dark. Many reach the point of despair and depression, not understanding why, and turn to various substance abuses: alcohol, prescribed medication to dull the pain, illegal drugs, eating disorders, feeding that big wound inside that has never been grieved; anything that will help them to dull the pain. But any proved psychologist knows that until the woman deals with the root cause, until she expends the emotion and the grief of that trauma, she cannot have resolution. Abortion does not resolve itself by itself. She may run, she may run into promiscuous relationships, she may run in many multitudinous ways from her feelings, she may have suicidal thoughts. She may in fact do everything she can to prove that the abortion decision was right, she gets very active in pro-abortion legislation, constantly trying to prove to herself that what she did was right. But I say to you that the lack of peace tells us the truth of what is really going on. Many women need to prick that balloon that is pent-up grief, and then they will say, 'now I am peaceful', or they will be honest and say, 'I know my decision was wrong. Thank God, God forgave me'. But they need to deal with the truth.

Mother Teresa, is quoted as saying, 'God gave us the family as a sign of His love' and I believe He gave us the family and He certainly gave us children as a sign of His love. Yes, the family is imperfect, and yes we make a lot of mistakes, but He wants us to love all of His creation. The act of intercourse by two people may be a mistake: it may be out of wedlock, it may be an extra-marital affair, it may be a rape. But the act of God's creation is never, ever a mistake. Mother Teresa said in Oslo, when she accepted her Nobel Peace prize, that the greatest barrier to world peace was not problems in the Middle East or Northern Ireland or South Africa or any one of the hot spots, it was abortion. That when we as human beings can desecrate that very life within us, can allow the creation in God's image within us to be torn from us, then we are living absolutely without conscience, and we allow any host of other trauma upon ourselves.

It is no coincidence, that child abuse has dramatically increased since abortion has become so liberalised. RU486 has been toted as the answer, to post-abortion syndrome. We will just give the woman the pill, she will self-abort, she won't have to go to the physician's office, so there will be less recognition of what happened, and it will all be a piece of cake. A French woman, Dr Obenis, reported in France in July 90 where the pill is legal, that half, of her study of twenty four women, were quoted as saying that they found it emotionally difficult and very trying to view the remains in the toilet or in the shower or somewhere at home, after they had taken RU486. The researchers who support the use of the abortion pill are reporting that there is no real danger physiologically with this pill. But I warn you, psychologically it is a nightmare that is about to come on women. As I have worked with women, many have looked at the aftermath of the abortion; nobody has asked them to, but they have looked, and I believe it is because of that deep inner desire of wanting to know, wanting to see their life. With RU486, she needs to determine that she has fully expelled the aftermath. We have given her the gun herself. Not only is she now going to be the one who made the decision to abort, but she becomes the abortionist in her own home. That is not a gift to women, that is a trauma. A woman aborting her child is trauma, it is wrong, it is evil. What is about to come upon us and her own suffering, we have not yet been able to imagine

However, there are some winds of change in the United States. The Webster case in the United States, issued by the Supreme Court, has begun to reflect the truth that I feel most Americans believe; abortion needs to be restricted. We have been terribly liberal in the U.S., and they let stand with the Webster decision, the fact, in the Missorri Statute, that conception is where life begins; they also allowed that any woman or man, being required to participate in an abortion, but who in good conscience did not want to, could in fact say no. Webster opened the door to encourage states throughout the U.S. to start to restrict abortion.

In June 1990 the Supreme Court issued statements saying that parents, of course, should be notified and that in general the family unit should be upheld, and that parents should act and counsel their children, their minors, with regard to abortion. In Pennsylvania, the Abortion Control Act, is being litigated regarding informed consent for women: that women will in fact be encouraged to look at all the real things that happened with abortion, and that spouses must be notified before a woman chooses to abort.

What does this mean for those of us who have fought against abortion for so long? Those few little pieces of news, at least in the U.S., are good news. They are news that places that have had such liberalised abortion, are beginning to realise the trauma that women are suffering. I encourage everyone of you who works towards life to take heart from that, to have hope with that, to do the work I feel all of us are called to do with the post-abortion woman. Take her with love, walk with her as she realises the truth of what happened, help her to bind up her broken heart.

I have had the privilege of working with many women who have been healed of their abortions, who have named their children, who have with guided imagery seen their children in the arms of God. And afterwards many of them write a love poem, many of them write a love letter to their children. When they in fact get through their denial, they come to the reality of what was really in their womb. One woman wrote me this poem after her healing:

'I knew before they spoke it, as women often do,
That a life had formed inside me, though I had prayed it not be true.
In an instant I was not alone, and fear stood by me constantly,
It attacked my thoughts in dark black moods, How could this have happened to me?
I do not want this baby, there is no other way,
"Get rid of it", were words I heard, and then it seemed a small price to pay.
The whiteness of the ceiling, bright lights and sharp cold air,
Are vivid in my memories, I never knew I'd care.
Years went past with only fleeting thoughts of what yet might have been,
And never once did it dawn on me that act had been a sin.
It never seemed to me that way until one awful night,
A nightmare broke into my sleep and I screamed and I cried with fright.
I could see the Lord standing beside me at that table, in that place,
And I saw His eyes, and I head His voice. And tears were streaming down His face.
In a broken voice he said to me, "My daughter, tell me why. I worked with love to make that child. How could you have let it die?"
Since that meeting with my Lord, He has healed all my wounds and forgiven my sins.
But I'll never be completely healed until abortion ends.'

# Commitment to Care

## Dr Phillipe Schepens

Modern medicine was actually founded in the fourth century BC by Hippocrates. Humans and their families always gave their life and health into the hands of their physician in full confidence. This was and is only possible because Hippocrates gave to his disciples the mission of keeping themselves only at the service of the human beings, who sought their helping hands. The health of the individual man is the physician's supreme law. Physicians had and still have therefore to follow Hippocrate's famous oath, and I quote the most important part, of that particular oath: 'I will use treatment to help the sick according to my ability, but never with a view to injury and wrong doing. Neither will I administer a poison to anybody when asked to do so, nor will I suggest such a course. Similarly, I will not give to a woman something to cause abortion. Into whatsoever houses I enter, I will enter to help the sick, and will abstain from all intentional wrong doing and harm'. It is clear that people could only put their trust in a physician who pursues such principles. The individual human was so important for Hippocrates and his followers that he explicitly prescribed not to make differentiation between man and woman, child and adult, citizen and foreigner, freeman and slave. Tensions between physicians and patients existed even before the time of Hippocrates. Nowadays, when the progress of technology has never run faster, the tensions are stronger than ever. The ethical discussions and topics of abortion, euthanasia, genetic manipulation, ecological pollution of air, water and food, contraception, extrauterine fertilization, organ transplantation, experiments on humans, torture and other similar so-called psychiatric treatments, are at the centre of politics. Discerning between what is good and what is useful, between what is permitted and what is possible, is every day a more difficult aim to achieve for many. If we want to secure the future of medicine at the service of the human species, we have to look closer at today's exact position of the physician in our society.

The physician today is submitted to temptations which constitute threats, both for the integrity of his profession and for the human species itself. I group them in three types.

The first temptation, for the physician, is the temptation of money. Whoever loves money more than the well being of his patients is an unworthy doctor. This kind of inversion of priorities is universally known and understood.

The second temptation is, for the physician, more elevated than the previous one. Pure science, own experimentation, own investigation, are put on a higher level than the health and the well being of the patient. This constitutes a clear yielding to the lure of our hyper-developed and over-technologised world. Science and technology, technological progress—they must remain at the service of humanity, not at the service of the personal strivings and ambitions of the researcher. This means to me a necessary condition for the further development of our civilisation. Science is absolutely unthinkable without conscience. Ethics must prevail over technics. This is more than ever true in medical sciences, since there, it is man himself who is the subject of research. The one who researches on human life must stick to the service of that life. The only human-dignifying attitude in that field will be an attitude of utmost respect for every single human life, without any discrimination based on age, race, illness, political or religious belief, etc. To exploit or discard human individuals, is to treat them as objects in strong contradiction to the nature of medicine. Whoever loves science and research more than the well being of the patient is an unworthy doctor.

The third temptation is even more elevated than the second temptation. The physician opts for the service of society and its rules, government, party, ideology. The service of the patient as a suffering individual comes second. The physician becomes the healer of the diseases which afflict society. He shares then the structures of power. He becomes an executant of the will of the leaders of the nation.

These three temptations appeal for the physician to put himself above other people. They flatter his pride. More money means more power, more science means more glory and therefore also more money and power. To share political power means more influence and more power. It is more important than the well-being of the patient. This does not imply that those physicians who fell into temptation are immediately bad doctors. There are many gradations, but to say 'yes' to those temptations means that the physician renounces his ideals which are first of all and unrelentingly the service towards every human being, his patient.

Exaggerated craving for money or for research or for social and political domination are three aspects of the same exaggerated egocentrism. Pride is here at its summit. The intellect is at the service of itself, of the cast of the ruling party and not at the service of man, of the suffering fellow human, of the patient.

These three temptations must be avoided if the medical profession is to remain at the service of the patient. The humanitarian and the Hippocratic character of medicine must not only be stressed in word and deeds, it must be perceived as clearly as possible in every single medical act. This cannot be stressed enough, especially in the teaching of medical and paramedical students. The medical studies, almost exclusively concentrate to create a medical technician who knows a lot about the function of the human organism and its disturbances. The fact that this good man works on the human being itself seems to be of lesser importance. The difference between man and animal seems to fade away. This must be changed. Physicians are the shepherds of liberty. It is not enough to say, 'I am against abortion, I am against euthanasia'; we have to offer alternatives, we have to help women in need, we have to help dying people in need, because for the dying, there is always an alternative to killing them.

It is of course easier for a physician to kill the people he can no longer cure. Many physicians do find it a bother to have patients they cannot heal because they think it is a failure of medicine. But this is not true at all, because medicine is not only concerned with curing people, but also with helping those you cannot cure. Ultimately we are all bound to die one day, with or without doctors. We cannot prevent that. We can postpone it, but that is all. So death is not a failure of medicine, but good medicine is to help the people we cannot cure.

Abortion and euthanasia, are always supported for the one and only reason that this particular human being, the child, or the elderly person, stands in the way of others, is a nuisance to others. That is the ultimate reason, maybe a very brave reason, maybe a futile reason. If we want doctors to really follow the Hippocratic and humanitarian vocation, the doctor must remain at the service of every member of the human family, no more at the service of the ruling class than at the service of the poor, no more at the service of the woman than at the service of the unborn. Therefore, in our opinion, not only abortion and euthanasia, (by euthanasia I mean the killing of unhealthy people), but also experimentation on human beings are major wrongs of modern medical practice, since they all discriminate, kill or harm, while alternatives do exist. It is useless to give hormones to women when you have natural family planning, which is completely harmless. Why take those hormones to prevent children being born, while there are other healthy alternatives? Of course there is no money to be made out of the teaching of natural family planning; prescribing hormones which are costly products, benefits the pharmaceutical industry, and I denounce that kind of collusion between medicine and the pharmaceutical industry.

One of the main principles of medicine is 'first do not harm', *primum non nocere*. I think that today's medicine must stick to that, as our forerunners did during the two thousand four hundred years since Hippocrates.

Further, what do those gynaecologists think when practicing a systematic search to kill unborn handicapped children by amniocentesis and/or corionvillae sampling. Once a so-called defective baby is found, the parents are informed and told in their natural and normal desparation that by aborting this particular baby, they can be free of this burden from their families. They say it is better that this baby is not born. Better for whom? How can the doctor judge over the happiness of another person? How can you deliver a death penalty to an innocent? How can you reconcile this attitude with both the Hippocratic oath and with Article Three of the Universal Declaration of Human Rights, which says everyone has the right to life? Does a handicapped baby not fall under the universal declaration of human rights any more? I accuse those doctors of perpetrating the most subtle kind of racism. What they are really doing is leading the way to chromosomial racism. They discriminate on a chromosomial basis. Anyone who has, for example, a third twenty-first chromosome which gives downs syndrome, or a fragile x-chromosome, or another impairment which gives a handicap, is, when detected, irrevocably killed by abortion when the psychologically vulnerable parents agree. The parents are the only ultimate guarantee when they say no to the proposal of abortion for their unborn handicapped baby, they are the only defenders left of the poor child, and if they agree abortion takes place. I call that eugenism in its most brutal form. There is supplementary evidence that they also do not refrain from killing completely normal babies when they know they are carriers of a recessive impaired gene which may end the next generation, as for example in the case of Hemophilia. Those people yield to the third temptation; they try to cure society rather than the individual, as the individual could be a so-called threat to society, and because a handicap is, in their eyes, a threat to society, they will kill him.

To treat a disease by killing the patient is indeed the most deviant way of performing medicine.

Such problems are the reason for the founding of the World Federation of Doctors, who respect human life. We are already about three hundred thousand doctors in some sixty countries. We want all doctors to respect human life so that we, the WFD, are no longer necessary. I ask you to motivate your own doctors. You have the right to know what your doctor thinks about life and death from an medical ethical point of view, for you put your health, sometimes your life in his or her hands.

# 5. YOUTH OF TODAY . . . PARENTS OF TOMORROW

## Education and Alternative Lifestyles

### *Rachel Tingle*

Early in 1985, I received a phone call which was to lead me into an area of work which I had never for one moment contemplated. It came from the late Raymond Johnson who was at that time research director of the evangelical Christian organisation CARE. Raymond explained to me that CARE had been receiving letters from some Christian parents and teachers in London who were concerned that, in various ways, it appeared that an attempt was being made to promote homosexuality through the educational system. He asked whether I would be prepared to spend several months researching exactly what was going on.

It was, quite frankly, just about the very last thing I wanted to do but eventually, and fairly reluctantly, I agreed. The results of some of that research are now available in a booklet called *Gay Lessons* which was published in Autumn 1986. What I want to do now is to summarise some of my findings and lay the background as to why Parliament should have felt it needed to make changes to the legislation governing schools' sex education, and should have also felt it necessary to bring in the now notorious Clause 28 of the 1988 Local Government Act.

From my research, I found that there seemed to be an entirely new campaign, spearheaded by a relatively small group of people, to use whatever means they could to promote the ideology of the gay movement. I should stress that this ideology goes far beyond demands that homosexuals should be treated fairly under the law, and it is not at all the same thing as an objective treatment of homosexuality in sex education lessons (both of which I would support). Rather, it is an attempt to so change people's ideas that they come to accept homosexuality as completely normal, or even, in some ways, to be preferred to heterosexuality. Correspondingly, any idea that heterosexuality is the normal and natural form of sexuality is referred to as 'heterosexism'—an 'oppression' which, like racism and sexism, must be overcome by education and political action. As a bulletin produced by the GLC Women's Committee in June 1984 stated;

> 'heterosexism is plainly and simply an oppression. Like other oppressions, it is perpetrated by a dominant and powerful group, in this case, heterosexuals. Like other oppressions, it works both on the institutionalised level, and through individuals . . . Like other oppressions it stinks.'

Furthermore, the publication *Tackling Heterosexism*, also produced by the

GLC Women's Committee (in 1986) argued that heterosexuality is not natural, but simply acquired. It says:

> 'In the same way, it has become clear that heterosexuality, like the assumed superiority of men, is not natural but acquired. The fact that the majority of men and women may choose (heterosexuality) as their preferred form of sexuality has more to do with persuasion, co-ercion and threat of ostracisation than with its superiority as a form of sexuality.'

To repeat then, most of the campaign I am talking about, was not so much aimed at encouraging tolerance and fair treatment of homosexuals. Rather, it was a campaign aimed at totally overcoming the idea that heterosexuality is 'normal'.

In the Autumn of 1985, the Greater London Council (GLC) published the document, *Changing the World: A London Charter for Lesbian and Gay Rights* which had been written by a working party of lesbians and gay men and which was sent to all local authorities in the country. It cost £44,000 to produce, but this needs to be set against a background that the GLC had already spent over £1,000,000 in the previous three years in grant aid to lesbian and gay projects. This document stated categorically that it aimed:

> 'to bring about a change of attitudes amongst the public, to dispel ignorance and foster positive attitudes towards homosexuality.'

Amongst its 142 recommendations, like those of the document *Tackling Heterosexism*, were many which were aimed specifically at children and teenagers. After all, it is easier to change attitudes when people are young than when they get older.

Let me mention just six of the many recommendations of those two publications relating to the young. These were:

1. The Inner London Education Authority (ILEA) and other local education authorities should make a positive commitment to challenging heterosexism in schools and colleges in the same way that anti-racist and anti-sexist programmes have been launched.
2. Heterosexism awareness training should be introduced as a compulsory part of teacher training courses.
3. In sex education lessons, there should be positive information on homosexual lifestyles.
4. Resources should be put into developing materials and changing the curricula in order to challenge heterosexism in lessons at all stages in the education process from primary school upwards.
5. Material should be available in school and local authority libraries which treat homosexuality in a positive way.
6. Openly gay teachers should be employed in schools.

It is important to be aware that, in London at any rate, such proposals did not remain merely recommendations on paper. ILEA set up what is called a 'Relationship and Sexuality' project to:

> 'educate against ignorance and prejudice with regard to homosexuality both in the formal and hidden curriculum.'

By 1987 it had organised a series of training courses on ways of challenging heterosexism with a wide range of ILEA staff like teachers, inspectors, and librarians. And in April 1986 it published an eighteen page *Positive Images* resource guide to books, videos and music about homosexuality which were regarded as suitable for use in secondary schools, colleges of education, and the youth service.

But althogh the tiny group of people staffing ILEA's Relationship and Sexuality project may have thought this material suitable for use with children, many of you here would, I am sure, be of a quite different opinion. It includes, for example, a novel called *The Milkman's on His Way* which is the story of the awakening homosexuality of a seventeen year old Cornish boy called Ewan. After a series of experiments in mutual masturbation with a heterosexual friend, Ewan is initiated into the joys of gay sex by a 23-year old London teacher. His first experience of anal intercourse (on a Cornish beach) is described in graphic detail. Ewan eventually goes to London, where he becomes a milkman and, more importantly, establishes himself as a pretty promiscuous member of the London gay scene.

Also included in the *Positive Images* guide is an extraordinary video called *Framed Youth: Revenge of the Teenage Perverts*. Because of its informal style and the use of pop music this will have instant appeal to many young people. It is, however, deeply subversive of normal family values. Throughout the video heterosexuals are made to look old-fashioned and rather stupid and, by the clever interlinking of scenes of boxing matches, missiles, nuclear explosions, and Mrs Thatcher, normal family life is made to appear as aggressive, violent and ultra-Conservative. On the other hand, the use of scenes of pairs of girls, or pairs of boys kissing and cuddling each other, makes the homosexual lifestyle look great fun and enormously appealing. What the video (like virtually all the rest of the material) does not do, however, is to show the other side of 'gay' life—like the extraordinarily high rates of promiscuity amongst male homosexuals; the precarious and unstable nature of so many of the relationships; not to mention the increased risk of certain diseases, and so on.

In other words, many of these books do indeed present *positive* images of homosexuality, but the question is whether they are presenting *truthful* images. Truth and objectivity are, of course, essential to good education, and if these are sacrificed one enters the realm, not of education, but of propaganda and indoctrination.

This is also true of other less obviously sensational material, like that produced by the London Gay Teenage Group. Their publications, *Something to Tell You, Talking about School, Talking about Youth Work* and so on, are also misleading in that they perpetrate what can only be described as the myths of the gay movement, notably that at least 10% of the population is homosexual (there is no sound scientific evidence to support this) and that homosexuality is an unchangeable condition—which is certainly untrue. These books, like many others in the resource guide, also provide names and addresses of gay and lesbian groups for readers to contact if they so wish.

Whilst I do not want underestimate the stress and difficulties faced by teenagers with homosexual tendencies, the dangers of all this material, as I see it, is that it can attract children to homosexuality who would not otherwise be interested. Moreover, it can lead adolescents experiencing a fairly normal crush on friends of the same sex to:

(a) believe they are homosexual;
(b) endorse the view that this is both good and unchangeable; and
(c) by putting them in contact with gay and lesbian groups, lock them into a homosexual lifestyle, possibly for life.

I do no hesitate, therefore to describe the effect of this material as the *promotion* of homosexuality, potentially leading to an increase in the number of practising homosexuals in this country.

I have talked about the activities of the Inner London Education Authority, but a number of other local authorities, particularly the London boroughs of Haringey and Ealing, have also attempted to adopt what they call 'positive images' policies regarding homosexuality. In the forefront was Haringey which, in 1986, set up a fund for:

> 'curriculum projects from nursery through to further education, specifically designed . . . to promote positive images of gay men and lesbians'

and which planned for all council employees to attend heterosexism awareness training courses. Such policies were adopted without prior consultation with parents, and rapidly ran into fierce opposition from many parents who formed themselves into local action groups to resist the policies. But when the parents in Haringey attempted to put their case before meetings of the Educational Committee or the Council, really horrific scenes ensued. The parents were shouted down, spat upon and urinated upon; every conceivable obscenity was hurled upon them and threats of violence were made. One of the leaders of the Parents' Rights Group in Haringey and her daughter later received threats on their lives.

It was against this background, and because of growing concern about some of the books now being promoted for use in sex education lessons in schools, that there was such a groundswell of backbench concern in Parliament that changes were made to the law relating to sex education. Under the 1986 Education Act, it was clearly stated that sex education should be given 'in such a manner as to encourage pupils to have due regard to moral considerations and the value of family life.' At the same time, control of the *content* of sex education was taken out of the hands of local educational authorities and placed with the re-vamped school governing authorities instead. These can now decide whether sex education lessons should be part of a school's curriculum or not and, if so, parents now have the right to know what is going on in them. In this way it was hoped that boroughs like Haringey, Ealing and others would find it much more difficult to impose positive images policies via sex education.

It is important to be aware, however that the intention of those advocating a 'positive images' policy was that this should not merely apply to sex education, but throughout the whole school curriculum—for example, in history, English literature and even in mathematics. Partly because of this, Parliament also felt it necessary to introduce new legislation in the shape of Clause 28 of the 1988 Local Government Act. This makes it illegal for a local authority to 'intentionally promote homosexuality' or 'promote the teaching in any maintained school of the acceptability of homosexuality as a pretended family relationship.'

The homosexual community has found it convenient to describe Clause 28 as some sort of wholly unprovoked attack by a repressive, morally authoritarian right-wing Government. In fact, the clause attracted cross-party support and it came about, not because of any initial Government initiative, but because back-bench MPs responsed to the wishes and concerns expressed by ordinary parents in areas like Haringey who felt at the mercy of a few exterme left-wingers and/or gay-rights activists who had gained control of the council.

In my opinion, then Clause 28 was a victory for educational sanity. Since it was implemented it has, to some extent, prevented the worse excesses of the so-called positive images campaign.

All this may sound like a success story for people like you and me who espouse the values of normal family life—and, in some ways it is. But any complacency is wholly unwarranted. The ideology of the gay movement has not gone away; and all this material—aimed at children—which presents homosexuality as normal and good has not gone away either. Moreover, the Labour Party has committed itself, in its election manifesto, to abolish Clause 28. If this should happen we might expect to see a renewal of the positive images campaign all over the country.

# Drug Addiction: Causes and Cure

## *Don Mario Picchi*

Some time ago in Italy two posters appeared. One reproduced the profile of a woman's face and the other that of a man's face; on the first, one could read 'I have a *small* child. I needn't give any thought to drugs. What can he know about them at his age? I'll tell him about them when he is older, but there is time enough. Moreover we are understanding parents, ours is an honest and respectable family. My son will never take drugs. I hope.'

The second poster read 'Drugs don't worry me. If my son took to drugs I would know at once. I know him too well, even though we do not spend much time together now. Should he have a problem, he would talk to me about it. I am his father after all. My boy would never take drugs. I hope.'

Hoping is not enough. Good intentions, putting off, avoiding decisions, expecting others—the school, the police, the government—to protect our children, all this is not sufficient. I have met hundreds of parents who have all put the same questions to me: 'But what do our kids want? What have we failed to give them? They only had to ask. We granted them utmost freedom, they could live as they wished.'

Why is the family unable to tackle issues as serious as drugs and the problem, also linked to drug addiction, of the spread of AIDS?

My priestly vocation and my long experience among fragile and maladjusted youths who very often have lost all hope and were more scared of life than of death, have led me to consider man and woman as the real problem, focusing on the person and not on the drugs.

In this perspective it is easy to see drug addiction simply as the symptom of a deep inner malaise. The question then becomes: 'Why is the family unable to forestall, contain and alleviate the malaise of the new generation?'

Many answers have been put forward. Psychologists and sociologists the world over have produced intelligent, penetrating and comprehensive theories. But the answers I prefer to quote here were given to me by a group of my kids, former drug addicts who at the time were completing the programme we have for them. The programme demands on the part of them, as well as of their families, a strenuous and painful commitment which gradually leads, among other things, to a new and positive relation within the family.

I then asked them: 'What more would you have wished from your parents?' Marco's answer was: 'Love. I longed for love. They gave me freedom to the point that I felt non-existent for them.' Giuseppe: 'Understanding. I longed for a family in which I would feel recognised, understood, loved. Instead I felt I was at home only to eat and sleep.' Lucia: 'Communication. My parents were punctual, precise, orderly, and asked of us children to be the same. But they didn't talk, not even to each other.'

Another youngster, Paolo, answered: 'I wish they had slapped me at times. I might have revolted there and then, but at least there would have been interaction.' Maria-Teresa: 'Attention. My parents failed to understand that children are already persons, small but capable of judging grown-ups.' Luigi: 'Freedom. My mother's anxiety was as strong and oppressive as my father's continuous absence.' Michele: 'Acceptance. My parents were firm, deliberate, self-assured. I couldn't live up to them and as a consequence I felt different and unhappy.' Francesco: 'A relationship between equals. Instead I was given things, gifts, material objects, all substitutes of love which my family was unable to give me.'

The question then changes once more. Why can't parents communicate, understand, accept, listen, find the proper way of exercising authority, of balancing rules and concessions?

One possible explanation might be the following. Adults who have experienced years of economic hardship find it natural to consider material satisfaction a priority for their children; but they fail to offer stable points of reference and certitudes.

In a similar vein one might argue that parents, in part, because they are absorbed in their fatiguing daily routine and in part because they believe that in a highly competitive society their children should be provided with the very best in order to 'Keep up with the Joneses', have done this at the expense of the essential inter-personal relations. It is these relations however that alone can provide young people with the goals and the means of growing up and becoming adults.

The crisis of the adult model: maybe this is what it is all about. There are young men and women whom we look upon as self-seeking, irresponsible, aimless, exclusively dominated by the logic of pleasure-seeking consumerism. But when they say, 'I want everything here and now,' or, 'I may do what I wish,' the message behind these words is: 'I don't wish to grow up, I am not willing to become an adult.'

It is an ill-worded, disturbing and yet dramatic indictment: many of our youngsters do not wish to become like us. We do not represent a valid model. We are unable to offer them promising openings towards a better future.

Besides: how can we expect young people to stay away from illicit drugs when we ourselves abuse licit drugs such as alcohol and tranquillisers, induced as we are by the hammering pressure of publicity to cure our fears and anxieties with a 'magic' pill?

How can we expect young people to be honest, frank, responsible, attentive and serviceable within the family, when the family sacrifices communication and dialogue to the pursuit of success, wealth and reputation? When in the home the young are not taught to express and to share feelings, and education and care are delegated to electronic babysitters, when parents refrain from hugging their children and saying, 'I love you,' to them?

How can we expect young people to be consistent and irreproachable when so many politicians, administrators, intellectuals show signs of ethical and cultural corruption?

How can we expect young people not to intoxicate themselves with noise, rock music, violent emotions, when some of our towns and villages have no facilities for play, sport or even for vocational training and study?

How can we ask young people not to opt out, and seek unconsciousness, when the world's arsenals are still full, and aid to poor countries often takes the form of a sale of weapons? When a minimal distraction may cause a nuclear disaster or an ecological catastrophe? How can we ask young people to look upon their own future and that of their countries with confidence, if we have never faced with them the great mysteries of life, if we have never explored with them such issues as life and death, ethical values, non-violence etc?

I believe that juvenile maladjustment, which is both cause and effect of the suffering of so many families, originates from these unanswered questions. Problems such as drugs and AIDS, which are relatively new, have caught unprepared almost everyone, families in particular that find little support from institutions and social services.

Nevertheless there is still space for building up a new consciousness and for pursuing a better future. In what way? Let us be careful not to expect institutions, legislators, men in power, to find universal solutions.

I have never believed in great crusades, those that 'others' are always supposed to fight out. Instead I believe that the fight against drugs and its consequences really begins when we place ourselves in front of a mirror and ask what *we* can do *here and now* to gain greater respect of ourselves, our youngsters and our society.

The commitment cannot start from above. It must start from below; it concerns us all. It must start from our homes. When we are able to give up our magic pills and stop seeking chemical peace at all costs. When we teach our sons and daughters to endure frustrations. When we learn to smile and prove that we are still able to dream, to make long-term plans, to give. When we recover the value of the simplest gesture, accept our neighbour's limits, appreciate the contribution of others and avoid over-stressing our own contribution. When we drop our mask and the image of righteous respectability we have chosen to wear. When we own that we are not omniscient and infallible. When we let ourselves be seen as normal parents, with our qualities, virtues, defects, fears, wishes, deceptions. When we encourage children to build up self-esteem, when we are ready to listen to them and hearten them. When we don't fix ourselves in front of the TV for hours, but instead enjoy sharing with them our thoughts and our projects. When we do not hide from them the apprehensions which are part of *our* lives. When together we seek significant and spiritual contents which transcend us. When we help young people to live their youth not as an end in itself but as an investment for the future.

My experience with the great number of families I have met has given me the measure of the courage and the passion that such things require. It is indeed normal to experience fear. The fear for instance to allow our son or daughter to measure the distance between what we say and what we do. The fear of not knowing how to answer.

Maybe in our homes we do not address certain issues because we are somehow ashamed, because our convictions are uncertain, because we are unwilling to halt for a moment and seriously reconsider our way of life and what would be worth changing.

If money could have the better of drugs, many people would easily win the battle. Instead also the very rich man is dramatically powerless. Drugs mean barren selfishness: they can be overcome only by love, sacrifice, readiness to serve, humility and hope.

I often say to parents with whom I work daily: 'What we achieve in our therapeutic communities and programmes you can practise in your homes, your offices, schools, factories, groups. The way to do it may differ in form but not in substance.'

Some people consider me an utopian just because I firmly believe the world can change. I do believe it because every day I see it happen in the many young people who yesterday were on the streets, forlorn, ready only to hurt themselves and others. These same young people today are again masters of their own lives, capable of inter-relating with the world and with their own parents to start with.

If our homes are a place where an open and sincere dialogue is possible, our children will listen to us and understand us. We shall not be strangers to each other. Our families will start a silent revolution to bring back hope and faith in our society.

# From Hippocrates to Hypocrisy

## *Prof Bernard Nathanson*

I want to start by posing a whole series of questions. Ten days ago I admitted a thirty-three year old woman in labour. She had had one baby three years before. We admitted her to hospital at 7.30 in the morning in labour. At 9.00 the electronic foetal heart monitor discovered that the baby was in distress. The line was flat and she was passing what is called miconium, which is a greenish substance indicative of a foetus in distress. We advised immediate caesarean section; she refused, she was frightened of the procedure. We had her husband, her mother and her sister all talk to her, but she still refused. So we called the hospital psychiatrist, the consultant. He saw her, interviewed her at length and concluded that she was competent and rational and that her decision not to have the caesarean section was one that we had to respect, with respect to her mental competency. We called her clergyman and explained the situation to him. He came, spoke to her and she still refused. It was now 12.00 and the foetal distress had been going on for three hours. We called the hospital administrator and he in turn, of course, called the hospital attorney, the solicitor. They spoke to her to no avail, so they went to court and the judge convened a hearing in her labour room.

At 4.00 pm. The electronic monitor was still showing a flat line, the baby was clearly in severe distress, even in agony. We did an ultrasound examination and the baby appeared limp with only a few breathing movements. The heart was still functioning but not very well. The judge heard the evidence and decided that the foetus, in this case, was a dependant, and a neglected child within the meaning of the New York State Children's Code, and he ordered the ceasarean section. She still refused to have the operation. The monitor was still showing a flat line and the baby was still in severe distress. What were we to do?

Angela Carter is a patient who is dying of cancer but is pregnant. She has had heavy chemotherapy for her cancer and there is a 50 per cent chance that the baby is seriously impaired from the chemotherapy. She has less than forty eight hours to live. We wanted to do a caesarean section to save the baby. She was too heavily sedated to give us an answer, 'yes' or 'no'. We asked her husband, the father of the baby. He said he did not want a caesarean section, he did not want his wife subjected to any more cruelty, any operations, and he did not, in fact, want a baby who might be seriously impaired. We asked Angela's mother and she said to go ahead with the caesarean section. What were we to do?

In West Germany, business people with severe cash flow problems may now bank their kidneys. According to a story in a West German paper, Count Rene von Ardelmansvelden has founded the Mutual Benefit Association for Organ Donation and Human Replacement. He has obtained the names of people who recently have become bankrupt. He writes to them along the following lines: 'Dear Bankrupt, you are now a social leper driven to take out loans or live on social assistance. But there is another alternative. Sell a kidney through me to your transplant patients. Even if the recipient does not survive, you do, both medically and economically'. The mutual benefit is up to $46,000. Is this ethical? Is it permissible to sell a portion of your body? Are your organs property? Are you property?

Pamela Ray Stewart in San Diego in 1986, pregnant with her third child, was diagnosed as having a placenta previa. This means that placenta, the afterbirth, was lying in front of the baby—a very serious condition in obstetrics which may very well precipitate a massive haemorrage and foetal death. She in fact was warned by the doctors, having bled twice before, that she should not have sexual relations for the remainder of the pregnancy because it might precipitate another haemorrhage which could be fatal for both her and the baby. She used marijuana and cocaine, had sexual relations, began to bleed, and bled heavily. But she waited six hours to call her doctor. When she finally admitted to hospital, a caesarean section was done. The child was brain damaged, and died six weeks later. Pamela Ray Stewart was arrested by the police. She was charged as follows: It is unlawful for a parent to fail to provide medical attendance or other remedial care for his or her child. But the father of this child was not charged. Should he have been? Should he, the father, have brought charges against her for failing to tell him that she was not allowed to have sexual relations? If she is convicted on the charge, what punishment should she get? She has two children at home. If she is jailed, so is the foetus. But if she is jailed, would this not have a chilling effect on poor, drug-addicted women seeking pre-natal care if they thought that because they used drugs, they were going to be charged with abusing their unborn? Would that not drive them away from pre-natal care? And in a country in which abortion is legal, does the fact that a woman has refused an abortion implicitly (after all she has carried the baby to term), impose a special duty on her with respect to caring for her unborn child, for instance a duty not to use drugs?

Diane Fannensteel is a twenty nine year old alcoholic who, two years ago, had a baby suffering from foetal alcoholic syndrome. Foetal alcohol syndrome is a deformity of the baby in which the face is severely deformed and the baby is very small, and most important, suffers from mental retardation. She is now pregnant again. Judge Denhardt advised her to remain alcohol-free in this pregnancy, and she did not. She continued to drink. The prosecutor brought charges against her and had her arrested. Question: should she be jailed? Should she be put in prison? After all, drinking liquour is not against the law. But the foetal alcohol syndrome is rare. It may not happen with this pregnancy. What if this child is normal but we have had her in jail for the remainder of her pregnancy, and she has been incarcerated in that case without cause?

Here is a news clipping from the *New York Times*: 'Baby is conceived to save daughter. Bone marrow donor needed for girl, seventeen, with cancer'. A middle-aged couple from a Los Angeles suburb have conceived a child solely in the hope that the baby's bone marrow cells will save the life of their teenage daughter who is dying of cancer. The Aolas found out this week that they only have 4–1 odds that this marrow would be good, and would be received by their daughter, yet they decided to go ahead with the pregnancy. They said, 'We have been searching for a donor for our leukaemia-stricken daughter for two years and we haven't been able to find anybody, so this is the only other alternative, to conceive a child who will be immunologically close to our daughter and therefore the chances of the baby's bone marrow being accepted by the leukaemic daughter will be greater'. Is that ethically acceptable, to conceive a child solely to be used as a source for bone marrow for their other seventeen-year-old child, who is dying?

Melanie Baldwin poisoned her first child. Now she is pregnant again. The judge has ordered that after this child is delivered she be sterilised permanently. Question: is that ethical? Is it good law? Is it humane?

Researchers have found that the scientific data acquired by the Nazi doctors, who experimented with Jewish prisoners by subjecting them to hypothermia during the Second World War: they lowered naked Jewish prisoners into vats of ice water and carried out scientific observations on how the body temperature went down and they ultimately died. Now researchers have found that these data which the Nazi doctors compiled can be life-saving when applied to homeless people sleeping outdoors during the winter in the northern part of the United States. Is it proper? Is it ethical? Is it acceptable to use such data, acquired in such a barbarous manner? Even to save lives, is it acceptable to use data that those Nazi doctors obtained in such an inhumane way?

More questions. On June 12th 1986 the physicians in Ontario, Canada, went on a 25-day strike. No medical care was available to anyone in the province, about four million people. The doctors claimed that after paying their expenses under the rules and regulations of Bill 94, the Health Care Accessibility Act, which sharply restricted their fees, they could no longer support their families, and therefore they went on strike. Is it ethically acceptable for physicians to go on strike and to deny to people under their care any further medical advice, even life-saving?

Now all these questions fall under the heading of 'bioethics'. Let me clarify what we mean by ethics. We mean how we conduct ourselves with regard to the distinction between right and wrong. Bioethics is the area at the interface of philosophy, medicine and the law, and bioethicists are confronted with these and many other questions and try to find a Solomonic answer. I personally have been looking for a one handed bioethicist, because every time I talk to a bioethicist he says, 'Yes, it's true, what you say is correct, but on the other hand...'

Most bioethicists practising today practise in a purely secular, curiously bloodless, 'situational' basis. It is what is called 'situational ethics' and the first element of this is autonomy, that is self-rule: a compelling, domineering, overriding respect for self rule. This means a person having an absolute right, unless it infringes on the personal freedom of others. The second element in situational ethics is beneficence, the obligation to promote the wellbeing of others, and the third is justice, the rights of individuals to claim what is due to them, based on certain personal properties or characteristics. Situational ethics has no rules, it has no timeless strictures, no mention of decency, honour, goodness, godliness.

So what do we look to? Where do we stand—those of us who reject situational ethics, this loose, flexible, collapsible, multi-directional, all-purpose, stretchable ethic, ethics to fit any situation comfortably? What do we look to, those of us who really want something strong, dependable and reliable in every situation, so that we do not have to make it up as we go along? We can go to the Ten Commandments, which were probably the first codified rules in bioethics. They were the Ten Commandments, not the Ten suggestions! The first major bioethicist was Hippocrates. He wrote his oath about twenty five hundred years ago. Doctors no longer take that oath. It said as follows: 'I swear by Appollo the physician, Escalapius, Hygia and Panacea and all the gods and goddesses, that according to my ability and judgement I will keep this oath and this stipulation...' and he goes on to stipulate certain things, and then he comes to... 'I will follow that system of regimen which, according to my ability and judgement, I consider for the benefit of my patients and abstain from whatever is deleterious and mischievous. I will give no deadly medicine to anyone if asked, nor suggest any such conduct, and in like manner I will not give to a woman a pessary or recipe to produce abortion, and into whatever houses I enter I will go into them for the benefit of the sick and will abstain from every voluntary act of mischief and corruption. I will not divulge anything which must be kept secret. And while I continue to keep this oath, may it come to me to enjoy life and the practice of the art. Rejected by all times, should I violate this oath—may that be my lot'. Well, the oath has been rewritten. It is now a corporate version. I am not going to go through the whole thing. This was written a year or so ago, and it says: 'I swear by the American Hospital Supply Corporation and Health Maintenance Organisations that I will fulfil according to my ability and judgement this oath and covenant. I will apply dietetic measures for the benefit of the obese, the alcoholic, the smoker and the drug addict, but because these days everyone has the right to do his or her own thing, I will seldom be able to keep them from self-harm and injustice. As an internist, I will not perform an abortion. In fear of malpractice I will guard my life and my business. I will not use a knife unless I am a surgeon. Into whatever clinics I come, I will come for the benefit of the insured, keeping myself far from all except capitated care for the underprivileged, unless they are not covered, of course, by the group insurance. If I fulfil this oath and do not violate it, may it be granted to me to enjoy life and business and to be able to retire at the age of fifty in the sunbelt'.

Someone at the Boston Medical School concocted his version: 'As required by law, I shall share with federal and state agencies, insurance companies, professional review organisations and the like, all strictly confidential information. Like any businessman or businesswoman, I will observe all anti-trust laws. Should I and my colleagues, with only the most honorable of intentions, meet to act and maintain professional standards, may the Federal Trade Commissioners suitably punish us for our noble efforts. If I keep this oath faithfully, may I survive in this hostile medical environment long enough to discover an alternative career so that I may enjoy life, respected by all people and in all times, but if I swerve from it or violate it, may the reverse be my lot'.

Hippocrates, by the way, was the author of this statement: 'Life is short, Art long, the crisis fleeting, experience perilous and decision difficult'. Do these strictures, these commandments, the Hippocratic oath help us with the other challenges which become increasingly pressing as technology becomes more sophisticated? Let me fire some more questions at you. In 1985, baby Fay was dying of congenital abnormalities of the heart. A baboon heart was placed in the baby. Was it ethical to put an animal part in a human? Was it ethical to use the baboon's, who by the way, is almost an endangered species? Should doctors be allowed to practice procedures on dying children, that is children in coma or near death, so that doctors can sharpen their expertise?

Should parents be allowed, for example, to use siblings in severe illness? A clip from the *Daily News* of New York recently is datelined Chicago: 'Thomas Bosi is suing to force his two children to undergo tests to determine whether a donation of their bone marrow could save their leukaemia-stricken half-brother'. He and his wife had twins. They separated and divorced, the mother got the twins. He remarried, had a child and that child developed leukaemia. Now he is suing to force the mother to submit the twins, which are the half-brothers of his own child, to donate bone marrow to save his child who is dying of leukaemia. How shall the courts rule on that? What about sex change operations? We don't hear much about them but they are becoming more and more frequent. Are they ethical? Are they permissible? How about the human genome project? The human genome project has now been funded with 3 billion dollars in the United States, the object being to map out every single gene on every chromosome in the human body. There are one hundred thousand genes. Genes control everything in our lives, from the colour of our eyes to whether or not you will get cancer or heart disease in your life. In due time this genome project will be finished and we will have the capacity to take a cell from your body or from a foetus for that matter, run it through a computer and it will have a print-out of every single characteristic that you have. Question: Who will share this data? Will the government get these data and use them against us? Will your employers get these data? How about insurance companies? Will the insurance companies be privy to these data? How about the military? Your fiancé, do you want him or her to know that you are carrying a gene, let us say, for cystic fybrosis, which will affect your children? And how about you yourself? Do you want to know what your genes are predicting for you and determining for you the rest of your life? Would there not be a severe increase in suicides if we all knew exactly what was facing us in terms of disease? How about 'designer children'? If we have the capacity to map genes, we have also the capacity to change them, to engineer their change, and in the future in the year 2000, you will be able to order designer children; you want blue eyes? We'll get you blue eyes, we'll change the gene; you want red hair? Fine, no problem; You want a life span of ninety-eight years? We can do that, just manipulate certain genes: designer children.

That is what is coming. Some of it is already here. There were four calves born in Texas recently, and each of these calves has human genes in them. We have now come to the point where we are beginning to mix species. Is that permissible? Look at selective termination of pregnancy, where a woman is carrying twins, triplets, quadruplets, or quintuplets, two or three or four of those babies can be destroyed, and the pregnancy still go on so that she only has one. That is going on frequently in the United States now. Look at the question of sale of foetal tissues and organs. Foetal brain cells have already been implanted in people with Parkinsons Disease in the United States. Soon we will have the use of foetal tissue for non-vital purposes. If your sex drive is failing, why not get foetal gonads, foetal sex organs; if you are losing your hair, foetal hair; if you are losing your teeth, foetal teeth; and so on. There is beginning, a huge commerce of this. We have problems and questions in the new reproductive technologies: IVF, GIFT, ZIFT. We have problems with the frozen embryos which result from these technologies. Look at the Davis case in Tennessee, where the frozen embryos were said not to be property but to be human beings and were awarded to the mother. But this is something which is still going on. This was at a lower court level, and this will be appealed. Look at the question of organ transplant. Is a commerce in organs acceptable? If organ transplant is acceptable, such as heart transplant, should it be Americans first in America, Britons first in Britain? Who gets it? Who pays for it? What are the age limits for somebody to get an organ transplant, a heart transplant, say? Are there people too old to get a heart transplant? Are there other limits? Look at surrogate motherhood. Have you heard of the 'Callaghan proposal'? This states: 'Research and development of all new life-saving treatment should be halted. No one over seventy-five years of age should receive any life-saving treatment, and to partially compensate, the elderly will become eligible for government supported nursing home care, palliative medical care for chronic disease and other support services'.

Finally, there are questions surrounding the end of life: withdrawal of food and water for those who are terminally ill, chronically ill; doctor-assisted suicide. Have you heard about Dr. Kovorkian's death machine, which he used on a woman in Michigan a month ago? It has been suggested he really should have experimented to perfect the machine with himself, but unfortunately he didn't get around to that! Active euthanasia, which in Holland is now socially a legitimised procedure, will soon be legalised there.

What can we do? Whom can we turn to? Can we turn to the government? No. Governments are baffled by these things.

What can we turn to? We can turn to people like the man who said in his Nobel Prize speech, in 1986, 'Sometimes', he said, 'We must interfere. I swore never to be silent whenever or wherever human beings endure suffering and humiliation. We must always take sides. Neutrality always helps the oppressor, never the victim. Silence encourages the tormentor, never the tormented. When human lives are endangered, when human dignity is in jeopardy, national borders and national sensitivities become irrelevant'.

We can turn to a great and profound document called '*Humanae Vitae*', which said this: 'We owe these physicians and medical personnel the highest esteem, who in the exercise of their profession, value above every human interest, the superior demands of their Christian vocation. Let them persevere, therefore, in promoting on every occasion the discovery of solutions inspired by faith and right reasons. Let them also consider as their proper professional duty the task of acquiring all the knowledge needed in this delicate sector so as to be able to give to those persons who consult them wise counsel and healthy direction'.

These words to me are the most profound, the most reliable, the most solid infrastructure of any bioethical mechanism I can imagine.

Finally, if you are still perplexed, there is a word from Malcolm Muggeridge, who said this: 'There must, in other words, be another reason for our existence and that of the Universe, than just getting through the days of our lives as best we can. It has never been possible for me to persuade myself that the Universe could have been created and we, *homo sapiens* so-called, generation after generation, somehow made our appearance to sojourn briefly on our tiny earth, solely in order to mount the intolerable soap opera with the same characters and situations endlessly recurring, that we call history. It would be like building a great stadium for a display of tiddlywinks or a vast opera house for a mouth organ recital. To suppose that the distinguished believers were all credulous fools whose folly and credulity in holding such beliefs has now been finally exposed, would seem to me to be untenable, and anyway, I would rather be wrong with Dante and Shakespeare and Milton, with Augustine of Hippo and Francis of Assisi, with Dr. Johnson, Blake and Dostovesky, than right with Voltaire, Rousseau, the Darwins, the Huxleys, Herbert Spencer, H. G. Wells, George Bernard Shaw, Dan Wather, Michael Dukakis and Senator Edward Kennedy'.

# The Electronic Generation

## *Michael Keating*

Perhaps this article might better be titled 'A Stolen Generation'. I think that we are witnessing an attemp to steal an entire generation, to steal them from their parents, and from their God, and to rob them of their own happiness. A famous American rock musician described thus:

> 'I figured that the only thing to do was to steal their kids. I still think it's the only thing to do. By saying that, I'm not talking about changing people's value systems, which removes them from their parents' world very effectively.' (David Crosby, quoted in Rolling Stone Interviews)

One of the most famous British youth idols put it this way:

> 'We're moving after the minds, and so are most of the other new groups.' (Mick Jagger)

The process of stealing is not confined just to one country or to one part of the world. It is truly an international event. In some countries, such as the United States, the stealing job is very far advanced. In some countries it has indeed begun, but it has not yet proceeded so far. The important thing to note is that in almost every place it is on the rise.

My purpose in this article is threefold:

First, I will try to explain the broad outlines of this process that I have called the Stealing of a Generation,

Secondly, I will take a closer look at what is going on in the United States, which I think parallels closely the situation here in Britain.

And thirdly, I will make some comments toward countering this attempt to steal the hearts and the minds of the young.

If we look around us, we see a world that is unlike anything in the past. We are dealing with what is in many respects an entirely new situation. Even a brief look at the modern world should be enough to alert us that these are new and strange times. The population of the world is immensely greater than it has ever been before, and is growing at a phenomenal rate. Rapidly expanding technologies are uniting the world in universal technological culture that is sweeping away every time-honoured tradition in its path. An electronic revolution has made the communication of ideas and of images incredibly rapid, extremely powerful, and all-pervasive. Old institutions, old values seem to be crumbling on every side, and no one can say what will rise to take their places. Change, in every direction, is the order of the day. We are increasingly estranged from the past, and increasingly uncertain about the future.

In such revolutionary times, is it not reasonable to suspect something new to arise among those who have been raised in such a world?

In the midst of this seething change, something new has indeed arisen. Originating among the youth in certain of the most advanced countries, and especially in the English-speaking world, a new youth culture has developed. It has become an international phenomenon, engaging the minds and the loyalties of young people from East and West, in Asia, Africa and Latin America, from Singapore to Paris, from Los Angeles to Moscow. And upon what is this new youth culture founded? It is sad to say, but it is founded upon animal sexuality, rebellion against every form of authority, drug and alcohol addiction, and profound hostility to God. It communicates itself with great power in larger-than-life images of its superheroes, and in the pulsating sound of its own very potent music. It stands against every kind of human restraint. It exalts the wild, the perverse, the prideful, the sensual as the highest of human values. It despises morality of any kind. It is often fiercely violent. It is obsessed by death, by skeletons and skulls, by the world of the occult. It proposes profound self-centeredness as the way to a happy life. It prepares those under its sway neither for eternal life with God, nor for succesful life on earth. It is destructive of all that families hold important. Indeed, it is destructive of civilization, of all that allows people to live together peacefully and productively.

It would seem that such a culture would be attractive to no one. It is obviously a bundle of lies. But the lies are cleverly told, and they break upon the youth with all the convincing power that music and screen can bring to bear. The young have not the wisdom and the experience of life to see that they are being lied to. They are being told that death is life, and they cannot see the deceit. So they drink deeply from the draught of death. And many of them are dying.

Is it accidental that at this unprecedented time in history, when the majority of the world's population is so young, and a period, when for the first time in man's history the possibility exists of creating an international culture rapidly, is it accidental that a powerful culture has come about, one that is so enthrallingly captivating to young people? Is it accidental that this new culture seeks as one of its primary goals to separate the young from any ties of loyalty or affection to their parents and to the world of their parents? Is it accidental that this culture is so profoundly antagonistic to God, and so abusive of the family? I suggest not. I suggest that we are seeing an attempt by the enemy of the human race to steal away an entire generation, a pivotal generation, a huge generation, a generation whose choices will affect the future in ways that we cannot see, but in ways that must be of great consequence for good or ill.

The origins of modern youth culture are to be found in some of the technologically advanced societies. An increasingly technological world has put a certain strain on the youth years. There was a time, and still is in many places, when the distiction between the world of youth and the world of adults was not so great. In a simpler society, the youth would enter the adult world earlier. They would be (more or less) responsible, and sometimes necessary, members of their society. They would likely have significant relationships with older people. The challenges of adjustment that naturally attend youthful years were thus encountered in the context of stable relationships and clear expectations. With the advent of a more complex society came the need for more training, and this not only for a few, but for the majority. Young people in a technical world have little to give their society until their late teens. Often a university degree is required, and this pushes the entrance into the adult world back into the early-to-mid twenties. So here was a group of young people in a ticklish spot. No longer children, and resenting being treated as such, capable of adult behaviour (such as having children) and passionately desiring to be taken seriously, yet they were not treated as adults, and had no real responsibilities except to themselves and to their training. They were hangers-on between two worlds, not children and not adults. Their period of adjustment into adulthood was thus lengthened and made more difficult.

It was among this group of young people that modern youth culture was born. At first the adults were careful to control the youth world for the benefit of the young. They invested time and energy in passing on their way of life, their morality, their faith, and their human competence to the youth, rightly seeing the importance of these years as a time for young people to gain the moral character and the abilities necessary to deal with a complex world. Schools were the most obvious example of this. In various ways, in families, in schools, in the Church, the youth were well connected to the wider adult society, and gained a good measure of wisdom and protection from their elders.

But especially in the last thirty years or so, the youth world has been under severe attack from adults who have tried to wrest control of it for their own purposes. Why would they want to do that? Sometimes it is because they wanted to change the society. The strategy might be stated as capturing the youth to capture the future. More often it is because they wanted to get rich. They saw that young people had more and more money, and little to spend it on but themselves. They found that the way into the pocketbook of the young was to appeal to all of their most base desires. In any case, the capture of the youth world in these countries was largely accomplished.

It is important to see that youth culture is not devised by the young. Youth, on the whole, have neither the ingenuity nor the resources, nor for that matter the desire when left to themselves, to wage war against the whole of adult society. They tend to follow adults. The adults many of them began to follow led them down a path of human spiritual destruction. So problems with youth are often not primarily youth problems. They are adult problems, and family problems. The youth are caught in a snare that they did not make.

Let me explain how this capture of the youth world was accomplished. First, and this is very important, it was made possible by virtual abandonment of the youth by their elders. As family life has grown increasingly weak, as marriages have broken up, as people have assumed a more selfish attitude toward their time and money and have been less willing to spend it on children, the young have been left in a world by themselves. Parents let them do as they pleased, schools relinquished their responsibility to educate the character and morality of their students, 'chaperon' became a bad word. And all this was done in the name of freedom. The result has been the worst kind of slavery, as others have rushed into the vacuum and have taken their places as leaders of the youth world.

To get at these abandoned youth, it was necessary to gain control of the most significant youth culture carriers. The carriers of youth culture are the roads, if you will, that the culture uses to gain entrance into the lives of the young. Of these, the most significant were four: (1) the family, (2) the schools and education, (3) the peer group, and (4) perhaps most important in this process, electronic media, and especially music. (It is hard to exaggerate the importance of music in the youth world. It is not too much to say that music almost defines the boundaries of youth culture. It creates a world in which young people live, and provides them with their most exciting and most compelling models for life.) In any case, all of these strategic points, these carriers of youth culture, were assaulted and fought over. Some were largely captured. Over some, and I am thinking here of schools and family life, the battle is still raging, but the defence grows ever weaker. The result has been that young people now often inhabit a world of their own that can make them seem strangers in the very homes of their parents (unless of course their parents decide to join that youth world themselves, which is happening more and more.)

Once the key carriers of youth culture were captured, they then became the means used to fill the youth world with hellish doctrine. It is a dark business to study this culture. It is filled with blood, with futility and despair, with self abuse, with irrational lusts, with the neurotic and the diseased. Many of the heroes of the youth world are themselves seriously unhealthy people, psychologically unstable, often exalting all that is sick and sinful. How strange that this time of youth, a time so naturally characterized by high hopes and lightness of heart, by thinking too well of the world, by a kind of freshness and joy, should be thus perverted into a time of darkness and death. How sad that the heroes of the youth world should be so depraved, as one popular singer whose New Year's resolution was 'to absorb larger quantities of alcohol, a larger intake of illegal substances and spread disease throughout the world.' (Nikki Sixx of Motley Crue)

And so the young have become increasingly rebellious toward their parents and teachers, toward God, just as they have been taught to do by their heroes. They have learned to drink in wild frenzies, and to become addicted to drugs, and to abandon themselves to pleasure. This has been a tragic situation for us in the United States, and there is hardly a family in our country that has not been touched by the desperate behaviour of teen-aged youth.

The next step was for this youth culture, now in possession of the youth world, to pursue an expansionist policy up and down the age scale. The youth were a kind of beachhead, an unprotected flank, through which to attack the whole of the society. Increasingly we have seen all of our society being made adolescent, as little children are taught to be sexy and sophisticated, and middle-aged people are encouraged to forget duty and commitment, and to pursue fun and fulfillment in a new hair style or a new wife. Partly through graduation, as young people have moved into adulthood, and partly through clever marketing, youth culture began invading the wider society. The same attitudes of rebellion and violence, of sensuality and self-centeredness, of lack of regard for anything but today's pleasure, could be seen echoing throughout the adult world.

Then comes the export business. And this is where we here begin to be affected. From its home in a few countries, this youth culture has become an international affair. It is remarkable to see how all-pervading it is. It crosses every boundary. It finds its way into every part of the world. As soon as there is a little money to spend, and a little electronic capacity, youth culture makes its entry, and tries to steal the hearts of the young. Let me mention just two examples that might stand for a general pattern.

I have a young friend from an island in the South Pacific. He has been studying in New Zealand, and he recently made a visit back to his home after being away for a few years. He told me that the youth of his island have changed radically in that short time. Drug use is on the rise, vandalism and fights with police have gotten worse, and the young have become disrespectful toward their elders, a particularly grave symptom among his traditional people. I asked him why the change? After all, his island home is quite remote. They just began receiving television last year. His answer? American rock music. It recently made an entry there, and the youth of the island have gone wild over it. In the process they have picked up more than a new style of music. They have taken on a new way of looking at the world.

I have another young friend from the Central American country of Costa Rica. He spent three years in the U.S. working on a university degree. Upon his return to Costa Rica, he was shocked at the change in the young. He was so concerned that he decided to go into youth ministry to help them. He told me that the young people in his country are doing everything they can to catch up with the American youth. They haven't caught up yet, but they are changing rapidly. And this is true in many places. The same glittery heroes, the same appeal to barbarity, the same hostility to God, can now be found among the youth of all continents, and its influence is on the rise.

And what is happening to the young who are captured by these clever lies? They are having a very hard time. They are being taught the lie that slavery to sexual lust is deep joy, but they don't experience it that way. They are being taught the lie that alcohol and drug abuse enhance life, but they experience the opposite. They are being taught the lie that the whole world is having a fun party, that everyone is beautiful and sexy, but their experience of themselves is different and difficult. They are being taught the lie that rebellion against God brings freedom and peace, but they experience only bondage and turmoil. They are being taught the lie that they will find fulfillment in selfishness, but they experience only pain and emptiness. And being too young to see that their supposed heroes are lying to them, and are perhaps even blind to their own deception, they think that the problem is within themselves. The life they experience is the opposite of the life they are taught to expect, so they grow depressed and despondent. They become cynical and jaded. And often enough, far too often, they find their escape in chemicals, or they end their lives outright. The last thirty years, years of incredible affluence and unlimited opportunity, have seen an increase in the suicide rate among teens in the U.S. rise by 300%. This kind of statistic screams at us, that something is desperately not working.

So how are we to respond to this? Is my intention to paint a dismal picture so that we can become experts at moaning and wringing our hands? Hardly that. Is there nothing that can be done? On the contrary. There is much to be done. But we need to know what we're facing, if we want to make an effective response. This sad story of the stealing of a generation is not an inevitable story. It need not happen this way. God has not abandoned them or us, and he also has a strategy for this generation. I want to make three comments, toward dealing with our situation.

The first is to note the great importance of strong family life. The youth become vulnerable when they are abandoned, and that abandonment is usually the result of a breakdown of family life. When the family is strong, loving, and stable, when the youth have significant relationships of respect and love with their parents and other adults, they find the extremes of youth culture less attractive. I have found it to be generally true, that the stronger the life of the family, the less the ill effects of youth culture on their children. It is the youth whose family has collapsed around them, or whose parents have forgotten them amidst their own concerns, who are most likely to look for fulfillment by diving headfirst into the youth world.

My second comment is to note the strategic importance of what I have called the youth culture carriers. Besides the family, which I just mentioned, these include the schools, the peer group, and the various forms of media. We need to pay attention to who is controlling them, and for what purposes. We need to help our children to steer clear of the great harm that can come to them through false education, or bad friends, or perverse movies and music. I have often seen parents confused by the way their children change before their eyes, as their son becomes rebellious or sullen, or their daughter comes home pregnant. But often enough there should be no surprise at all. Often enough the children are doing just what they have been taught to do by their heroes, or by all their friends. As parents we must put aside a certain naiveté about the youth world, and offer our children protection in these areas.

My third comment is to suggest that the ultimate solution for the youth of our day lies in turning their hearts to God. I have found that there is great hunger among this generation, a hunger for truth, for deeper meaning, for God. Indeed, they often pursue their youth culture idols, their rock and screen stars, because they think they see in them something beyond the mundane, something seemingly spiritual, something that will take them out of a world hemmed in and darkened by its tawdry materialism.

And so we find ourselves in the midst of a battle, a battle for the hearts and the minds of a whole generation. The casualties are mounting. A secular youth culture is loudly proclaiming its message. Cults and sects spring up like mushrooms, promising spiritual fulfillment. But their triumph is not inevitable. We can successfully fight against this godless culture, if we do not abandon our youth, if we stand by them, and protect them from those who would steal them away, if we counter the attack with determination and with faith. The consequences of this battle are enormous. A whole generation hangs in the balance.

# Families Mean Fathers

## *Dr Patricia Morgan*

The anthropologist Malinowski pointed out long ago how the moral traditions and laws of all human societies decreed that a woman and her offspring was not a socially complete unit, that the human family consisted of a male as well as a female, and that children should be brought into the world with both a male, and a female link, between the child and the rest of the community. Such links are infused with a sense of continuity to embrace both male and female, the living and the dead, and give cohesion to family, kin and society.

Just as it was the capacity to make, enforce, and follow rules that made human society possible, so human mating and reproduction have been universally governed by laws, moral rules, and beliefs at every stage. Our development is such as to need social regulation and social stability for the prolonged care and socialisation of dependent children. It is 'institutionalised fathering' which highlights the crucial difference between human and non-human reproductive relationships, for here we find created in the family a new type of bond for which there is no prototype in the animal kingdom. Fatherhood does not come into being through biological, natural events, but is established purely by rules, by social provision and, as such, it exemplifies the rule-making and rule-following that is basic to the emergence and existence of human society. It is the expression, not the corruption, of all that is quintessentially human.

The necessity for the marriage tie demonstrates how the father is made to look after his children, to a large extent because it is his duty. Fatherhood imposes radical restrictions and self sacrifice on men who, as feminist Germaine Greer has realised: have to deny themselves the ' . . . anti-social satisfaction of seeing how many children they can sire, and cultivate instead a desire to be actively involved in the few they may sire'. Male participation in child rearing is part of that process of group collaboration and joint action upon which all human survival and success has depended. In turn, fatherhood bears witness to the way in which human life, as opposed to animal existence, is a system of mutual obligations and interdependencies. For, in the human family, altruism—most fully expressed in parental relationships and all the processes of parental care with their obligatory sharing—becomes a binding moral force. It involves rules of conduct which emphasize the willingness to forego selfish gratification for the sake of others and underlies the feelings of solidarity which underlie cohesion and control in all societies.

The human family has to endure since family bonds are necessary for the transmission of culture from one generation to another—a function as important as the propagation of a people—for neither could survive without the other. Every society stands or falls on what it can pass on to the next generation—material and otherwise, and this involves a lengthy process of education of great complexity. Inseparable from social relations, it includes the inculcation of conventions, the building of attitudes and sentiments and the development of morality. Since it enables their skills, energies and resources to be harnessed in the interests of the next generation, the involvement of men in families would seem a remarkable human invention.

The savage attack on the family of the past couple or more decades is, of course, essentially an assault on fatherhood. Seen as the prop and product of oppressive forces, the family's foundation as a social institution through the incorporation of men, became the fall from grace; a global enslavement of women and children powered by the thirst for domination and possession. More than useless appendages, fathers are malign growths on families, so that as we progress, the male contribution must be led to disappear. In its place is a world of 'self-sufficient' mothers who have children entirely on their own terms and men do not seek to protect or provide for the children they spawn.

Otherwise, fathers only have their uses insofar as they take on their 'partner's' childcare and household chores so that she is not held back in the competitive struggle. If they do not then they are simply behaving irresponsibly or are 'uninvolved'. One implication of this is that men currently contribute little that is of any worth or significance to childrearing—so that there is nothing to lose or disturb if they get stuck into those chores. Or anyway, they might make a positive contribution to childrearing if they became like mothers—except, again, there is that uncertainty whether it is optimal child development that is the criteria of performance here, or the maximisation of the woman's career prospects—which is rather different. However, it all reflects a deep contempt for men's role in families as much as a long-standing dismissal of their relevance to child development which pre-dates the modern rise of feminism.

Yet, this all flies in the face of the plethora of evidence that fathers are an addition, not a subtraction, to every area of child development and child welfare: that their involvement means a qualitative, as well as a quantitative difference to all domestic relationships through the establishment of the family as a social group—and that their functions are often gender specific.

Beginning with life itself, perinatal mortality is consistently higher for illegitimate children compared to legitimate ones in advanced societies. These are not statistics one would expect if men really behaved like the feminist stereotype: brutalising the family and taking the lion's share of resources. But, they are not new and neither are they explicable in terms of economic factors or the maltreatment of the illegitimate child and mother. We even know for example, that the number of infant deaths in the last century in 'fisher families' where the father was obliged to be away from home for long periods were double those where he was not.

Indirect effects of quite impressive scope and consequence are shown in the way in which father involvement significantly enhances development and well being when children are with mothers as well as their fathers. The father's positive relationship with the mother enables her to perform better as a parent in every respect. From the earliest days, it increases her effectiveness in the care and feeding of her infant; enhances her relationship with the child and helps her foster the child's psychological and intellectual development. Not only is there an association between high father involvement and secure boy-mother attachment, but it is one indication of how the tie between mother and child is itself more difficult to establish and maintain without the presence of another interested adult. Such information highlights both the complex nature and interdependence of relationships within the family system and shows how human beings were meant to be part of social groups, not living and bringing up their young alone.

In any enterprise, including child rearing, standards are maintained, performance improved and excesses checked through the expectations and responses of other people, who tend to bring out the best in each other when they work as a team. Those on their own do not receive the same kind of feedback for their efforts which tell them what they are doing is right and worthwhile; without the collaboration, confirmation and correction of others, confidence, standards and any sense of purpose easily decline.

Marital breakdown and single parenthood are associated with heightened levels of child neglect and abuse, with only one third of children on abuse registers living with both their original parents at the time of abuse. Parental absenteeism often means the presence of unrelated males in the home where, if she does not remarrry, the woman may associate on a regular or intermittent basis with one or a succession of men. Girls in these circumstances experience a fivefold increase in sexual abuse compared to those living with both natural parents. In case this seems to show how men are unfit to be near families, it must be emphasized how mothers too are more likely to illtreat and neglect their children where fathers are absent or otherwise poorly involved. Moreover, abuse also occurs outside the home, and the risks of children falling victim to it is affected by family circumstances. Paternally deprived boys are more vulnerable—not only to be overly influenced—but also abused, by dominant peers.

In turn, one of the more practical advantages of being a group is that this makes available a division of labour which is not possible where one adult is left to perform the tasks and functions otherwise distributed or shared between two. Because child rearing makes so many demands, the greater options open to two people compared with one ensure that more of these can be met. Two parents can not only supplement each other, but each may compensate or help to make up for any of the deficiencies of the other; with one parent, more hinges on the attributes of that single person. Conflict in one-parent families is more damaging for children than high levels of conflict in two-parent families. This is an aspect of the way in which the nature of the relationship with the remaining parent becomes more crucial to the development and adjustment of the children of lone parents, than is the children's relationship with either parent in two-parent families. A second parent may be able to protect the child, or provide a buffer, against the disorientating effects of domestic conflict or poor relations between the child and the other parent. This is something which, by its very structure, the one-parent family cannot provide.

Indeed, if the home is critically dependent upon the viability of one adult, that person's physical or mental illness can obviously devastate that home in ways which would be unlikely were there two parents. More one parent as compared to two-parent families, are apt to find themselves in circumstances which have moved beyond their capacities to cope so that they become no-parent families, and the children go into institutional care. Particularly in lower social groups, the presence of a father seems to be vital to the sheer physical existence of a home at all.

Children who have been in care do less well at school than those who have never been in care. The results are not simply due to the effects of being in care itself. Both reception into care and the adverse outcomes associated with this owe much to family insufficiency and are attributable to lack of parental attention and interest, conflict and stress at home.

All the indices of maternal and paternal participation in child-rearing measure not only the amount of contact a man or a woman has with their children, but something about the cohesiveness and philosophy of the family. And both cohesiveness and ethos are located in the family as a social group and hence, a little moral community. This provides the focus and reference point for both spouses where the father's and mother's involvement with the children is part of, and sustained by their commitment to a common life and the maintenance of a domestic environment in which this can thrive. But parental absenteeism is often marked by low levels of general family integration and involvement of the young with adults in a household. Contrary to the expectation that the one parent will compensate the children for the loss of another parent's attentions, this is not what often happens. Parental attitudes are as important as time and energy, and it is not simply that when the adult has to do more this puts pressure on what they can accomplish—but the domestic ethos itself changes without another committed adult. Thus, divorce is often seen as a gateway to a new life for the parent, which can leave children feeling that parental attention has been almost totally withdrawn. The position of children from previous unions may become untenable where there are new partners, so that they may be forced to leave home. In turn, the never-married mother may be oriented towards a singles' lifestyle in which her own interests and relationships absorb her time and energies in ways that are at odds with the interest of the child.

Conflict is not only more damaging to children in one-parent homes, but it is more common. It is not only more likely to occur between mother and child, but the making and breaking of relationships with boyfriends, or the comings and goings of cohabitees all multiply the occasions for domestic crises and disputes.

It is not only a child's basic care and welfare, but also their linguistic, educational, intellectual, moral and social development which are dependent upon the adult attention they receive. As the ratio of involved adults drops, attention is more thinly spread and the absence of one of the two primary socialising agents means that it is far more likely that the children will be comparatively disadvantaged in one or more respects. Underachievers, delinquents and drug takers have long and repeatedly been found to have poor relationships with their fathers, who are more likely to be rejecting, hostile, detached or simply missing. Conversely, the availability of an active, involved father makes it more likely that individuals can realise their potential, since father involvement contributes uniquely to child development, independently of any other characteristics of parenting. Anybody who seriously wished to consider the possible repercussions of hastening the exist of fathers from the home might do well to look at the now sizeable body of evidence demonstrating how they exercise a very strong influence over children's intellectual development. They might also attend to the most stable findings to emerge from investigations of child rearing practices: that father absence is consistently linked to delinquency or other irregularities in moral development. Among the places this is to be found are the large scale longitudinal studies from both sides of the Atlantic.

In addition to documenting a wide range of negative outcomes among children from mother-only families, studies show that income sometimes accounts for part, but not all, of some of these effects. Even in respect of school drop out rates, where the income influence could be expected to be high, economic factors barely explained half of the difference between children from mother-only homes and two parent families. In turn, the effects of parental absenteeism or detachment are consistent across racial and ethnic groups. However, the detrimental effects are most clear cut and far reaching for lower class individuals and for males: attainment and performance are affected before intelligence and the earlier, the more long term and the more complete the parental absence the more negative the effects. Moreover, the differential rates of paternal involvement and absenteeism between ethnic groups also go far to explain the different outcomes between children from the various ethnic groups.

That it is the father who plays the important role is demonstrated by the way in which delinquents in intact families are more likely to come from homes where the father is hostile, or rejecting or uninterested. John and Elizabeth Newson, for example, looked at the effects of different levels of father involvement in intact families at four different ages in their long-range, well-known analysis of more than 700 Nottingham children and found that father participation from an early age was significantly related to lower criminality and, from middle childhood, the child's aspirations and educational achievements. Data from the National Children's Bureau's longitudinal study tells a similar story of how a child's educational attainment at school is closely related to the father's interest in the child's progress irrespective of social class—and even such small matters as the willingness of the father to discuss his child with the teacher had large measurable effects.

Two-parent households provide increased supervision and guardianship not only for their own children and property, but also for the community. The supervision of peer-groups and gang activity is not simply dependent upon each child's family, but on a network of families. Where there are communities of intact families, laws are easier to enforce. But where the institution of fatherhood is undermined, government finds itself faced with a task of maintaining order far beyond its abilities.

If the extent of a child's relationships with adults is the measure of his integration into society then much the same applies to adults—for father absence encourages drug use and delinquency not only through its negative effects on emotional well-being and household discipline but its corrosive effects on community structure. If boys are not involved with men, then men are uninvolved with families, and atomised individuals are far more likely to end up a nuisance to themselves and a threat to others compared with those who have secure and respected ties.

Certainly, a paucity of home ties not only mean that juveniles gravitate towards their peer group, where they tend to mix violently with each other and similar groups. The peer group boy's problems are exacerbated by his lack of an accessible role model from whom he can learn how to delay gratification, and control aggressive and destructive impulses. He is not in intimate association with somebody who might be able to demonstrate how more appropriate behaviour befits a male.

There is hardly a more erroneous and dangerous notion than the one proclaiming that a less violent and more law-abiding generation could be reared without the influence of men. What we can predict with some certainty is that any rise in the number of boys without close ties to males with socially acceptable standards of behaviour is the very thing likely to generate a brutalised and violent masculine style, as boys detached from men endeavour to stabilise their sexual identity in crude, uncorrected ways.

Research indicates that conscience development and delinquency, are areas where the father's, rather than the mother's, role is of primary importance. It is common to find poor father–child relationships as antecedents of delinquency, even where there are normal or good mother–child relationships. A combination of paternal dominance in discipline and high levels of paternal affection bear the strongest association with male children's sensitivity to their moral transgressions. But paternal detachment is not simply related to delinquency and drug abuse via matters of values and social ties. Observational learning, or modelling, is important and a boy's perception of his father and other males is crucial to the development of his own concept of masculinity. The development of sex-appropriate behaviour is difficult, if not impossible, to separate from wider social expectations and other rules of behaviour. Even if the behaviour of the sexes was to become identical, boys would still have to see how it was appropriate to a male. The teacher is gender specific, even where the message need not be.

Part of the way in which fathers play crucial, gender specific roles in the development of children is not only through what they are, but the ways in which men parent differently from women. Given this, it is a grievous mistake to conclude that because a father is not behaving like a mother, or doing child care and other household chores, he is therefore contributing nothing. We have seen how it is his relationship to the mother and his own involvement with the child which is predictive of the *mother's success* in dealing with her child—not the degree to which he actually participates in child care. Responsibility for child care chores is a measure neither of parent–child attachment nor parent–child involvement and is not significantly associated with any of the child's characteristics. Some of a father's most important contributions cannot be remotely represented in terms of any servicing functions. This is illustrated, for example, by the way in which fathers discretely monitor and police the relationship between mother and son so that this may be sustained in a mutually satisfactory way instead of deteriorating into the kind of mutually antagonistic struggles often described for mother-only households.

The most influential and beneficial fathers who take their role seriously, and consciously involve themselves closely with their families tend to spend more time with the children. Equal rights activists, or course, condemn this as a cop out from responsibility, accusing the father of only doing the 'nice bits' of childrearing to avoid the chores. Yet, he is engaging in what are well known as developmentally beneficial activities, and an increase in his workload outside or inside the home is likely to erode this time spent in ways which are so strongly associated with children's performance in socio-cognitive tasks, or problem solving skills. Put simply, the central role of the father is as playmate rather than caregiver.

Like mothers, fathers are more comfortable and successful parents to their infants and older children when they receive encouragement and emotional support. And where, in healthily functioning, flexible family units, wives positively support and enhance men's fathering they do this not by insisting that men should do, or take over, what they do, but by allowing them to function as fathers in ways that may be quite different from their own. Hence it is in such a complementary system that both parents have a recognised and equally respected role to play within childrearing. In turn, it is through the development of their own distinctive contribution that men may most reasonably and fruitfully be asked to be better fathers—instead of being labelled 'irresponsible' for not releasing women from day to day charge.

But this demands the secure incorporation of men in families—something which return us from the details of childrearing to the matter of social organisation—since it is only through the existence of certain values, rules and institutions that men become involved in families. Certainly, the male contribution to childrearing will disintegrate where there is no accepted role for male parents; no affirmation from the surrounding society and nothing to regularise their contribution to family life.

Without it, more children reared without fathers means more children at risk from poor care and abuse, together with all the implications for society and the individual alike of increasing educational and cognitive defects, drug use and crime—in a context where the disengagement of men from families represents general social dissolution and fragmentation.

# Good Children

## *Lynette Burrows*

I have often thought that the neutron bomb was the very model of a modern offensive weapon. It was, if you remember, a bomb that killed people but left the buildings standing. The ultimate designer weapon, invented with estate agents in mind and only affecting people who would have died anyway, leaving the business behind.

It is this ability to kill eveything living whilst leaving the outward edifice still intact, which makes it for me such an exemplar of our age where so many of our institutions are still standing—looking much as they have always done but with nothing living left inside.

From the outside, they still seem to be there but they no longer seem able to do what they were originally painstakingly built up to do; religion to provide a basis for morality; schools to educate; marriage to make a secure and indissoluble union; the family to educate and protect its members in a freedom not found anywhere else.

It is so much easier to destroy than to build, as Attila the Hun discovered to his delight, and his cultural heirs today have had a field day using almost all his personal qualities except courage. In consequence of their actions, much of the living content that enabled institutions to function effectively, because they were taken seriously, has been remorselessly killed and carted away by a culture that has a deadly aim when it comes to picking off anything that cannot defend itself.

One wonders, in passing, if our fearless contemporary iconoclasts will continue to be so brave now they have run up against a more aggressive protagonist in the form of Islam. One suspects that they will, for the noblest of motives, decide to leave well alone and light again on softer targets.

The family, of course, has always been a relatively soft target for professionals dressed in a little brief authority—especially those families at the poorer end of the social scale.

However, I am not one of those who believe that the family as an institution is in any terminal danger largely because it is a natural institution that all history shows us has survived every disaster as well as deliberate attempts to suppress it. It is far stronger than any of its opponents can ever be and that should be a comfort; and yet, it must be said that a determined onslaught by those powerful enough can certainly make life for the family unnecessarily difficult for the majority and impossible for the unfortunate few.

So on those grounds alone, it is well worth, I believe, making the most determined efforts to rebutt some of the attacks on the family that aim to change it in a way that would make it acceptable to liberal opinion and unworkable for the rest of us.

The area I want to address is the one which concerns discipline within the family, firstly because that is where a well co-ordinated attack is being launched by various professionals and, secondly because it is too important an area to allow it to be high-jacked as a passing fad by a handful of academics who, when they have found something else to interest them, will wander off leaving others to sort out the mess.

As we are learning to our cost in many areas, unless children are taught discipline and the respect which is inseparable from it at home, no other agency can really supply the deficit.

In the absence of firm, confident discipline, grounded in love and concern in the home and at school, all kinds of previously uncontentious activities like watching football or having a party, a carnival, or even a drink, have become occasions in which the heavy hand of the law has to be invoked to keep order because the young people involved simply do not know how to behave themselves and cannot be trusted not to create havoc for others and often severe penalties for themselves.

Now psychologists are very interested in this new phenomenon of the wild and dangerous young person and have come up with an explanation which is very curious: so curious in fact that it reminds one of the remark of G. K. Chesterton that whereas a tradition represents the common experience of the majority of people who are sane, psychological theories all too often represent the views of a handful of people who are mad.

How else can one explain the process by which a person, upon seeing something very new, reaches for an explanation, to something that is very old and was never found before to have caused the phenomena in question. Psychologists, like the rest of us, are surrounded by new social phenomena such as divorce, pornography and a mass media which systematically educates young people in a vocabulary of violence and sex in a hitherto undreamt of scale—and yet they calmly tell us that it is normal, parental discipline that is the seat of violence in children and are calling for it to be made illegal in the home, just as they have made it illegal at school.

It is as though a group of scientists, noticing that the seas were suddenly all polluted, the sun hidden behind a dense green cloud and that cows were beginning to grow feathers—were to mount a campaign to stop people going to Church on Sunday; on the theoretical grounds that since prayer was widely believed to change things, obviously all change was due to prayer and so must be stopped.

Before addressing directly the question of discipline and the need for it, I want to talk about the history of ideas in the child-care field because, not only are they frequently sensational in themselves, but they do put in context some of today's theories and clearly demonstrate that when it comes to deciding who is most likely to be right in these matters, the domestic tradition of mothers and fathers at home has been both more rational and more moderate over time.

So let us begin with one of the earliest writers on child-care, the great political philosopher, John Locke, who took it into his head to write in the 17th century about the care of new-born infants despite being a life-long bachelor who only dabbled in medicine. He confidently advised that a weak, new-born infant should be smeared with cinnamon, butter and wine and have slices of warm meat placed on its head and anus. Following him, any aspiring doctor who wanted to be considered 'in with the in-crowd' in matters of child-care, excelled themselves in advocating remedies along the same lines and babies were force-fed butter, cake, bread soaked in wine—and those wretched pork slices again!

It goes without saying that most women did not follow his advice but, such was Locke's influence that, fifty years later, another doctor, William Cadogan, protested in a famous document, at the number of infant deaths resulting from bizarre and unnatural medical practices. So great was the death-rate, he said, of children whose parents were unfortunate enough to be able to afford a doctor, that childhood itself was regarded as an illness from which few recovered.

Some time after him, in the 1780's there was the enormously influential Jean Jacques Rousseau who was the prototype liberal parent who professes wonderfully civilized, but unrealistic views on child care and then makes sure that they are not around to carry them out. He maintained that children were naturally good and needed neither instruction nor correction from adults at all. No doubt in order to avoid the temptation to do either himself, he placed all five of his children into a foundling hospital as soon as they were born.

Despite this rather unsatisfactory track-record as a parent, his many followers claimed that he had 'changed the view of childhood' and created the 'unfettered' child that still haunts the mythology of education colleges and many an unruly, unproductive, classroom. This particular little brute, it must be said, has never found much favour with those parents who do not place their children in foundling hospitals.

However, after fifty years of the unfettered child produced by Rousseau's philosophy, one is perhaps not surprised to learn that professional opinion had changed again and, for most of the last century, child-care experts were obsessed with what they called the 'natural depravity' of children.

This necessitated frequent whipping, savage beatings and, for those who preferred emotional punishments, long periods of solitary confinement and disgrace. Child-care experts today would call it 'withdrawal of approval' or the even more fun-sounding 'time out'—but it is the same emotional punishment although carried to an extreme that today's experts seem to think only parents are capable of. In factories, schools and workhouses and orphanages all over the country, this idea of the naturally wicked child was the basis of much of the cruelty and violence shown towards them.

Again, these dominant, professional ideas did little to change the ordinary, more moderate domestic tradition of child-care which was based, as Thomas Aquinas said of common-sense, on the recognition of reality.

Parents have always known that children are born neither good nor bad but, because they are all born with a very definite self, there is always the permanent, life-long tendency to become self-ish. It is the rigour and vigour of the love relationship between parents and child which has the power to teach, through admonition and example, the way to reconcile this natural selfishness first with the needs of the mother, then the family and finally with society at large.

As we turn the corner into this present century, professional opinion had so far moderated as to favour merely over-regimenting children with strict routines rather then half-killing them with punishment, but already a new theory was looming on the horizon casting a shadow that lay across child-care for more than fifty years—and a miserable shadow it was too.

Step forward John Watson—guru extraordinaire, who earlier this century was so famous and influential among his colleagues and is now almost forgotten.

How lucky psychologists are that their mistakes are not immortalized in concrete and breeze blocks like those of architects. They at least do not have to clutch convulsively at their shirt-fronts murmuring 'We were all wrong' every time Prince Charles comes in view.

At least, psychologists can simply pretend John Watson never existed especially when they are using his methods to advance a new theory.

His discovery, as expressed in his best seller of 1928 *'Psychological Care of Infant and Child'* was that 'mother love was a dangerous instrument that could ruin a child's chance of happiness'. He tells parents, 'Never kiss or cuddle your children, never have them in your lap; if you must, kiss them once on the forehead when you say goodnight. Shake hands with them in the morning.' He was also dead against any encouragement of children except for the most extreme and successful endeavours.

The reasons that he advanced for being so devoutly against physical affection have a strangely familiar ring about them and indeed are exactly the same as those now being used to discredit physical correction.

One is not allowed to kiss and slobber over anyone else in society without their permission, he said, so why should it be permitted in the case of children. Or again, parents do not show physical affection to their children because they know it is natural and good for them, but only because it was always done to them and, the poor souls only know how to reproduce the experience of their own childhoods.

Since this argument is now being deployed against parents who smack their children, one is perhaps entitled to ask why, in that case, parents do not favour outside toilets and rickets for their children since they too featured in the childhood of many poor people.

Finally, he was able to point triumphantly to 'extensive research' that demonstrated that physical affection shown towards children produced 'moral individualism' in adults including a greater tendency to sickness and depression.

It would be funny if it were not so tragic, how quickly other professionals absorbed Watson's theories and made them the basis of their beliefs and practices. The reason, alas, is not hard to see and it has a relevance to us today. By producing a plausible-sounding theory that attacked what was common practice in every home—he provided every child-care professional who wanted it, with a cause to interfere in almost every family in the country.

What an opportunity for empire building it provided since, if parents were so incompetent about so basic a matter, there was obviously great scope for professionals to educate them. They were not slow to see the advantages of this boost to their power and prestige and, in no time, the bandwagon was positively groaning with the weight of experts encumbered with Watson's theories that gave them the right to lay down the law to parents and to be impressively authoritarian when dealing with families.

Under this malign influence, foster parents who might show unseemly affection for the children with them were strenuously opposed by psychologists who preferred institutional care for even little children until the 1970's.

For more or less the same time, doctors and psychs would not allow parents to visit their sick children in hospital on the grounds that parental love would upset them. Indeed I was recently told by an editor for whom I had written an article on the subject, that he had not realized until then why it was that, when he was ill in hospital as a child, for six months, he was allowed infrequent visits by his next-door neighbour—but not from his mother.

People have forgotten all about these inhuman and damaging policies now, and doctors and psychs are not anxious to be reminded of them.

But we should keep the whole Watson phenomena in the forefront of our minds as we are confronted, yet again today, by a new and ridiculous fashion that this time seeks to invoke the law on its side—actually making it illegal for a parent to physically correct a child on the theoretical grounds that it teaches a child to be violent rather than as parents have always found, that it teaches them not to be violent.

The economist Friedrich Hayek said that 'Without a theory, facts are dumb' and this strikes me as a profoundly true observation of the way ideas are disseminated.

The average, ordinary, careful, mother who devotes herself to her children until they go to school probably knows just about all there is to know about children by the time she has had a couple; our cultural tradition fills in the gaps and married women talk endlessly and necessarily about what their children do and why.

It is a breadth and depth of experience and knowledge that no professional person can ever match, however much time they spend examining odd corners of behaviour or studying facts and figures. They simply do not put in the hours that a mother does without the benefit of nannies and 'home-helps' that enable the professionals to have the time to assemble such theories as they can garner from second-hand experience.

But mothers very seldom bother to develop theories to explain their children's behaviour. Why should they, after all? In most human affairs, it is the person who actually does the job and is experienced who is considered the expert, especially where anything live is concerned.

Women, on the other hand, have to suffer the effrontery and condescension of being told by men and women whose principle career is not in the home, that their traditional methods, tried and tested a million times, over generations, are wrong and—to quote from the leaders of the End Physical Punishment Campaign—they don't work!

Perhaps it was ever thus; didn't Socrates reproach the sophists of his day for being clever enough to teach but not having enough knowledge of anything that needed teaching? Certainly some of the people laying down the law in child-care today remind one of an over-confident taxidermist claiming to know all about lion-taming on the grounds that he's stuffed a few in his time.

The fact is that analysing anything common-sensical is rather difficult—and for the fairly obvious reason that, because it is a common perception, one never needs to. Shared experience has established the truth of something and though it is widely affirmed, it is never proved because it does not need to be.

This is the hole through which creeps anyone looking for a startling theory with which to make their name.

So, for the benefit of those people who find themselves bemused or intimidated by such theoretical expertise, I should like to spell out the two reasons which lie behind the universal practice of smacking children.

Firstly, it is for simple correction that is quick, minimally painful and emotionally short-lived. Before the age of reason, in those crucial years of learning in a dangerous world, it is easily understood by the child. It supplies the basic model of all correction in human behaviour; that impulsive behaviour is restrained by fear of the consequences.

But it is even more precise than that, because by inflicting a small amount of pain and shock, the mother is duplicating the methods inherent in nature to teach caution and control to a young creature. Throughout our lives pain is a simple warning that carries no overtones of punishment. It is nature's way of telling us, through bumped heads or grazed knees, to develop our senses and our skills. Mothers simply build on a child's natural receptiveness to the message carried by the signal of pain.

Secondly, it is the means by which a child's aggressive instincts are trained. These instincts are perfectly natural and indeed necessary for personal and collective security—but they are out of fashion at present and some people like to pretend that if they ignore them they will simply go away. They won't! and they need to be trained if they are not to become purely self-serving.

This training is done by mothers in the first instance and it is very important that they do it because I think it helps to imprint firmly in young minds, respect for womanly authority that is not based upon any real muscle power. Many a shambling six foot youth with arms like a gorilla will tell you that they would never dare be rude or disrespectful to their mothers, and by association, to other women—even when they tower above them—out of an ancestral memory of the symbolic power of that hand which once controlled their naughtiness and gave them clear limits to the pleasure and excitement of aggressive feelings.

In smacking a child for bad behaviour, a parent is not simply meeting violence with violence, as the modish opinion claims. What they are doing is demonstrating a central fact of life; that there are two kinds of aggression and the difference between them is crucial. There is the illegitimate sort which kicks another child and throws temper tantrums as a way of dominating others; and there is the legitimate kind which the parent uses to stop wrong-doing, which is moderate and has a moral purpose.

When physical correction is used at an early age therefore, it instills a doubly valuable lesson. It shows the child that its aggressive feelings are shared by the parent and are not something terrible that only he has; it also shows him how they must only ever be used for a good reason.

Children understand this intuitively because they have a very strong sense of justice and they quickly know when they are in the wrong. This is why they accept punishment without resentment—provided it is not excessive—they know that the same power that stops them from being destructive also protects them from the aggression of others. This must be why most children do, in fact, grow up well-adjusted and law-abiding.

The ones who come unstuck are those who come from randomly violent homes where excessive violence is the norm because they have never learnt the difference between legitimate and illegitimate aggression. It is not surprising that they grow up to be dangerously violent themselves.

At the other end of the scale is the child who is never smacked and is often called by other people—never its parents—a spoiled child. These too are often noticeably spiteful and aggressive for the same reason that they too have never had their aggressive instincts effectively trained.

I suppose many parents throughout the generations must have wondered why a good, civilized talking to was not sufficient to curb bad behaviour, particularly of their sons—and regretted the necessity for a good wallop every so often; but I believe there is a sound reason for it.

Even small boys know perfectly well when they are behaving badly—that is mostly why they do it. They are looking for opposition because they are unconsciously practising their ability to cope with it. They actually need the experience of a quick, muscular response that tests their courage; and are frustrated and infuriated when all they get is a rationalistic nag about how anti-social they are being.

They know that what they are looking for is a physical response because they have an instinctive drive to develop their strength and their aggression is reinforced by resentment when they don't get it.

These observations, or ones very similar, have been made and are made by most people who deal with children in their natural habitat, wherever that may be. Certainly every respectable survey that has been carried out recently confirms that the vast majority of parents believe physical correction is necessary although they will not have a ready-made theory to explain why. It is what Dr. Johnson called 'the dumb certainty of experience'.

To deny parents the right to make such a judgement based on their own experience is really a devastating piece of arrogance. If the judgement of ordinary people is not to be trusted in this most fundamental area, what possible cause could there be for trusting them with a vote in politics or even the right to give evidence in a court of law. The poor creatures are obviously too stupid even to tie their own shoes.

This is the inescapable interpretation of the attitude of those professionals who are now attempting to coerce parents into not smacking their children, as they have coerced teachers, against their better judgement.

They will probably never admit or even see that their theories, contradicting our tradition, but backed by a powerful bureaucracy have already caused a tremendous amount of harm; creating conflicts in the family, hooliganism in society and anarchy in many schools.

They are like those absurd and untruthful dictators that have so recently crashed in their ruined kingdoms in Eastern Europe—still talking about the peace and plenty their ideas have brought whilst all around them chaos and discontent multiply. As things get worse, all they can talk about is more of the same.

It is ironic, is it not, that at this time in our history when people talk more than ever before about women's rights—a group of influential professionals should seek to challenge every woman's rights even to act on their own judgement within the home.

It is a wonderful example, I think, of the basic fallacy of feminism which is that the quarrel is, or ever was, between men and women. As one can see demonstrated so clearly here, tyranny is always operated by the powerful against those without power, and it makes not a jot of difference whether it is a man or a woman who is wearing the foreman's hat.

So, instead of allowing so many upstart academics to dictate family policy to those people who, throughout our history have been responsible for the management of the home, let us assert the experience of generations of mothers, so undervalued today that it is scarcely considered a proper job at all; and give due respect and attention to what dear Mr Micawber called the 'immemorial skills and the lofty character' of mothers.

# Preteen and Teenage Sex and Environmental Influences

## *Prof Melvin Anchell*

This article is a psychoanalytic look at some environmental influences—*especially school sex education*—that effect preteen and teenage sexual behaviour.

The facts to be presented are based on

1. Established psychoanalytic principles,
2. My personal observations of young patients whom I have treated psychoanalytically,
3. Case histories of other clinical investigators, and
4. Any source of data that can be clinically substantiated with everyday patients.

My discussion will first consider some environmental influences effecting 10–12 year old sexual behaviour and will follow with the effect of these influences on the sexual behaviour of pubertal and adolescent youths.

A distinctive characteristic seen in 10–12 year old children is an increase in activity to adjust to the realities of the adult world. This increase in activity in 10–12 year olds to adapt to grown up realities differs markedly in boys and girls. In the boy, his adaptations to adult realities are directed outwards, towards his environs, giving him an objective aggressiveness which the male uses throughout life to master the environment and to achieve utilitarian goals. In girls, their increased activity to become grown-up is directed inward, towards the psyche.

Prepubertal boys' and girls' activities directed to becoming independent and grown are greatly influenced by (1) identifications with parents, (2) family values and standards and (3) by consciences instilled in the minds of young people by parents.

However, when the 10–12 year old reaches the age of 13, that is puberty, psychological changes occur which push parental influences into the background, and identifications with individuals outside the home begin to play major roles in influencing the behaviour of teenagers.

If environmental influences are in accord with previous parental teachings, new adaptations to life are made harmoniously, and pubertal-adolescent maturation progresses smoothly into early adulthood. When, however, the environment is out of sync with parental teachings, parents' and the child's conscience are rapidly deprecated in the minds of most youths. Under such circumstances, leaders in the contravening environment replace the authority of parents; and the consciences of young people are decimated by the beliefs and teachings of the new leaders.

In the sexual development of 10-12 year old children, 'secrecy and curiosity', which are loosely attached filaments of the human sexual instinct, provide the sensual pleasures normal for this age group.

In girls sensual gratification derived from secrecy and curiosity is shared with other girls of the same age. The clandestine secrets of pubertal girls are always investigated privately before sharing the findings with a girlfriend. The privacy used in acquiring sexual information is a first step in life leading to individuality and independence.

Pleasures derived from sharing secrets with other girls are the only 'prepubertal' sensual activity. In all other respects the 10-12 year old girl friendships are normally non-sexual. The privately investigated secrets concern physiological sexual matters and are not related to sex with boys. Sex between girls and boys normally plays no part in the lives of 10-12 year old children. Prepubertal boys regard close friendships with girls as unmanly; and girls adopt an 'I don't care' attitude.

Today's school sex education given to prepubertal children completely shatters normal sexual secrecy pleasures and compassionate girl friendships by catapulting 10-12 year olds into a world of ready made, instant sexual information. Such school interferences usurp girl-to-girl friendships with their harmless sensual secrets and at the same time disrupt the beginning development of individualism and independence.

Many aspects of gangsterism, prostitution and criminality in 10-12 year old children result from the violent interruption of normal pre-teen sexual growth with premature sex acts foisted by school sex teachings. Since the advent of school sex education, promiscuity, pregnancies and venereal diseases are no longer uncommon in 10-12 year old children.

Almost invariably pubertal and teen youths separated into two parts by family and environmental differences will develop, in some degree, attitudes offensive to the family. For example, youths brought up in sexually moral homes become critical of the family when taking school sex courses that glorify all types of physical sex while at the same time 'damning by faint praise' the affectionate nature of human sexuality stressed by parents.

School sex courses at all grade levels can teach one thing only, and that is physical sex. The vitally important, life-sustaining affectionate component of human sexuality cannot be learned from a school textbook. Unfortunately, notwithstanding family allegiances, teenagers all too often favour the school sex teachings making it almost impossible for them to make sexually mature adjustments in later life.

By the age of 13, prepubertal 'girl-to-girl friendships' gradually lessen as the girls grow older and go their separate ways. Puberty is also a time when sexual energies that have remained dormant during the latency years of 6-12 are once again reawakened.

The reawakened sexual energies in pubertal boys are direct and are centred in the male genitalia. The reawakened eroticisms of the 13 year old girls follow a MUCH different course.

Because teenage female biological and psychological maturations are not completed until late adolescence, and because the female genitalia remains anaesthetic to anatomical sex until at least late adolescence, nature has provided the young girl with a natural aversion to the sex act. Contrary to the teachings of sex educators, both sexes—if left undisturbed by school sex teachings and the pornographically-oriented entertainment media—are normally chaste during puberty and adolescence.

Though the teenage girl has a natural aversion to engaging in the sex act, her sexual desires, however, may be as intense as the boy's. Teenage female eroticisms involve (1) the desire to love and be loved, (2) kisses and caresses, (3) tender words of love, (4) sexual fantasies and (5) sometimes thoughts of pregnancy and motherhood—but unlike the male, the girl's sexual eroticisms are not inseparably entwined with the sex act.

The dichotomy between the adolescent boy's capability for the sex act and the girl's natural reluctance to sexual intercourse may seem strange; but Nature always has a reason for what it does. The teenage girl's reluctance to the sex act serves to strengthen the affectionate and spiritual nature of sex. Through affection and sexual spiritualization both sexes learn to regard 'sex and the sex partner' with utmost importance.

Spiritualization of sex leads to the idealization of members of the opposite sex. Idealization of a special someone makes life complete. The answer is not that 1 plus 1 equals 2, but that $\frac{1}{2}$ plus $\frac{1}{2}$ make 'one whole person'. This is the basis for monogamous love which forms the foundation for Western civilization.

It should be noted that sexual fantasies are important for adolescent sexual development. The fantasies primarily consist of an ardent desire for love with someone of the opposite sex. Such fantasies are (1) natural, (2) beneficial and (3) gratifying, but they are not meant to be carried out in real life.

To paraphrase the impression of many sexually educated youths: 'If they are teaching it to us in school, they are telling us to go ahead and have sex—for what other reason are they giving out free condoms?'

It should be clearly understood that under usual environmental circumstances, teenagers are normally chaste preferring to engage in platonic relationships. Some reasons given by youths for becoming sexually active in today's world are:

1. To prove that they are grownups
2. To surpass older siblings and friends
3. To gain prestige from classmates by engaging in school condoned sex
4. To take revenge on parents who are accused of thwarting independence, and
5. To take advantage of the sexual permissiveness overlooked by schools.

Another school sex education related catastrophe is the ever increasing numbers of adolescent lesbians in the United States. Students in sex classes are taught that all perversions are normal.

Given this assurance some disappointed girls, who find no gratification in genital intercourse, and feel they have been used and abused by providing indifferent males with sexual satisfaction, turn once again to the more earnest girl-to-girl friendships they recall from pubertal years. However, exclusive relationships between adolescent girls—devoid of boys—differ from the 10–12 year old girl friendships. Erotic feelings are more intense during adolescence and may push girls into homosexual activities which arrest further heterosexual development.

The greatest harm done by today's school sex education is that all sex courses, from kindergarten through high school, destroy natural sexual growth. In humans, unlike any other creatures, three phases of sexual development occur before adult sexual maturity in reached: the first phase of human sexual development occurs at birth and lasts through the fifth year of life; the second phase begins at six and continues through the age of twelve; and the third phase of human sexual development starts in puberty around the age of thirteen, and is not completed until late adolescence.

School sex teachings at all grade levels disrupt sexual growth during the three phases of human sexual development. The instrusion of an adult—whether a sex teacher or not—into the sexuality of children is a form of child molestation that can be just as harmful as an actual attack by a child molestor.

Sex education proponents are resolute in their resolve to involve themselves in the sexual development of children and young people, and to inculcate physical sexual matters into youths' minds. The illiterate sexual intermeddlings of sex teachers in the developing sexuality of children and youths could actually be considered *comical* if it weren't for the egregious harm that is done to students and society.

The sex 'educators' have no compunction in overriding any data that is not supportive of their sex education theories. For example, a recent international survey on approximately 30,000 thirteen year old students from a number of nations clearly showed—'American students come out at the bottom of the heap scholastically.... and revealed a marked weakness in higher order thinking skills...'.

Such research is disregarded by sex educators who insist that 'immature juvenile students' formulate new sexual standards and values and use their own judgements in determining whether or not to engage in sex—and if so, what sex acts to commit.

In developing new standards and values, the students are implicitly or openly cautioned not to heed thousands of years of tried and tested, life sustaining findings, nor pay attention to teachings of parents, because these sources—students are made to believe—are prejudiced, puritanical, outdated and erroneous. Instead, students are taught to rely on the 'sex is for fun' approach and on the sexual propaganda of homosexual activists.

Sexually educated young people are not a new breed of youths who, under the guiding patronage of a progressive educational system, have managed in one generation to change five thousand years of human sexuality.

The new breed simply represents misled children who have been rushed into 'sham sex' by benighted sex educators. Parents and the public may listen and even see, but rarely can anyone who attended school prior to today's sex education, possibly fathom how deeply sex-educated young people have been led into wanton sex. For example, recently, a major Chicago newspaper casually reported that 80% of freshmen to senior female students in a Chicago high school are pregnant. Can any parent over thirty truly imagine what is happening in education to create such disasters?

By some means or other, sex teachers in the United States, have summarily seized the right to teach children and youths:

1. How to mate in every possible way,
2. How to override inborn mental barriers against perversions,
3. How to rely on contraceptives and abortions,
4. And how to engage in all sex acts without guilt.

These are the characteristics of pimps and prostitutes.

To justify their coup, educators frequently use the argument that parents don't feel comfortable teaching sex to children and prefer leaving such matters to school teachers. At the same time, some teachers complain that they are being imposed upon by parents... especially those parents who expect schools to uphold Judeo-Christian sexual morality—a morality, incidentally, that

1. supports the struggle for existence,
2. sustains civilised lives,
3. is in line with all enduring religions, and
4. a morality whose life sustaining nature is sustained by psychoanalytic observations.

At no time, do educators remotely explain 'who decided, and for what reason' it became suddenly fashionable to teach physical sex and perversions to school children living in the late 20th Century!

Aside from evading these questions, sex educators shun the most fundamental psychoanalytical facts that unequivocally show that school sex education from 'kindergarten to 12' causes irreparable harm to students throughout life. For example, when the psychoanalytic fact became widely known that sex education destroys sexual growth and personal developments during the latency years of six to twelve, Mary Calderone, the leader of SIECUS, simply decreed that the Latency Period in six to twelve year old children did not exist. Subsequently, followers of SIECUS and Planned Parenthood dismissed from further consideration the pernicious harm done to six to twelve year old children by school sex teachings.

Not only do sex educators disregard scientific psychoanalytic knowledge, but when it suits their purpose, they likewise turn their backs to the findings of their very own principal sex investigators. For example, Alfred Kinsey is one of the sex educators 'leading lights'. In his sex questionnaire studies, Kinsey found and reported that the average teenage female had an intense aversion for engaging in the sex act. Nevertheless, his finding is rejected by sex educators, and students in sex classes are taught that it is usual and gratifying for young girls to engage in sexual intercourse. To avoid appearing abnormal and rebuffed by their classmates, many female students arrange to lose their virginity to someone when they become fourteen.

Another 'guiding light' sexologist highly used by sex educators is Dr William Masters. SIECUS's Mary Calderone, virtually deified Masters for his sexual experiments in which he used prostitutes, as well as paid and unpaid volunteers. Recently, however, Dr Masters might have had a change of heart for he denounced homosexuality and homosexual sex acts in a magazine article.

An ostentatious cliche used by proponents of school sex education is: 'If they don't learn it in school, they'll learn it on the street anyway'. Such justification for teaching children carnality is as logical as trying 'to control a fire by dumping more fuel on the flames'.

It is true, that there are 'street smart' pubertal girls, who, not infrequently became trapped into sex acts by identifying with sexually loose older females and by emulating sexually uninhibited heroines seen in many of today's movies and television shows. *But* sex education is *not* the solution for these young girls who play out their provocative coquetry on the street and who feel secure because they realize that they have no real desire for sexual intercourse. However, when their seductive coquettishness becomes too intense, it may free some men from any scruples they have concerning a juvenile.

In this way, all too often, 12, 13 and 14 year old girls, who frequently make themselves look older, encounter their first sex experience. The first experience is, not infrequently, followed by others on the basis of the girl's feeling: 'Well, now everything has been lost anyhow—what is there to lose?'

Some sexually active girls regret their sexual involvements, but, nevertheless, continue sexual offenses against themselves as a form of self-punishment.

1. Prostitution
2. Venereal Diseases
3. Illegitimate children

are frequent consequences of their remorse.

A generally known psychoanalytic fact concerning human sexuality is that the female is prone to follow the conventions of her culture. If her social order regards chastity as a virtue, she becomes chaste. If her society espouses free love, she may readily assume the characteristics of a promiscuous woman.

The brusque truth is that today's sexually emancipated female is not an example of 'new progressive social changes which have made her a free individual.' She simply represents a woman—or girl—who has become a slave to the demands of her society.

Some girls resist this sexual enslavement by returning to their families. School teachers frequently label such girls as 'immature and family dependent', but in reality these chaste young females develop into fully mature women who become ideal spouses, mothers and home makers.

Conversely, some other girls accept the sexual expectations society makes upon them, and take on the characteristics of the male's sexual aggressiveness. Many rush hungrily from one man to another and learn to equate love with fornication. Such females keep searching for the 'Grand Passion' all their lives—even when they are happily married.

A variety of subconcious defense mechanisms are used by many modern females to fend off the sexual flummery imposed upon them. For example, some girls turn to intellectualism as a means of defence. This particular defence reaction against sexual impositions may seem sound; but, unfortunately, intellectualism—unless the girl is born with a surfeit of intellectuality—feeds upon the affective life of feminacy. That is, a girl's intellectualism or objectivism gets much of its energy from female emotions, leaving her largely depleted of rich, warm feminine feelings.

Other defense reactions against unwanted anatomical sex can be seen in girls who:

1. excel in sports, or who
2. take up professions and business careers, or who
3. become activists in various ideological or political groups, or who
4. join communes or cults as a means of escape.

However, sports, play, work and intellectual pursuits are *not* adequate substitutes for a close, emotional relationship with a person of the opposite sex.

The goal of a boy should be to become a man and that of a girl to become a woman. The development of the feminine woman involves female maturation processes that are not completed until late adolescence.

Premature sex during adolescence disrupts natural feminine maturation, as does too early a motherhood. The demands made upon a young teenage girl by pregnancy require that she use all her energies for the pregnancy and for the caring of a newborn child. Infantile mothers fail to develop real motherliness, even under the most favourable conditions, and a too early motherhood leaves little physical energy for developing the girl's personality which remains incomplete.

In humans, unlike animals, when affectionate needs are not met and physical sex is all that remains, sex becomes meaningless and life becomes empty. This psychoanalytic maxim is readily apparent in the suicides of 'sexually educated, sexually active' youths. Suicide now ranks as the leading cause of death in young people under the age of 21 in the United States.

Over the past 25 or so years, a sexual revolution has been destroying western civilization by vilifying human sexuality. The effects have been truly devastating. Assuming this scourge has not, as yet, brought us to the 'point of no return' what can be done?

First, I believe, society must re-establish its social conscience, a conscience that—as just a generation or so ago.

1. will not sanction free love and perversions,
2. will not permit gutter sex to be spread publicly by a pornographically oriented entertainment media,
3. and a social conscience that will not tolerate schools acting as child molestors.

Sexual revolutionists, by corrupting the meaning of 'free speech' and by stretching the boundaries of sexual indecency, are persuading much of the public into accepting social degeneracy.

Fortunately, however, civilization is not a one way street. Restoration of a social conscience can

1. stop the decline of our civilization and
2. help it climb back out of the abyss into which it has been flung by those determined to make Western Society a bastion for pagan sexual hedonism.

In conclusion, two matters stand out:

First: Life-sustaining sex completely depends on an affectionate, monogamous, man/woman long lasting, love relationship. Such relationships are essential for the survival of civilizations based on families composed of individuals living by consciences, instead of barbarians living by instincts only. And secondly: For the benefit of all mankind, it is just as important to eradicate the psychological venereal diseases that are rife today as it is to eradicate physical venereal diseases, such as AIDS. Both arise from the malignant abuse of human sexuality.

# 6: THE WAY AHEAD FOR FAMILIES

## The Elderly: New Answers

### *Peter Benton*

I would like to examine this issue of the care of the elderly in relation to the family in the context of the new phase which is gaining currency in the social service arena, and that is care in the community. That, of course, does raise some questions: What care, for whom and when, and what is the community? Indeed it also raises the question in my mind of what is the relationship between the community and the family, and what is the family. The concept of the family has different significance to different people, and certainly those of us who are concerned in the Health Service with 'receiving back into the community', whatever that may mean, people who have sometimes spent fifty or sixty years in the mental health institutions in Britain, are aware that the Victorian and the Edwardian family could be quite a fearsome organisation. Some of those people who spent fifty or sixty years in mental institutions perhaps went there in the first place for conditions that would certainly not be treated that way today. In fact, some I fear were just perhaps looked on by their family as a little untidy!

The concept of the family is one that has many vibrations, many aspects that I think we ought to think about rather carefully. I have five children, and I know that many people also have large families, but I think we are also all aware of the implications of Christmas, shall we say, for those who do not have close family relationships. I am told by them that Christmas is rather a lonely period. So this issue of what is the family, is one that poses a lot of questions.

With those initial thoughts, I am going to draw from my observations on the particular community in which I have had some experience over the years. It is a community in North London. I am Chairman of the Enfield Health Authority, and we have just last year asked the University of Sheffield to do a detailed study of elderly people in Enfield: their conditions; what they need and what they receive, in the form of care and from whom they receive it. It is not really very helpful to deal in exact figures, but perhaps it might be fruitful to run through what it is we have observed about the condition of the elderly in Enfield.

Enfield is a borough partly leafy and countrylike, but partly quite inner-city in some of its characteristics. The population is just over a quarter of a million, 21 per cent is of ethnic origin, from Bangladesh, Africa, Caribbean, and a number of people from Cyprus—Greek and Turks. Only five per cent of the elderly are ethnic, that is people over sixty-five, and only 1 per cent of those elderly people we look after in hospitals come from that ethnic community. It seems quite clear that the family structure of these immigrant groups is very strong certainly in the Bangladesh area and also amongst people of Greek and Turkish origin.

The first rather dramatic figure is that of thirteen thousand very elderly people who look after themselves eighty per cent live alone. Of the seventeen thousand, the total population of the 75s and over, most of them look after themselves with just the help of family and friends. In fact, only about one quarter of that group get any sustained help from what you might describe as the professional carers.

So the community has a tremendous role to play in caring for the elderly, and when you consider that the cost of keeping a frail old person in a hospital bed is around £15,000 a year and even in the charitably-run old people's homes with a moderate level of care, it is not less than £10,000 a year, you can see that not only are we looking at any important social issue, but we are also looking at an important economic one too.

I give you these facts in the context of a new philosophy, which has been much talked about and much thought about, and indeed sometimes much criticised: the concept of 'care in the community'. As I understand it, the National Health Service is concerned about the cure of patients, and therefore regards an elderly person who comes into one of our hospitals as somebody who should be cured and returned back to normal living in the community with the family. Thus, although this is our primary concern, there are a number of people, about less than one percent who are over 75, who do become very confused and need psychiatric and nursing care beyond what could be expected even in a Local Authority Home.

So that is what we are about and that is what the Health Service is about. What is the community? The idea that some people have, that the community is just the Social Services Department of the Local Authority, really is not a very sound one. In Enfield, less than one in four of the people in the over-75 age-group actually receive any regular care from the Social Services department. But the community is also not merely the nuclear family. I believe that the community is the neighbours. I think it is neighbourliness that actually makes it possible for three-quarters of quite elderly people to live more or less happily in their own homes. It is this rather broader idea of the family, the family that is not exclusive ('this is us and you are not it') but the inclusive family, the family that draws others to it, the family that is so strong in its own stability and its own loyalty, that it can look outwards, and provide neighbourly support.

I would like to turn to what the public policy should be if these are the circumstances. What is the role of the public services? I believe they should be concerned, first to understand what constitutes value in the eyes of the client, and turn their minds quite openly and freshly to how can that be promoted.

For the over-75s, that value represents independence, personal dignity and the ability to lead one's own life. So in this concept of public service, I believe the goal should be that objective.

The question now is how is that to be done? In the old days the idea of a geriatric policy was to create beds in old people's homes, but I think anyone who has been to see even the best of old people's homes, realises how far short they fall of the ideal. We are contemplating, and beginning now to implement, a new strategy. It is concerned with supporting the broader family, and is focused on an observation that there are two trigger-points which make even the most devoted carer look on an elderly relative or elderly friend as a burden that has suddenly become intolerable. These two trigger-points are incontinence, and severe and continued mental infirmity. Anybody who has looked after old people will know the strain of constant care. In our strategy we have identified five points, and I would like to point out that I believe each one of them makes good humane sense but also good economic sense too.

The first, and it sounds very simple, is to make incontinence aids freely available. In Enfield we have quadrupled the supply of freely available incontinence aids, and we now spend some £80,000 a year on providing them. The second, and here my neighbouring Health Authority in Barnett is the pioneer, is to use our hospital laundry service to provide a sheet washing service for patients or individuals who live at home and suffer from incontinency. The third is to encourage all sorts of bodies to provide a sitter service. I did this with my hospice group some years ago, and we recruited for the North London Hospice area some thirty individuals, very carefully chosen and trained, unpaid volunteers who spent hours sitting with dying people, so that the carer was able to go away just for a break, to a restaurant or to visit friends. I believe that there is a tremendous need for such a service. We know that it is provided by some bodies—it is provided to some extent by Age Concern—but I believe that the 'sitting' service, is very much the service that every citizen should be prepared to provide as a good neighbour to the elderly person next door or in the next street.

Fourth, we have established day centres in the Health Service, as has Age Concern. I think this is another good neighbourly need, as is transport. Elderly people can spend a day in a Day Centre and the carer can get away, at least for a few hours. Lastly, extremely important, is the provision of 'respite beds' for holidays. In the London borough of Enfield the Local Authority now provides respite-beds for some two hundred families a year. This makes good sense not only for the carer because it gives them respite to go and have a holiday, but also for the old person because it means that they are welcome for a longer period with their family. To spend two weeks care and avoid having an old person rejected and landing on the authorities for fifty weeks a year makes extremely good economic sense. The provision of respite-care does seem to me to be an area that has been somewhat overlooked and has got tremendous opportunities to come. We could also look at respite where some neighbour comes and lives in a family's home for two weeks while the regular carers get a break.

Our strategy then, recognises that true value in the eyes of an elderly person is to maintain personal independence and personal dignity, and that comes from living at home with the ability to develop one's own life. The best way to promote this is not for the authorities to regard the family as competition but as the major basic force. This means the family in that outward-looking, inclusive sense: the family that welcomes others into the stable community that a good marriage forms. There are other benefits, too, for the citizen, and one lesson we learnt in the North London Hospice group was that if somebody dies in hospital from cancer, it takes much longer for those left behind to get over the grieving process. The process of feeling that you have done your very best is extremely important in the recovery of a normal happiness after the tragedy of a cancer death.

I believe the same point is also true in caring for the elderly. I have no doubt at all that the rejection of an old person as being too burdensome is deeply damaging to the carer who has taken that decision, even though in many cases it might be regarded as absolutely inevitable. So this policy of providing care when it is most needed, to mitigate the terrible pressures of these trigger-points of incontinence and mental infirmity, seem to me to bring benefits to everybody. The essence is to augment and supplement good neighbourliness, which itself depends upon stable family units.

Our objective in public policy should be, that elderly people should maintain their independence and their personal dignity, and also that the strong and stable outward-looking family is crucial for the concern for the care of the elderly.

If that is the message for public policy, what is the message for every citizen? Love thy neighbour.

# Supporting the Family in a Secular Society

## *Prof Thomas Langan*

When traditional social supports break down, only creative intelligence can supply to construct new forms of healthy, developing human existence. Never before has the family been confronted with such rapid, radical change of social conditions, so never has there been so great an imperative for thoughtful adjustment and creation of new institutional forms.

Little can now be 'taken for granted'. The reasons for everything have to be explained. A concerted effort has to be made to educate the young to a sense of enthusiasm for and commitment to family life. Many are frightened by the evidence of family breakdown they see all about them. Family life as *vocation*, as something normal but which requires commitment and effort and which, in the best of circumstances, is humanly fulfilling has to be explained to young people, many of whom have never experienced more than a truncated and perhaps disastrous form of family living.

Even those who have experienced a good family life are often unaware of what this will demand of them in their turn when they become parents.

Single parent families and the divorced may well need help in explaining to their own children that a full family existence remains the norm and is, despite the problems in their own case, an attainable goal.

The human and social disaster constituted by sexual promiscuity and cohabitation without the commitment of marriage has to be thoroughly explained. Its effects have to be worked against—one of the worse being that many otherwise available young people are no longer marriageable.

When the society actively encourages egoistic self-gratification, the task of convincing young people that unselfish commitment to spouse and children is the better way becomes much harder.

When divorce rates approach fifty per cent—and remember these are among the people who did care enough to get married—then you know that the character of many is not strong enough to respond to the demands of married life.

How much attention and promotion does career receive among the young, compared to family? Something must be done so that a balance is achieved. Young people are legitimately, but often too exclusively, interested in career.

Even when the children are treated to the example of devoted parents generously raising several children, the parents unthinkingly can so reinforce the society's message—that career success is all—that they invite their children, without even realizing it, to give too small a place to family in their priorities.

And even good, solid intact families can 'spoil' children. Over-indulgence, lack of discipline, furthered by poor quality schools, encourage children to close in on themselves too much. They then may lack that generosity and courage which serious commitment requires.

What all these dire considerations tell us is this: It is not just the children who need a strengthened education in family. It is many, if not all of the parents! (None of us is ever finished with our education as people; we even learn much, I am sure, on our deathbeds.) Above all the parents need encouragement and help to 'buck the trends', for instance to limit energetically the inroads television, videos and films make on the consciousness of their children. But that means not just issuing fruitless interdicts, but determination to provide interesting family activity in place of dreary mindless sitting in front of the 'telly' or going to the 'flicks', for want of anything better to do.

But that takes great motivation, energy and imagination. First the parents have to become alerted to just how serious it is to deliver their children over to the evil forces of the popular culture. Inventing a sound family culture to replace the siren call of these easy enticements is demanding. It is a work calling for help from an entire community.

If both parents are working, or even if father is pursuing an absorbing career and coming home completely exhausted, is mother going to have the energy, the commitment and the ideas to invent enriching, interesting family routines all by herself?

If it never occurred to the parents that raising a family is something more than what you do just with the little time you have left from pursuing your careers, then you can be sure little is going to happen to make that supposedly Christian family any different from the rest.

As a Christian community, as 'church,' we need a concerted, well-thought-out, across the board attack on the problem of fostering the family. The Holy Spirit can always be counted on to move us, but one form of his help is to use the intelligence the Father has given us and the Spirit illumines to follow concretely the Son's Way of Love.

In that spirit, I would see all of the following elements to be important:

— education, and this at four levels, as I shall explain;
— career guidance;
— community support.

## A. *Education*

The four levels at issue are: 1. from the pulpit; 2. in the school; 3. in the family; and 4. in marriage preparation classes.

*1. From the pulpit.* Priests should regularly and fully explain the apostolic role of raising a family, and exhort young people and married couples to assume the full responsibility of what is a glorious (and demanding, and I would say, were it not also natural, *heroic)* vocation. Christians should be exhorted to put family before brilliant success in career. Exhort the whole community to share some of the burdens which fall on families, and bring out the concrete nature of the needs, so that people see that Christian charity can take this communal form of making family life prosper in the local church.

2. *In the school.* This need by itself justifies the sacrifices necessary to have Christian schools. Nowhere else will the reality of family be integrated into the formal education of children. On the contrary, state schools most often tend to be anti-family in subtle, and sometimes not so subtle, ways. The Christian young person should be disciplined and encouraged to excellence, but the criteria by which excellence is measured should be, not those of 'worldly success,' but those of holiness. Needless to say, holiness for the contemporary schooled Christian integrates the developed, cultivated intellect into the life of the whole person. That is the central role of the school.

3. *In the family*, first by example, but also through parish programmes in parenting, which help parents with ideas and programmes of family prayer and instruction. The family that prays together and which undertakes to discuss what it is to live together as family, what it means to protect children and to be a loving support to the old, which discusses the nature of careers, and which, above all, sets out on a path of family spiritual development, of learning to improve the family's ability to pray, of improving the spiritual quality of their celebration of the great feasts together, such a family has at its core the very best, the most loving and impressive education.

4. *Finally, through marriage preparation.* The Archdiocese of Toronto recognized this as a golden opportunity to educate those who are about to found new families. We worked out a programme of instruction, provided by married couples who themselves are excellent 'role models', demanding about eight weeks of discussions one night a week. At the core of the programme is explanation of the sacramental nature of Christian marriage, and marriage as vocation. The centrality of family prayer and of growing together spiritually is emphasized. The demanding nature of marriage is not hidden from the young couples. This programme has been well received. Every couple marrying in the Archdiocese must give a year's advance notice, so they will be able to follow this obligatory programme. About sixty married couples have been formed through training courses to give marriage instruction. Ours is one diocese which has seen the potential of this form of education and has taken it seriously.

## B. *Career guidance*

Young people need to be encouraged, as they wrestle with their vocational decisions and begin to discuss marriage concretely, to face squarely one of the great dilemmas of our time: harmonizing career and family.

Nothing is to be gained by oversimplifying the issue. For instance, 'Father enjoys the great career, mother, hopefully not too over-educated, stays home and raises the children.' That is a fine solution for some, provided this is genuinely the mother's response to a call. On the other hand, it is also oversimplifying the problem. It is a further oversimplification to forget that they need Daddy to be available, too, and both parents need one another's very active support.

A few truths stand out in this otherwise murky mess of problems.

> 1. *Those contemplating marriage should face these career-vocation issues directly and openly.* Marriage is not truly human if it is not open to children, if God grants them. It is a great pity for a young

couple to enter marriage determined to limit their family to the perfect little boy and the perfect little girl, so their careers will suffer minimal interference. But if this 'Yuppie' structure is what they have in mind, it is better to be honest and open about it with one another, and to see the unchristian lack of generosity for what it is, rather than live a lie.

2. When, thank God, the couple is genuinely Christian in their generous openness to having children, then they need to be honest in facing the fact that it is extraordinarily difficult to reconcile big family and big career. An important distinction separates 'job' and 'career'. By job I mean a paid position with limited hours, something you can 'turn off' when you leave the work place. The problem with careers is that they put never-ending, 'bottomless pit' demands on one. Someone needs to explain to young couples these facts of modern life. Parents should raise these issues. Christian schools should talk about them. Marriage preparation courses should raise them.

Who would want to deny intelligent, educated women the opportunity to pursue exciting, fulfilling careers? Especially when the motive is more apostolic than for mere self glory, as it always can be, and which professions like medicine, teaching, and social work actively encourage. At the same time, I shudder at the thought of a young medical doctor handing her baby to the Nanny or the day-care and promising some hours of 'quality time' on Saturday, as she rushes off to an important consultation at the clinic. It is already intolerable enough to see Daddy kiss baby as he rushes to the airport, disappearing for the next three days.

These are very hard problems. There are many variables in each case, and a few principles. *The responsibility to see that the children receive all the love and attention they require is equally that of both parents*. Responding adequately to the call demands great love and generosity. The children never cease needing much presence, endless concern, even after they have graduated from university. (The writing of this paper was delayed three mornings in a row while my wife and I helped our youngest, just graduating from university, wrestle with a vocational decision.) But the time of the day when it is needed and the forms it takes vary with the stages in the child's life. It should also not be forgotten that brothers and sisters to some degree also should be helping one another.

It may be less of a strain on a family if the parents both have strictly limited jobs than if one is so absorbed by a career he offers little help to the parent who is devoted entirely to tending the children. It also makes a difference whether grandparents are near by and willing to contribute.

Whatever the complications and ramifications, true Christian love manifests itself, among other ways, through honesty and openness in recognizing the gravity of the issues, all the facts of the case, and the need for generosity on the part of all parties—including the children—if a satisfactory Christian life is going to be led in the family.

## 3. *Community support*

Most of us, not being called to become Desert Fathers, require community for our spiritual development.

Family is not enough, for several reasons. First, a family is too narrow a bit of humanity, and it can be very monolithic and tribal. The worst egoism can be the multi-headed Hydra of a family out for its own aggrandizement. Secondly, Christianity, the religion of love, is apostolic, it is always reaching out; and hence any good Christian family, through its openness, is going to help form community about itself as nucleus. Thirdly, even if the Holy Spirit has moved you to raise children who continue faithful in the Church, they cannot marry their brothers and sisters. In the increasingly isolating urban milieu, they may find it most difficult to know young people who share their sense of the faith and their commitment to marriage.

Is there any reason why the parish cannot serve as the core of this community? It would be wonderful if it could. But then groups within the parish have to form, families need to be doing something seriously together, especially aim at furthering their spiritual development together as families and as individuals. Somehow, a sufficient number of families have to become convinced of the need for developing an ever more intense prayer life and of mutual charity and support so that serious growing together will occur.

More commonly what we see happening is the formation, frequently across parish boundaries, of prayer groups, which may then develop into a fuller kind of community, as bonds form and common needs are identified. Over the years, a considerable variety of movements, such as: Communione e Liberazione, Focolari, Communauté Emmanuel, the various 'charismatic' Covenant Communities, and the tens of thousands of Communidades de Baje in Latin America have sprung up out of the recognition of different kinds of real need.

The difficulties such groups can face are beginning to be recognized. That is a vast and important subject in the life of the church today. Without prejudging any aspect of the issue, I simply want to call attention to the reality of the need, in the most isolated form of life man has ever seen, life in the vast metropolises of today, and to share my conviction that we will see much more of such inventive creating of new forms of community, and to suggest that a central goal of such activity ought to be to encourage and actively help families.

## *Conclusion*

If we address the challenge of family with all the energy and intelligence and confidence in the Holy Spirit all of this presupposes—in one word, with Christian hope—then what we are going to witness in the next years is not only a reversal of anti-family trends, but a renewal of Christian society. Do you not agree that there are good grounds for this hope? How much more do the mass of sensible people have to see of the foul fruits of nihilistic society before they begin actively searching for something else? And we are ready to show them an alternative: Families that function, families that radiate love and joy. Consider an encouraging statistic. The U.S. Census discovered in 1980 that the divorce rate among families where both parents are present, and where there are children, and where the family prays together, is one in 1,250 families. It is our apostolic mission to get this message out to all, despite the lack of cooperation of the nihilistic media.

# Leisure, Youth and Family

## *Myriam Puig Abulí*

'If termites could talk, they'd no doubt use the word "progress" to describe the condition of a house right up to the moment it collapsed', Joseph Sobran once wrote.

Our century is the century of 'progress', of intense life. But this intense life is nothing but an agitated life, because the sign of our time is the 'rush' and the most important discoveries of which our civilization is proud of are not discoveries of wisdom or sapience, but of velocity. We may say: 'This computer is no good any more because it is too slow' or 'With Concorde we may go from Paris to USA in 3 hours less...'. But why, For what?...

What is the meaning of life and where is happiness?... 'Oh well let's do something now', says the man of today 'and then see what happens'.

No; it is not the rush, or in the tumult of people, or the uproar of the cities, or in the haste of hundreds of urgent things, where we recognize beauty or we allow it to flourish. Solitude, silence, ease, are needed for any birth, for any being, for any rising. If you think about it, any creation, or work of art has been preceded by a long period of incubation of leisure.

Newton sitting under the tree, Archimides in the bathtub, Plato in his Academy. Chinese painters take hours crushing graphite in silence before they do the painting which most of the time takes only a few minutes.

Yes, peace, silence and ease. The book from which you read a page and then stop to allow the interior voice to arise within you, the painting that you contemplate, consider, and that even makes you forget to continue. The fabulous panorama of a sunset....

Let us allow that interior song to arise from within... But how do you think you can listen when every sense is contaminated with noise? We are surrounded with a confusion of sounds, colours, forms, sensations, ideas, images in a rush. At the age of 10, every child knows the makes of cars, the names of all football players, or TV stars of not only his own country, but even of the rest of the world.

We should try to forget that we always have ten things to do at the same time, and even today we are in a hurry. Just for a moment, let us rest, listen, try to sit here as if nothing else was happening, as if all of a sudden time didn't exist any more and in the immobility of the minute, the eternal came to us.

This is my task today, to talk about leisure, the *'atium'* of the ancient Greeks. We have a sensation of void and unease, which *originates in the fact that man has lost the notion and even the possibility of leisure.*

This existential vacuum is usually latent and becomes manifested through activism, the disease of many executives who work, work, work and make this a substitute for their lack of sense, their lack of values.

They try to abate the inner vacuum with noise, velocity, activism. 'The more a man ignores his sense of life, the more trepidating rhythm he gives to this life.' 'I don't know where I am going, but I am certainly going fast'. This man flees from himself and he finds men in the same situation with whom he cannot communicate. People have never been so close to one another as today, and at the same time they have never been more isolated. The modern city permits the necessary noise to abate the feeling of loneliness. There are numerous machines and electronic instruments to help. Diversion and amusement and men are not really accompanied but at the same time they are distracted and they don't feel their isolation. Modern society shouts, cries out, to pacify the inner voice that shows the lack of communication with others and they also shout to avoid the necessary silence to be with oneself and to relate to the eternal Truth.

According to an American survey, the amount of leisure time enjoyed by the average American has shrunk 37% since 1973. (Leisure time had dropped $8\frac{1}{2}$ hours a week, from a median of 26.2 hours in 1973 to 17.7 in 1985). Over the same period, the average working week, including commuting, has jumped from under 41 hours to nearly 47 hours. In some professions, particularly law, finance and medicine, the demand often stretches to 80-plus hours a week.

All this raises the question: Wasn't an automated and computerized society expected to reward citizens with ever increasing leisure? Maybe not. All the time-saving devices may actually make people work harder. Simply to remain competitive, professionals find that their lives are one long, continuous workday, squeezing out any leisure time. 'It is ironic', writes the social theorist Jeremy Rifkin in *Time Wars*, 'that in a culture so commited to saving time we feel increasingly deprived of the very thing we value'. People *feel* more harried by their life-styles. 'There just isn't enough time to fit in all the things one feels have to be done'.

Yankelovich's poll for TIME and CNN found this sense specially acute among women in two-income families: 73% of the women complain of having too little leisure, as do 51% of the men (30).

More seriously, this shortcut society is changing the way the family functions. Parents know all too vividly the effects of the stress they endure in order to keep up their lives. Addiction to a speeded-up schedule can lead to a physical breakdown from hypertension, ulcers, heart disease, or dependence on alcohol, cocaine and cigarettes. The effect on the psyche is subtler and more insidious. People find themselves growing impatient and restless, and it seems harder to think logically about a problem. They tend to forget things more easily and then they buy computerized diaries to help them recall appointments. Even if two hours miraculously open up one evening, they may be spent watching TV, since people are too tired to do much else. 'A lot of people talk about sleep. They talk about sleep the way a hungry person talks about food'.

More ominous are the effects on children. 'You've got to hang around with your kids.' Yet hanging-around time is the first thing to go. The very culture of children, of freedom and fantasy, is collapsing under the weight of hectic family schedules. 'Kids understand that they are being cheated out of childhood. There is a sense that adults don't care about them.' Adults may care a lot, but in ways that are often distorted by their own zealous professional lives. Eager parents arrive home late and pour a day's stored attention onto a child who is more ready to be tucked in than talked at.

Children are scuttling from karate classes to play dates scheduled by Mommy's secretary. Their social lives out of nursery school rival those of their parents in complexity.

'It may be that the same loss of leisure among parents produces this pressure for rapid achievement and overprogramming of children'. If parents see parenting largely as an investment of their precious time, they may end up viewing children as objects to be improved, rather than individuals to be nurtured at their own pace.

No combination of innovations, inventions or timely hints will restore the family to its imagined bygone tranquility. Only a dramatic change in both attitide and economics would offer a genuine respite. But at some point individuals must find the time to consider the price of their preoccupation and the toll on the spirit exacted by exhaustion. With too little sleep there are too few dreams.

Workers are weary, parents are frantic and even children haven't a moment to spare: LEISURE COULD BE TO THE '90s WHAT MONEY WAS TO THE '80s' reads the title of an article last year in TIME magazine. 'Time has become the most precious commodity in the land'.

These paragraphs summarized the important perspectives on a topic many people either don't comprehend or are afraid to address: What really is the 'good life'? Are we methodically destroying our culture, families, relationships, health and ability to be content with ourselves? And for what? To pursue additional possessions, status and the fast lane? We must redefine happiness and concentrate our time on what really counts.

Aristotle in his Nicomachean Ethics (Book X, 7, 1177b4–6.2. p. 432) said: 'Happiness is thought to depend on leisure; for we are busy that we may have leisure, and make war that we may live in peace.' ... ( ... )

Or, in other words, 'you work to live and not live to work'. A paradox that moden society has not captured yet.

For this reason, reflection on Leisure is urgent because it will help us to conquer it from within. A quote from George Eastman will give some light on this: 'What do we do in our work-hours determines what we have, what we do in our leisure-hours determines what we are.'

Leisure is as important for achieving amusement as it is for becoming recollected, to permit the internal dialogue about the meaning of life. It will allow us to find the culture of the heart and the values of which our civilization is so much in need. Leisure is a form of that silence needed to perceive reality. Leisure is like the silence in the conversation of people who are in love.

If from this talk you think about this, and this reflection produces the desired change and you start being a spectator of your own events and not a mere actor, my journey would have been worth it and I will go back home with the feeling that a new person has been recovered from this zombie-orientated world.

Seneca said that 'men busy in many things forget about living'.

We should work to have leisure, to dedicate ourselves freely to those activities that we like and that produce in us an expansion and development of the spirit. This elevates us.

The ancients used the word *otium* not as the opposite of work but as the opposite to the useful, productive, commercial, servile, slavish work that they denominated *neg-otium*, the negation of otium or activity not-servile which was the activity of the philosophers.

In Greek the word leisure is *eskole*, Aristotle used this word to refer to non-productive, activity, in material terms, and also to the place where knowledge is acquired. The latin word *schola*, from where the english word school comes also originates with this word *eskole*. Education and learning need leisure, 'otium' as a requisite. Only the free man, relieved from immediate pressures or needs can create art, science, philosophy, etc. Leisure is a requisite for research and any kind of intellectual undertaking. It is necessary to recuperate the meaning of life, to seek for the real freedom and the only truth that will help in the fight against the 'progressive' mentality. And to restore the real meaning of the word 'progress' which can only be progress in human dignity. The progress that will being us closer to our goal: the pursuit of virtue and happiness and the knowledge and love of God.

So we have to realize the importance of leisure, especially in these times when men seem to have lost the sense of it and are working more hours.

In his Politics (8,3(13337b)) Aristotle wrote that '... nature herself requires that we should be able, not only to use leisure well; for, as I must repeat once again, the first principle of all action is leisure. Both are required, but leisure is better than occupation and is its end; and therefore the question must be asked, what ought we to do when at leisure ...'. 'The principal problem is to know what to do when we have leisure'. 'Leisure itself gives pleasure and happiness and enjoyment of life, which are experienced not by the busy man but by those who have leisure'.

At this point we are, or should be convinced of the necessity to educate for leisure, but I would like to insist that to educate parents must be present, knowing that free time depends on the effort and willpower you put into getting it. And these will depend on the priorities that we give to our time and leisure.

And if leisure is important in the adult's world, it is essential in the children's world. If their leisure is a gratifying experience this will separate them from the dangers of boredom, drugs, and even of delinquency. Remember, some things are just worth the time.

We need *leisure to know our children*, to know each one of them, his/her ways, reactions, gifts, affections, in order to be able to guide them and allow them *to develop their capacities and abilities*.

If a couple or each parent separately and then together reflects, meditates on each child individually and is able to identify his/her positive and negative aspects, he/she will be able to encourage certain behaviour that emphasizes the positive and to prevent or avoid other behaviour that underlines the negative. Also if they know and accept their children they will be able to correct them. Discipline is only possible through love. If you know your strengths and failures and those of your children, you will be able to understand them and to help them.

And for this, we need leisure time, because it implies reflection, looking back and meditating a great deal on the way we are doing things and how we could do them better.

We need *leisure* to allow children to *acquire self-confidence and security*. It is an excellent moment to induce children to develop a sense of their own value, that will equip them for success and future happiness. This is self-esteem, that is not presumption or petulance but a quiet and calm respect for oneself, the sensation of one's own value. When we feel it deep inside, we are happy with being ourselves. And the idea that a child has about himself influences his choice of friends, behaviour, the person whom he will marry. It affects his creativity, integrity and stability and decides if he is going to be a leader or a follower.

This is the best heritage that parents can give their children: *a good sense of self*. It is more important what you are, than what you have.

We need *leisure* to help children *compensate for developmental delays* in certain areas. Children reach certain conclusions about themselves by comparison of themselves with other people and also by the reactions of other people towards them. The *fact* of any incapacity is less important to a child than the *reactions* that such incapacity generates in others.

We all have developmental delays for which we have learned to compensate. For example, it is very common to see people with problems in visual memory read out loud to compensate for their incapacity by using the auditory memory. We may help children with certain inabilities by using games that will encourage compensations or the development of the capacity itself. For example to improve visual memory we may play matching-games, etc....

We need *leisure* to discover inclinations, open horizons and to help the child face different situations, to solve problems. To induce good reading habits that will take root for the future.

We need *leisure* to foster personal relations, to relate to others and learn from this relationship. This is a fundamental aspect, with great repercussions in the formation of the child because long periods of his free time will be spent with friends. It is important to help them develop friendships, particularly in this age where friendships are so difficult, because we don't take the time to cultivate them. Aristotle used to say that to have a friend you had to consume several 'talegas' of salt, those 'talegas' were small bags that people used to salt their food and you can imagine how many meal-times you need to spend with one person to consume several bags of salt. This is a very important aspect on which to meditate. Because another by-product of our hectic pace can be loneliness. We remember the days when we could call a friend for sympathy and get a lift after a bad day. Now we may only reach an answering machine. We interact with many people, but do we have time for friendship?

We need *leisure* to create, to teach children, and to show them the artistic manifestations of the human spirit. To stimulate their expressions and creativity and encourage them to express themselves in painting or other forms of art. The importance of art in the formation of personality is without question, and we may see it when we analyze the paintings of children and see there expressions of their internal conflicts.

We need *leisure* to put the child in contact with nature and show him its variety. Here we may discover abilities, inclinations and even future career orientations.

We need *leisure* to teach children how to pray, how to live a full sense of the feast that takes its origin in religion. We have to restore the day of the Lord to its full meaning which is to celebrate the Gift of Creation and the reality of Redemption, and to give our children the spiritual weapons necessary for life... Religious belief facilitates an understanding of human dignity, helps a child to learn moral values and his own personal value as a creature of God made in His own image. It generates a conduct based on moral standards and fosters the desire to participate in the solution of social problems that afflict other human beings. It helps people to be self-transcendent and not self-centred.

We need *leisure* for amusement, and there are two principal forms of amusement: games and entertainment.

In a game man is essentially active in relation to the things he plays with. In entertainments he is mainly passive and receptive. It is precisely for this receptivity and passivity that entertainments (films, theater, TV) have such a profound influence in the formation of man.

After or next to the family, television is probably the most important influence on child development in our society. Children in the United States view an average of 3 to 5 hours of television daily. By high school graduation, the average adolescent will have spent more time in front of the TV than in the classroom. By the time today's child reaches the age of 70, he or she will have spent approximately 7 years watching television.

The popularity of TV is easy to understand: it informs us, entertains us, and keeps us company.

On the other hand it has been difficult to document the effects of such extensive television exposure on children. However television viewing may be linked with violent and/or aggressive behaviour, obesity, poor academic performance, precocious sexuality, and the use of drugs or alcohol.

It hinders the normal *activity* of the child, promotes a *passive attitude*, this slows down willpower and stimulates an inability to pay attention to the things that require effort. (Our time longs for people with willpower and sense of commitment, I wonder if the scarcity of this type of person could be related to TV). It impedes communication. We don't have a family circle any more, it is more a family semicircle where everybody keeps silence to listen to the TV. It promotes selfishness and loss of interest in the feelings, activities and things of others. You don't communicate your feelings, activities and things because they seem so unimportant compared to the things that you view and also because everybody there is listening to the TV.

The primary danger of the television screen lies not so much in the behaviour it produces as the behaviour it prevents—the chats, the games, the family celebrations and arguments through which much of the child's learning takes place and his character is formed. Turning on the television set can turn off the process that transforms children into people.

Thus, it is essential that parents help their children use television as a positive creative force and help them avoid television's negative influences.

*What to do:* End your passivity about television. Be assertive. Television is more than a way to eliminate boredom. It frequently acts like an uninvited guest, teaching your children lessons that you don't suspect. It is essential that you know what your children are watching and that you help them to understand and learn from what they see.

Approach a television programme as you would a film. Decide which show to see, and talk about it after it ends.

*Set limits:* know how many hours of television your children watch. Limit and guide your children's viewing to one or two hours a day.

*Plan:* When you limit TV time, your children will need to plan their viewing to get the most enjoyment out of their time. Do not use television to reward or to punish your children. Such practices make television seem even more important to them.

*Participate:* Watch television with them and talk about the programmes. The worst programme might be a good experience for your children if you are there to help them get the right message, while the best programme might be wasted without your encouragement to think, evaluate, and question what was seen.

*Express your views:* When you are offended or pleased by something on television, write or telephone the network or the programme's sponsor.

In today's world parents find themselves at the mercy of a society which imposes pressures and priorities that allow neither time nor place for meaningful activities and relations between children and adults, which downgrades the role of parents and the functions of parenthood, and which prevents the parent from doing things he wants to do as a guide, friend, and companion to his children. But it is the moment to struggle and to change this trend. First, by changing ourselves, then by helping others do the same. To value and share our free time will certainly contribute as a bridge of communication today and in the future.

If we all reflect about leisure, and it helps us to enrich our lives and our communication with others, I am sure the whole of humanity will benefit.

# Together for Happiness

## *Christiane and Guy Scheen*

The course of our life together has been decided by the presence of our little girl, Cateline, at the heart of our home. When she arrived, we promptly called her our sun-child.

At that time, we had been married for four years and were already parents of a beautiful little girl named Céline, a perfectly healthy child. The birth of Cateline in 1978 made our existence shift.

Cateline was a deeply physically and mentally multihandicapped little girl. She had no autonomy, no balance. She could not stand or sit. She could not speak and had no motor coordination. Swallowing posed serious problems. She could not chew and was epileptic.

Living with her during the two first years was a period of great trial: depression, fears, anguish and guilt feelings all mingled. A time marked by despair. We struggled blindly, tortured by questions which all parents, after the birth of a handicapped child, have to confront. Why us? What did we do wrong? What is the meaning of all this? Is our life finished? Could we still be happy?

These beginnings were very difficult both for Cateline and for us: for Cateline, because she had very little means to survive. For us, because one is not prepared to face such a trial, which literally tortures one's body and soul to the depth of one's self.

Cateline freed in us new and unsuspected energies to love, to bear things with courage, a capacity for compassion, and an openness toward our fellow-men and every suffering human person.

She became our teacher in the full sense of the word. She taught us patience, attention to the beauty of little things, the spirit of gratefulness. She helped us to seek the quality of a relationship, to go beyond the outward aspect of everything. She engendered in us a love of others and of ourselves.

Her face-to-face with the Lord was the mysterious source of her inner peace. How? We didn't know. But the fact is that again and again she revealed to us how absurd is the belief that intelligence is the only way leading to the Lord.

Year after year, Cateline splashed light on our whole family. Living herself in total dependence, she endlessly taught us surrender and trust, the two tests of the unity and the harmony of the couple and of the family.

Because she lacked so many physical skills, she made it possible for us to look at our deficiencies with greater serenity, to accept our limits without collapsing, and to discern the values to follow and the life-choices to make.

As far as these are concerned, they were plentiful. Her re-education was extremely demanding. In 1983, in order to be more available, Christiane and myself thought that it would be good that I stay at home, consecrating myself fully to take care of her. I became a father at home. I must confess this decision was at first difficult to make. But it only enriched our life.

In the heart of this tempest, we were touched and raised by a word from the Gospel.

In John 9, 1 to 3, Christ meets a man blind from birth. The disciples ask the Lord: 'Rabbi, who has sinned? The man himself or his parents, for him to be born blind?' And Jesus answered: 'Neither he nor his parents; he was born blind so that the works of God might be revealed in him.'

Thus the Lord came to the rescue of our boat battered by the storm in a heavy sea. He did not let us sink, and go under. He said: 'Let's go to the other side!'

By this word of the Gospel of the man born blind, indeed, the Lord came to us and said that He was present and working in our little girl, in her great handicap. And in our blindness, we started to discover little by little the wonders of the Lord in our little girl, so harmed and wounded in her physical and mental wholeness. Progressively, in our valley of tears, we reaped a plentiful harvest of happiness. We were able to identify with and to sing the words of the psalmist. 'Those who sow in tears, will reap with songs.'

First the beauty of our child struck us: her blond golden hair, the extraordinary sweetness in her face, the light in her blue eyes, her sparkling and penetrating look. She would make us grow in such a way...

We were not looking any more in our child for what she did not have but we discovered who she was and welcomed what she could give us.

We were spinning out perfect happiness with our two children! And our adventure did not stop there.

Cateline did not only open our hearts, and that of her big sister, to the dimensions of the world of handicapped children. By now, we knew that she belonged to the Lord. Through his voice, we were led to the work of adoption of handicapped children through the 'Emmanuel' Community. Through this work, we welcomed first in 1984 our third child, David, a small Columbian boy suffering from cerebral palsy, and then in 1988 two more twin girls from Brazil, Anne and Sophie, suffering in various degrees from deafness and blindness.

Of course, life with a handicapped child by itself entails a series of medical and social problems of integration and school adjusting and many such others that one has to face. It is not an easy life... And it is the life of every family that struggles for its 'different' child. But how much satisfaction in return does one get when one experiences the blossoming of the child in what he is and what he has, when you see him smile at you!

Thus Cateline, probably deemed 'useless' in the eyes of the world, helped us to become again like clay in the hands of the potter. She had no actual power... and yet how many lives did she transform around her merely by her presence. A true encounter with her was experienced secretly in the mystery of her silent look, of her open and welcoming hand, and in our heart-to-heart relationship with her.

Cateline revealed to us that suffering in itself did not have any meaning, but only Christ could inhabit it and convey meaning to it. She taught us so many deep truths about herself and those like her, about ourselves and about life itself. Her radical poverty made us richer in what is essential and we learned that each life, no matter how fragile and damaged it may be, remains unique and able to give and receive love. She has so often been a sign of hope for those who had lost it.

Then one day, when she was ten, after a long agony, she passed away, as if to tell us that now her mission had been accomplished, and our way marked out. It seemed to us that the ground was giving way under our feet. We were losing what made our life.

But beyond the tears and pain caused by her death, we soon experienced, in a flow of graces, that our sun-child continued to partake, more than ever, in our life, and the seemingly insignificant mustard-seed that she was, had fully grown into a strong tree. (MT, 13, 31) On this tree, again and again, we take refuge, to be ourselves rooted in the Lord and allow ourselves to be sent into the world, in the work of Adoption Emmanuel, alongside its Belgian founders, Pol-Marie and Christiane Boldo.

Emmanuel SOS Adoption is called to shelter at birth, or as soon as possible, the abandoned handicapped child, in order to provide a family for this child by means of adoption.

The work is open to all who say 'yes' to love and to life, whatever their religious or philosophical convictions. In practice, however, most of these adopting families, that we call Emmanuel families, are Christian, and when they decide to devote themselves to their adoptive child, they feel challenged by his small threatened life. They strive to be consistent in their faith to the end, to face the demands of love and of the Gospel.

They are normal families. They are not specialized in adoption nor perfect, but they are happy to share their happiness with one or several children, disadvantaged both by their abandonment and their handicap.

They make this choice in joy, but also with humility. They are conscious of their own limits and deficiencies, but wholly surrendered to the goodness of their master and Lord, in whom they have absolute confidence.

Each one of these family vocations will unfold according to its own rhythm, will be shaken by specific fears and know moments of dizziness. At the same time, each one will be provided, from the very heart of God, with an amount of graces, and will write, in the empty space of this life project, his own holy history.

Each one will indeed come one day to the point of jumping in the abyss to exclaim with Saint Paul: 'It is not me who lives, it is Christ who lives in me.' Or again: 'It is when I am weak that I am strong.' And what peace, what joy, what happiness then settle in the heart!

Over 120 children have been sheltered in this way in Belgium. But the Emmanuel work also exists in France, Switzerland, Canada and soon in Luxembourg.

We are usually called in to hospitals to the cradles of new born babies, abandoned because of a handicap. For the most part, they are Downs babies. When we welcome them, we know that the Lord awakens somewhere in the heart of a family a call to receive this child.

Emmanuel also believes in the mission of evangelization by these children. The true wealth in the eyes of God is that of the heart, and these little ones have it in abundance. They remind us of the true nature of man, which is to be a 'relational being'. They open us to the existential dimension per se, which is to love and be able to let ourselves be loved.

When they let themselves be received by us, these children make of our lives pathways of truth, the same truth that makes us free and which day after day gives us both the strength to continue and to live from this truth.

These wounded children to whom we allow ourselves to be given, in spite of all that weighs us down on this road, make us discover the kingdom of God being realized in the present moment.

With these children, the families are able to sow and reap love, and to gather in God's granary. They are preparing for a future that sings the happiness of man and the glory of God.

# Europe and the Future of the Family

## *Archduke Dr Otto von Habsburg*

In Europe in 1989 we went through an absolutely miraculous turn of events. It was exactly two hundred years after the beginning of the French Revolution that a revolution came about which carried just as much impetus as did the events in France, and may turn out to be a great blessing for all of us, because Europe is now becoming a unity, and this for a huge number of reasons.

First of all, we had the drama of Central and Eastern Europe. That is the area which had been surrendered to Soviet influence at the end of World War II. The 1989 turn of events there was considered by many as an absolute surprise and it was to a certain extent—although it could have been forseen, because for quite a few years Communism had been dead. If you want to have today a talk with a convinced Communist, I don't advise you to go beyond the outer border of the West. You might find some fossils still in our countries, but not beyond them.

This collapse of Communism had many roots. First of all, the movement of ordinary people against Communism. Let us not forget that this is not a new movement. There was the courageous revolution of 1956 in Hungary. There was the Prague spring of 1968. It was always known that ordinary people did not accept the tyranny which was imposed on them. President Reagan of the United States, in one of his earliest statements as President, had called the regime of Communism the 'evil empire'. At that time there was an uproar in the whole world by all our professional intellectuals, saying that this uncouth cowboy did not know what really went on in the world. I myself had slight doubts sometimes whether that was the best description. But in the last two years I have been a lot in the countries of Central and Eastern Europe. I have participated in many election campaigns. An election campaign has one colossal advantage over everything else—you get into places that you don't get normally. And there I saw that Reagan was right—this was an 'evil empire'. The way people were destroyed, the way environment was destroyed, is something which staggered the imagination. And perhaps for me the greatest memory is of discussions with people of middle age or old age who say 'they (the Communists) stole forty years of my life', and that is true. These people have lost years of their lives, and that is one of the greatest elements of embitterment.

Then, of course, there is the collapse of economy, which is due to the fact that there was a fundamental contradiction between Marx and the modern economy, because the modern economy is based on speed, and Marxism is based on limiting speed, that is to say, on fixing, on laming the economy. And that led to this colossal collapse which we now see in the Soviet Union, where it is tragic because the Russians have traditionally been an extremely gifted nation in matters of technology. But even the greatest genius cannot defend himself, cannot develop within the framework of a Marxist system.

And finally, let us not forget that the Soviet Union is the last colonial empire in the time of global decolonisation. The Russians today make up less than fifty per cent of its population, and as it goes on to progress, this imbalance will increase because Russia has a birth rate as bad as ours in the West, while the Islamic and Eastern areas of the Soviet Union have birth rates which correspond to those of the developing world, so that very soon the Russians will be a minority in their country. They are already a minority in the army, and that makes for the approaching collapse of the whole Empire.

At the side of this, we have from the West the tremendous success of our European Community, at least in economics and now also in politics. We are already in the Community the first economic power in the world, and that will be even more the case by 1992. This will necessarily have political consequences which we are in the European Parliament are already feeling today. We are going to have to take political decisions about this.

The great changes that have come about mean that all of Europe is now full of hope. But we also have tremendous dangers. The first of these is a political danger. We are still the neighbours of one of the last superpowers of the past, namely the Soviet Union. This Soviet Union is about to explode, and we should clearly realise one thing. We suffered, you will remember, from the catastrophe in Chernobyl when that large nuclear centre exploded in Russia. But a major power which collapses is just as much a chain reaction as was Chernobyl. We might therefore have to face, and fairly soon, a political Chernobyl, for which we must be ready. And if we are not as ready as we should be, this is mainly due to our moral decline which can no longer be denied; a moral decline which, in my opinion, is the consequence of the sins of the nineteenth century and of the first half of our century, namely of the time when the religious essence, which makes up for the glory of Europe, began to be ignored. It was a tragedy, because even if men no longer speak of religion, our cities speak of religion with their cathedrals and their churches, and therefore this collapse of religion was something that hurt the very soul of Europe. But I do believe that if we look ahead, there is every reason not to be too saddened. We have one fact which we should not underestimate. André Malraux, the great French political writer and poet, once said, 'The twenty-first century will either be a religious century, or it won't be at all'. And it is going to be a religious century, and for one specific reason: science is returning to God. Long ago scientists turned their back on the notion of God. They were very proud to be atheists. But nowadays, our top scientists all believe in God. They may not belong to an organised religion, but they have realised, out of the problems of our time, out of the greatness of their discoveries, that God is an absolute necessity, that He exists. And this, surely, is more important for the future development of humanity than even the nuclear fission.

But of course, while this is still a perspective for the future, and meanwhile we Europeans have to cope with our present problems. These include a collapse of morals and the mass elimination of children through widespread abortion. We are suffering, and we are suffering seriously, from the moral capitulation of many very good people, including church people, who simply say, 'We cannot fight this evil. It exists because everybody does it, everybody accepts it'. We know that in the European Parliament and elsewhere perfectly decent people have given up fighting, and they are probably worse than the evil ones who want to destroy us.

This leads then, in our European Community, to the continued downgrading of the family. It is frequently treated as no more important than other family-like organisations, like communities of lesbians or homosexuals and so on. This is an offensive which is now carried out very vigorously, to downgrade families completely.

Europe is becoming a void. We have no children. It is quite understandable that the people from outside come in and take the places which normally our children should have taken. And that is a point we must keep in mind, because, this general movement of population is something which could be avoided if we Europeans did our task, and help those in their own countries to attain the same standard of living we have attained here in Europe. So in reality those who want to give up the basic values of our civilisation, are the greatest enemies of the developing world too.

In that perspective, let us ask ourselves what we can do in the present situation, because it is no good bewailing a situation, it is what we can do about it which is really worthwhile. The first thing, and I say this out of the practical experience of a very old politician, is that we ought to dare to speak much more frankly, more openly, perhaps even, more brutally than we have done so far. Because I believe that we, and this applies also to the Churches, are dying of too much diplomacy, of too much 'kindness'. People have common sense about what is being said to them and they appreciate if they know that those who speak also mean what they say, and are standing up for their real values. They respect them, they may not like them, (and that does not hurt anyone very much!) but they will respect them. One can learn something in politics, from free-style wrestling. I once travelled on a plane with a wrestler, and he gave me very useful advice for my political career: he said that the 'bad' figures in wrestling, those that people dislike, are paid twice as much as the popular ones, because they attract people! So in politics, those who speak their mind attract the people more in the end, if they only have sufficient breath. So let us talk very honestly, let us talk very openly, and let us not care so much about our popularity. In my own experience, I have seen that men who dare to speak openly and to speak their mind, even though they are not liked, are generally elected.

In the second place, we are called upon to show solidarity. Solidarity, first of all with the nations of Eastern Europe which are now going to be reunited with us, or those which are still under slavery, like for instance the Baltic nations. They are Christian nations like we are, they are decent people. They have a right to support, they have a right to our solidarity. And let us not forget, their plight is a little bit the fault of the West. It was the weakness of the West at the end of the Second World War, which delivered them from one tyranny to another so we ought to do something to make them recover a little bit for what we have enjoyed for so many decades. We must also have solidarity with all religious believers. This means not only the Christians, but just as much the Jews and the followers of Islam—those who believe in God are all allies on the issues of family life. Let us make a common front and fight for life together.

Then, in my capacity as a politician, I urge you, all of you, to enter into active politics. You see, it is tremendous error, in our democratic countries, to believe you have done your task when you throw, every fourth or fifth year, a little piece of paper into a ballot box, and then don't care any more of what has happened with the persons you elected. Now, I have come to the conclusion that democracy is not a one-way thing. It is a task which is equally the task of those who are elected and those who elect them. Because I very much feel that people have to control those they have elected. I feel that very strongly in the European Parliament. That is to say, if the voters control their members, results would sometimes be rather different from what they are today. You see, we have somthing called 'roll call' votes. You can know exactly how your MEP has voted on a particular issue. And we have had a number of votes on issues connected with the family, and I would been have thankful to God if the voters had controlled the voting or non-voting of certain of our members, because that would create a discipline, and they would perhaps behave better than they behave today.

And so my message to you is, control your members of Parliament! I speak here of course as a member of the European Parliament. Control the Europarliamentarians—it would be very healthy for all of us.

We also need to talk about the influence of television. We should not necessarily deprive children of television. But we should see that we change television from within. Most of our families are trying to make what they call decent people out of their children, and unfortunately, in all too many of our societies, journalism and activities in mass media are not a decent activity. Let us realise something essential: radio and television is for tomorrow; it is the territory of missionary action. It is the most important territory of missionary action, because it is through there that one can change the system from within and bring it, with all its tremendous technical means, to be a strength for turning things from bad to good. And we can do so, if we only motivated more good young people to go into these professions.

And then, of course, we are also called to practical action. What do we want to do in favour of families? Now, of course, when you speak today, at least in certain countries like in Germany, on what to do for families, the first thing that is said is that we are going to give them material subsidies. It is now being generally recognised that to have many children is a sort of economic burden. And so some help has actually been passed, especially now under the present government. But I do feel that this is only a temporary solution and certainly not the best one. In some ways I feel that it is like treating cancer with aspirin. That is to say, you take away some of the pain, but you don't change the fundamental attitude toward families. And here I want to submit that there are two things we ought to do, because what we are interested in is to give families once again the status and weight they have lost in public policy. Let us have no illusions about it, today there is a general and a current hostility to families, especially against large families. Families today do not count very much in our political and public life. What we need first of all is, the principle which the jurists call the 'principle of subsidiarity', that is to say that the largest unit has never the right to take over a task which the smaller unit can perform satisfactorily. This ought to be possibly defended also in courts. And that would give the family that first base, because it is the smallest unit, and consequently it can have all the rights which it can actually handle in a satisfactory manner.

Then there is a second point I want to make, and a point which is certainly controversial. It is my own personal opinion, and I know that I am fairly isolated in this opinion, because I have noticed it several times in Germany, and I got a lot of criticism. Here it is. We must make the families politically significant once more because that is the only thing that is going to give them the weight which is needed. And I see only one way to this end. For many years we have been fiddling along in all our countries with the voting age. It is raised, it is lowered: twenty-one, eighteen years. I don't think that that is rational. I think that the right to vote is something that belongs to a person at the moment of his or her birth, and that smaller children have a longer interest than an old man like me who has already very little mileage left. And if we gave the children that right to vote, and the parents the right to exercise it as long as the children are minor, we would be certain that all the politicians would start running after the big families, because that is where the votes would be! I don't see any philosophical reason why that should not be the good democratic way towards a better family policy.

There is today in our Europe a wave of pessimism. People believe that things are going wrong and that they are going to be worse, and so on and so forth. When we look at things as they really are, there is no reason for pessimism. The wonderful thing about our time is that we have our future in our own hands. The events in Europe of the last two years have shown this absolutely clearly: where there is a will there is a way. In other words, we should not be pessimistic. Quite apart from anything else pessimism has never constructed anything. Instead, it simply kills the will to work.

We should be optimistic. Then we can turn to real and practical action. There was recently an opinion poll in Germany, asking how the generations stood with regard to optimism or pessimism for the future. The result showed that the older the people are, the more optimistic they are. This is quite logical, because when you reach my age, for instance, and you look back upon your life, there is every reason on earth to be optimistic, especially for us Europeans. When I was young, for every Frenchman the German, and for every German the Frenchman, was an hereditary enemy. When I was young, each one of us knew we would have to fight in a war between Europeans in his lifetime. And there were fortresses along the Rhine, and everybody accepted them as something inevitable. And if you tell that to the young people of today, they look at you quite astonished that this ever existed! This is a colossal achievement. We have had 40 years of peace. We have, in one generation, changed the mentality of two of the oldest nations of our Continent. And that is an achievement which has rarely been obtained in history, and it was achieved because there was good will on both sides and there was indefatigable action.

Let us not forget then, that the future is ours. Let us in that perspective go forward. We may have difficulties, we may have certain defeats. But defeats are there to be overcome. There can be a bright future for Europe's families, if we trust in God and take practical action.

# Family Policies or Social Collapse

## Prof Richard Whitfield

### Family Life: Key to the Social Ecology

Questions concerning the global ecology, the natural and physical environment, are now firmly on the political map and are beginning to affect our every-day lives, and that is, of course, very important. But, equally important is the sustaining of the basic social fabric of any society in the age of technology so that the individuals within it have a sense of identity, purpose and direction, thereby minimising the pain they experience themselves and the pain they may cause other people.

The basic mediating unit of the social ecology in all cultures and at all times has been the family—not just the nuclear family of course, but the extended family, surrogate 'relatives' and local community. No culture has survived throughout history unless it has had policies in place, whether written down or by habit or ritual, which safeguard family units. The 'bottom line' is that if a culture ignores and fails to safeguard the sustaining of relationships between men and women for procreation and child-rearing then it is destined for some form of internal collapse.

### Reliable or unreliable bonds

We now have much data about the ways in which the relevant safeguards for sound human nurture are not in place within western societies, and also now increasingly not in the developing world. (A result of the mixed blessings of outside influences upon tribal cultures.) The key to protecting the social ecology is to make sure that enough people within our communities both are and *feel* reliably loved. So the challenge for our international technological societies is to promote the means for the much more reliable transmission of secure love.

That unavoidably involves making moral choices, and for many of us raises spiritual questions about the nature and value of human life, about bonds between Creator and created, and about the limits of faith in ourselves and others. But nurturing mechanisms for the transmission of reliable love is very crucially also a hands-on business. Love is both experienced and transmitted between people. Feelings of reliable love begin in the womb through the process of secure attachment or otherwise of the developing foetus. Such feelings of reliable love, or otherwise, go on through the birth process (when the trauma of separation is first experienced) and crucially in our early years.

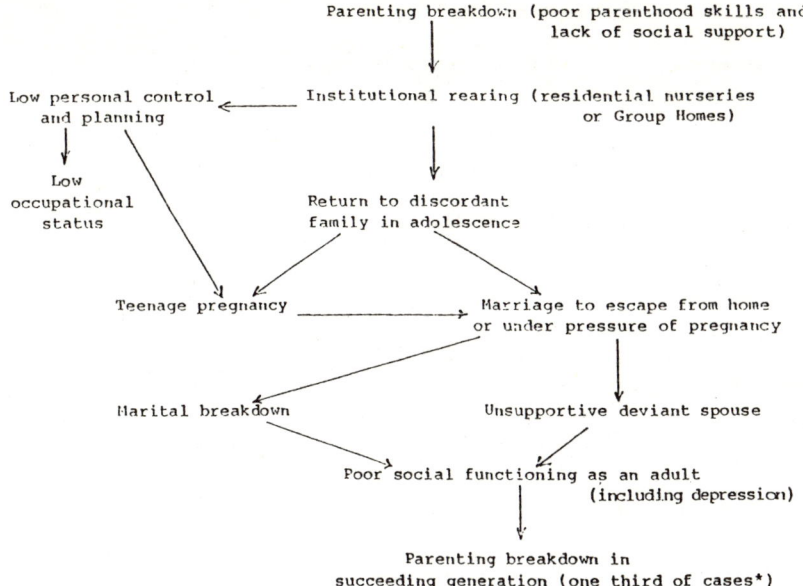

(* No cases in comparison group reared by both biological parents at home)

Fig. 1: A simplified map of intergenerational transmission of parenting breakdown in girls
[adapted from Quinton and Rutter, 1988]

Figure 1 simplifies such social research about the intergenerational transmission of parenting breakdown for girls, and shows how unsatisfactory nurture in one generation can be extensively transmitted into the next. We are now all too familiar about how such a pattern applies in a significant proportion of cases of child abuse, where adults who were themselves abused as children too often behave likewise towards children in their care. This figure shows that parenting breakdown was inter-generationally transmitted in about one third of case, while a matched comparison group of girls reared by both their biological parents at home became, in every case, 'successful' mothers with 'good enough' bonds with their offspring.

The probability (though not certainty) of inter-generational transmission of social and emotional deprivation applies to the converse, that is genuine affirmation and the sound nurture which children and others need. What Figure 1 represents is fundamentally adult insecurity about attachment and loving derivative from unsatisfactory childhood bonds.

Figure 2 is a positive chart showing a cycle of affirmation rather than deprivation. What we need, of course, is more of Figure 2 in everyones' lives! In an imperfect world this is easier said than done. But there are some guidelines.

From the moment of conception onwards there needs to be *commitment* surrounding the developing foetus and then the new-born child. The creation ideal requires these commitments to be provided by both a man and a woman

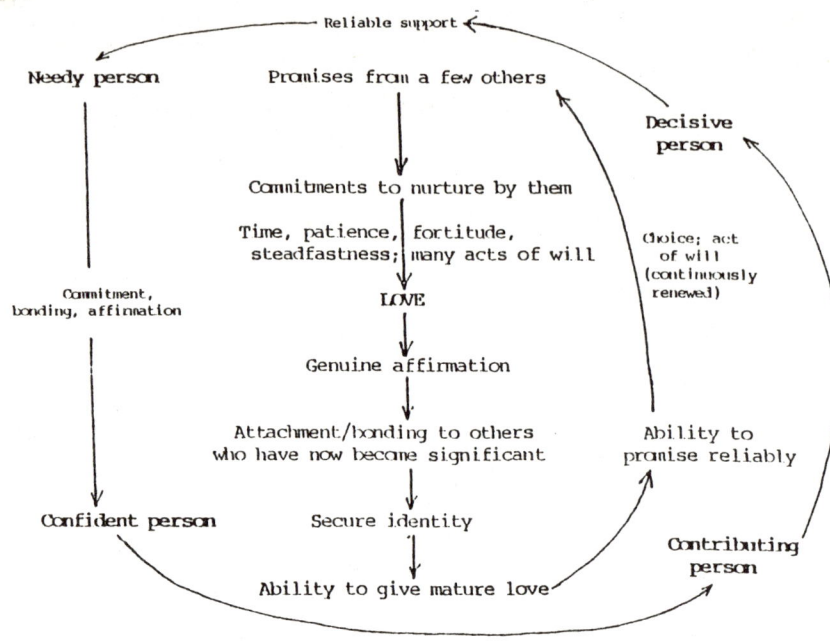

Figure 2: Lifelines involving love

together for the newborn boy or girl. Such commitments need not be necessarily based upon biological parenthood, but for every youngster psychological parenthood is what really matters for emotional and spiritual health. Now, of course, I speak of the basic family unit, the unit so fragile in modern societies, yet without which we cannot function.

## *Family bonds with marriage our best bet*

There have been many attempts to try and rear children by other means, but they have largely failed to deliver sufficiently the personal love, commitment and support, which all of us need, and the platforms which we all require to be able to extend such lifelines of reliable love to our children, to our friends, and to our relatives and neighbours. That is why the family is of crucial significance—not because family life is easy, let alone perfect, for some terrible things happen in some families—but because families are our best bet to secure the social ecology. There is no way to a better society if we ignore the emotional, practical and policy needs of families.

Within Britain our crisis is now severe. Two or three decades ago we believed that a few more divorces, sad though they may be, would not threaten society. No caring person could possibly advocate keeping people in impossible relationships. But how do we define 'impossible'? Few close relationships can avoid painful periods when things can seem 'impossible', for our feelings and behaviour can be fickle and unreliable indicators of relationship potential. Too many adults have found that 'the grass is not greener' in second and subsequent marriages, and that the challenges of step-family life are often even more complex. Yet our investment in sound preventative education and counselling remains meagre.

Of course it takes 'two to tango' over the rough patches on the 'dance floor' of marriage for a lifetime when unpredictable things do happen, but with the UK divorce rate rising towards 40% we can do better. Such a proportion of shattered illusions, hopes and tender feelings is not inevitable, and not in many individuals' or society's interests. We have to do better to sustain the commitments between adults so that lifelines of reliable love can be more safely propagated.

## *Family-sensitive policies*

The way forward involves all of us and our elected representatives in government and the voluntary sector.

Family policies must move to the core of our social policies. Work in our schools depends upon us getting cycles of affirmation into more and more children's lives. Our social work and health care systems, and the well-being of employees at work in every location depends upon such positive cycles also, for we cannot sustain a healthy workforce if too few feel securely loved and affirmed in their day-to-day lives.

Most of the great religions of the world have implicitly tried to support family values through the centuries to sustain the social fabric. As a Christian I welcome helpful insights into the human condition from sociology, psychology and the natural sciences. Yet experience tells me that the steadfast time, patience, fortitude, and the many acts of will (often involving real sacrifice) involved in Figure 2 cannot ultimately be sustained solely by our own innate powers. Many discover that divine grace is the crucial ingredient in forgiveness and perseverance in key relationships, particularly when they get into the tight corners, which sooner or later all of us experience. Confronting our full human nature requires us to confront our spiritual potential which is a source of hope and renewal in all despairing and painful situations.

## *Sexual behaviour and the ecological crisis*

Circumstances now demand a new urgency. Included among the many indicators of damaged relationships are the data on sexually transmitted diseases—now the most contagious in society apart from the common cold. Figure 3 is the November 1989 estimate of the pattern of spread of the HIV-AIDS virus in the UK; the graphs reflect an average incubation period of 10 years before the virus leads to symptoms.

Unless there are, without delay, major changes in human sexual behaviour in Western society (and the use of condoms offers hugely insufficient protection in view of the 'failure' rate for sperm, which is four times as large as the HIV virus), then our reproductive future will lie in tatters. If we ever needed a real solid medical and scientific reason for being concerned about family relations we now have it.

There are now nearly 1% of new born babies in America which have the AIDS virus at birth, while in the UK one quarter of HIV positives are heterosexually active. We and our children are likely to watch the projected exponential rise of AIDS cases among heterosexuals shown in Figure 3 over the next 40 years unless there is renewed emphasis upon chastity, abstinence and the moral ideal of 'one man, one woman for life'.

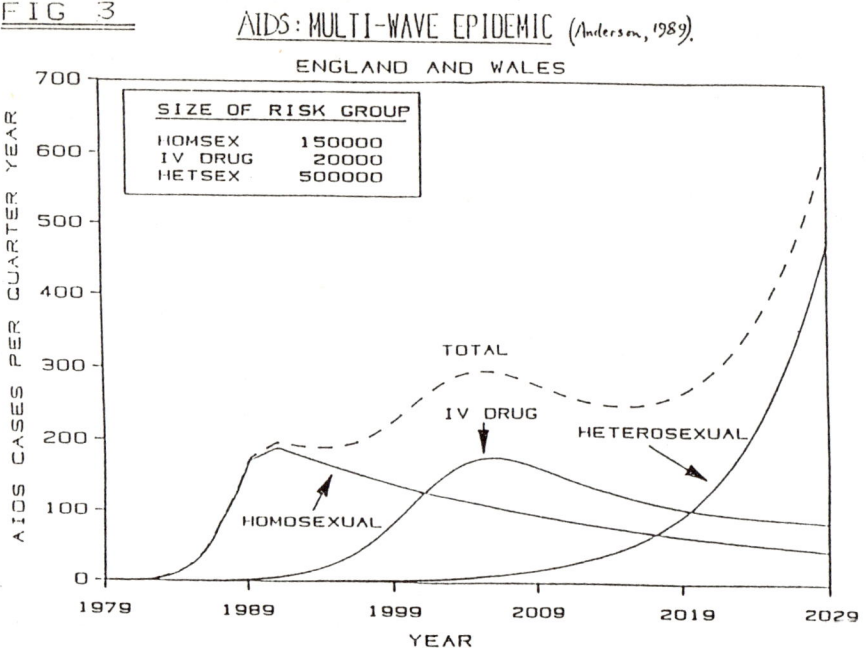

FIG 3. AIDS: MULTI-WAVE EPIDEMIC (Anderson, 1989).

However, before we make facile judgements about human sexual behaviour, we need to recognise that sexual permissiveness is related very much to whether people have prior solid experience of secure, loving bonds and a good sense of self-esteem. Those who move from one partner to another are often reflecting their uncertainty about bonding to anybody, and in sampling many partners they tend to get more and more lonely. Response to peer group pressures and norms also indicates an insufficiently established sense of self. It is the experience of many counsellors that people who have lots of partners end up extremely isolated. Their limited security is further undermined as potentially precious acts lose their meaning.

Hence the way we are bonding in marriages and rearing children early on and through adolescence is vital for social and personal futures. The HIV virus is a demographic and ecological time bomb now overlaying the world-wide crisis concerning the safeguarding of relations between men and women for safe procreation and reliable child care. We now need a new and more considered sexual revolution, and we have no time to waste concerning the educational and other social policy changes required to get it moving.

## Changing climate for commitment?

Already the climate is changing, but too slowly. Even some of our churches do not act with the necessary urgency, being somewhat asleep concerning changes in human relations and the associated social policy questions over the past thirty years, naively assuming that normal married family life would go on in our community without our taking special care to buttress it. We are already losing skills of childrearing which have been handed down from generation to generation simply because a high proportion of our youngsters today do not see effective parenting in operation. Good role models and learning by experience and 'watching' are vital here. Therefore we must seriously consider teaching these skills and sensitivities in schools and colleges. We are not in a 'normal' period of social evolution. We are at a major watershed where we either transform our models in an environment of high expectations, or we risk a cumulative spiral of transmitted deprivation which will pull our society down into chaos.

By about the year 2005 every new marriage on average in Britain will take into it one partner who comes from a broken home. Yet we know that the best prognosis for a good marriage is when a psychologically mature and stable man and a similar woman make promises and commit their lives to each other. They are aided in this by good, reliable nurture in childhood. When one or both parties becoming married are for whatever reason badly hurt inside, then there are likely to be specific difficulties to overcome so as to secure mutual trust; in part marriage inevitably involves mutual healing and some 'rescue' work.

FILE: IntCon

# Family—the Way Forward

## *Rt Hon Angela Rumbold PC CBE MP*
## Minister of State, *The Home Office*

'When Society requires to be rebuilt', wrote John Stuart Mill, 'there is no use in attempting to rebuild it on the old plan.' Today I pose the question—'Does the family need to be rebuilt?' and if so, what should we aim to do?

I think many people today do feel that the traditional family is being steadily eroded. As those pressures build up, I believe that the instincts of many are to reinforce and strengthen what is the oldest and best-tried institution in history—the family.

## Pressures on the Family

To begin with, geographical mobility weakens local associations and disperses families. Over the last 40–50 years it has become common for most of us to move to look for work, leaving the area where our parents settled to establish homes elsewhere. This very dispersal of families around the country and, indeed, around the world, means that there is less support when marriages and relationships come under stress. The extended family, so important in a time of crisis, loses its supporting role. And then there is the ever-rising divorce rate. During the 1970s the divorce rate doubled. If current trends continue, within a few years one in three marriages are likely to end in divorce.

Another major change has been the increase in the number of couples who live together outside marriage. Needless to say, this sort of relationship tends to be less permanent and less stable than marriage. Hand in hand with the growth of co-habitation has been a major rise in the number of children born outside marriage. In 1980, some 12% of births took place outside marriage and eight years later that figure had more than doubled to 25%.

There are more single-parent households and individuals living on their own. Here in the UK we have one of the highest proportions of lone parent families of all the European Community countries. In 1961, 6% of families with dependent children were headed by a single parent—today that is up to 16%.

For all the benefits of record living standards and unprecedented opportunity we now enjoy, it does seem that throughout the industrialised world people are faced with increasing difficulty in forming lasting relationships.

## Women and Work

I think that it would be foolish to expect that we can somehow recreate the family as it was, say, 100 years ago. But I firmly believe that we must create a climate in which people can discover for themselves the joys of family life—joys which far outweigh the ephemeral pleasures of more loosely defined relationships.

One of the major influences on the structure of the family in the post World War II period has been the steady rise in the number of women going out to work. At the same time, technology and economic progress have liberated us from some of the most dreary and time-consuming household tasks.

We must face up to the fact that over the next 10 years demographic changes are set to have a considerable influence on the family and on patterns of work. In the UK the number of school leavers will fall by a million between 1983 and 1993. As a result, employers will increasingly look to previously under-used sections of the community—older workers, the long term unemployed and women.

In an age when more women than ever are staying on at school and going on into higher education, it would be naive to think that all women will want to stay at home to bring up a family. On the other hand, it simply isn't on for the State—or indeed anyone else—to dictate when, whether and how much women work. That is a decision for individuals to take.

Increasingly, women are making the decision to pursue a career. Though it would be wrong to think that women's work patterns are identical to those of men. Many young women think in terms of work followed by marriage, family and the resumption of a career later. More than two out of five jobs are now done by women. A quarter of all self-employed people are women. In the next ten years 95% of all new jobs will probably be filled by women. So the trends of the last twenty years are firmly set to continue.

The fact is that women make a huge and invaluable contribution to our economy. But that does not mean that women are turning away from family life. On the contrary, more and more women are already showing that it is possible to combine work and the family successfully.

But this is not necessarily something new. Social patterns have changed before. The extended family helped in those conditions and I think there is more scope for it to help now.

## The Dilemma

Perhaps the most crucial question for women and for families in the 1990s will be how women can combine successfully the roles of workers and mothers.

I don't pretend that it is easy for any mother to balance the competing demands of work and family. Every individual will have to make quite difficult decisions to get the balance right. But I do believe that we must ensure that women do have a choice. We should remember that women have a huge—and rather underrated—capacity to combine work and family.

Since the War we have retreated from earlier conventions that the only place for a wife—with or without children—is in the home. It would be an absolute tragedy if, having given millions of women a real choice as to whether they go out to work, we erect new and equally repressive conventions—the notion that women *must* go out to work! Large numbers of young mothers want to stay at home to raise their children.

I believe, however, that we should make it clear that we firmly believe it is better for children to be brought up in a loving family with two parents—by that I mean the age-old union of marriage between man and woman.

At the same time we must be supportive of lone parents forced to bring up children without the help of a partner. Left alone for whatever reason, for however long, lone parents have to make a special effort to maintain the right environment for bringing up children. Out of hand condemnation is no way to create a healthy climate, helping them and encouraging the formation of strong family units.

## Dangers of Weakening the Family

The origins of some of our most intractable social problems can be traced to the weakening of the family.

Many young people leave home on the collapse of their parents' marriage or because they are unable to get on with the new partner, and this is clearly an important cause of homelessness. The fact is that the State can never fully compensate for the break-up of families. How can governments ever take on the responsibilities of parents?

Today, more than at any time in the past, we are aware of the terrible problems of child abuse. Some people claim that this shows the family is an oppressive institution. In reality, the opposite is true. It is frequently the non-natural father who is the problem.

## The Role of the Family

But despite all these problems, marriage remains a vigorous and popular institution. It is evolving—but reports of its demise are greatly exaggerated.

So why is the family so resilient? The simple answer is because it works.

Marriage is natural, the family is natural. Even if marriage didn't exist, individuals would quickly invent it because it is the best way of securing stability and happiness for children and parents alike.

We know all too well that the weakening of marriage and family links brings increased isolation, loneliness and unhappiness.

Marriage and the family teach responsibility, instil altruism and the ever important art of compromise.

They offer the best protection against the big State and over-bearing governments. The family is uniquely able to stand up against the unwelcome intrusion of bureaucracy and to provide support and comfort for individuals.

There can be no doubt that the environment in which young children are raised is the single most important factor in their achieving success and happiness in later life.

There is no more important contribution to a child's success in school than a stable home background.

A good family is the best start any child can have in life.

The reasons for the change in the structure of the family are not all for the bad:

- Many people live alone before marriage, mainly for reasons of mobility.

However, this is a positive sign since delayed marriage also brings a better chance of lasting marriage. Early marriages are more likely to break up.
- Although there is a high level of divorce and marriage break-down, we should also remember that remarriage rates are high in this country. Amongst men who divorced during the period 1977–1980 three in four remarried within five years. Marriage remains a popular institution amongst those who go through the trauma of divorce.

Most young people wish for and plan to get married and to have children within marriage.

Marriage remains an institution with strong support in our society. Seven out of ten people surveyed have said that they would like to see more done to safeguard the institution of marriage.

It is not hard to understand why. Anyone who has known the warmth of a family upbringing knows that is the best way to raise children. I believe it is in the family that adults are most likely to realise their potential and find happiness.

There is no more satisfying role—for men and for women—than bringing up children. I only wish more of our so-called opinion-formers would devote some column inches to the rewards and pleasures of parenthood.

The moments in a baby's first year which can be missed and never regained are too many to enumerate. I firmly believe that the first five years of any child's life are well worth a few financial sacrifices. Where it is possible, I do believe that this enrichment of both the children's and the parents' lives is a prize to be cherished.

## *The Role of Government*

I must first of all say that I am not here to set out an exhaustive record of Government policy. However, I will try to give some indications of the Government's general view.

First of all it is essential to emphasise the limited power of government. I believe the influence of government is often exaggerated. The impact of social policy and fiscal measures on the structure of the family is dwarfed by the effect of changes in social attitudes and economic developments. Government can no more legislate for family stability than it can for happiness. Although it can and must take responsibility for creating the best possible climate.

What any government would like to achieve is, of course, clear. It is to ensure that, as far as possible, children have a happy upbringing and a stable family life. The key ingredients in securing this goal are the love, care and affection of parents.

Sadly, the State cannot guarantee these things—but it does have a role. Government must ensure that financial help reaches those families in real need. It is important to target help where it is needed. Our 1986 Social Security reforms introduced radical new measures to direct help to families on low incomes. We are now spending nearly £10 billion on a whole range of benefits for the family, an increase of over a quarter in real terms since 1979. Family credit now goes to over 300,000 families—nearly half as many again as were helped under the old system.

We must also ensure that our policies encourage parents to act responsibly towards their children. Sadly, too many parents do not seem to understand that bringing up children is a life-time responsibility. Government cannot make irresponsible parents responsible but it can ensure that absent parents pay for their children. Men who abandon their families should not be allowed to walk away from their financial responsibilities—even if they want to escape their moral responsibilities. Hard pressed taxpayers, millions of them parents with children, should not have to pay through the benefits system for children deserted by irresponsible fathers.

My own belief is that taxation should be kept to a minimum. One of the great pro-family policies adopted by this Government has been the drive to lower, fairer taxes.

We must also make parents accept responsibility for their children's crimes. The first line of defence against mischief-making by youngsters is the good sense and responsibility of parents. The family provides the most important classroom for our children. Every parent is a teacher. All parents must be aware of that responsibility.

Schools, of course, have a crucial role to play. It is of the utmost importance that our schools teach personal responsibility. Our teachers have the awesome responsibility of preparing today's youngsters for the challenges, opportunities and disappointments of life. For it is at school that children learn to accept others' needs; to realise that compromise is often the only solution to a clash of wills; to learn that work is important and takes real effort; and to understand that playing as a team is as important as individual success.

Education about drugs including alcohol and their misuse, about being a parent and about religion and its place in our lives are also essential to a well balanced curriculum.

I know that many people are concerned about the dangers of divorce being too readily available. The Law Commission is looking at the question of reforming the divorce laws, to avoid a situation where divorce is available on demand. It is crucial that as many couples as possible have the time and opportunity to resolve their problems, before taking any irrevocable steps towards dissolving their union.

Throughout this talk I have tried to strike a balance between a realistic appraisal of the state of the family today and what is the best way forward. We have a very important responsibility for children *now*—they are the future of this country.

We must face this challenge realistically. We must admit that we cannot ask women who are educated, and have worked, to remain running a home which in itself no longer presents the overwhelming task of the past. But nor should women be made to feel that they have failed if they choose to stay at home to bring up a family. There are few tasks as important and as rewarding as raising a child.

## *The Challenge*

In an age when more women are going out to work and when the family faces new challenges, there is a pressing need for both parents—the mother and the father—to accept their role in child caring. Even today, women put in about 90% of the 70 hours a week needed to look after a child under the age of five. They also perform most of the domestic work in households even where both partners work. Few men, I would venture to suggest, are as considerate as Mr Denis Thatcher, who, when asked by a reporter on his first day at No. 10 'Who wears the trousers?', replied: 'I do—and I also wash and iron them.'

Whilst demographic changes will give women new opportunities to work, I also hope that technological and economic advances can be used to give women greater choice about *where* they work and how many hours they put in. Home-based and part-time work have a crucial role to play in providing the flexibility to enable mothers to raise a family and continue a career.

Of course, mothers will want more nursery and childcare places. Employers are accepting their role in helping to provide them, especially as *they* get tax relief in doing so, and employees no longer face a tax charge for using nursery places provided by their employers. But we must also avoid the emptiness of our small children being consigned permanently to crèches throughout their early years. The formative years of a child's development are the first five. Parents must be aware of this fundamental fact. Where trust, love, discipline and humour play their daily part, our children will grow up into balanced young adults. The choice of childcare for the parent who needs it, is almost as important as the choice of husband or wife. If it cannot be parents or grandparents, it must be in a loving, caring environment.

It is not only mothers who are set to play an ever more important role in the labour market. I firmly believe that more older people whose families have grown up have a huge contribution to make to our society. Employers must not ignore the huge pool of under-used skill, experience and talent represented by the over-60s.

I also believe, as you may have guessed from the importance I attach to the extended family, that care flows in both directions. I think much is to be gained by parents and grandparents sharing the upbringing of children—and children, in their turn, sharing the care of the elderly grandparents later on.

As education offers more to young people, so they will stay in the family. Between 1975 and 1988 the proportion of 16 year olds in full time education rose from 37% to 47%, and this trend is set to continue.

Much is written about the importance of happiness for the individual. Today I sometimes think the cult of the individual and his or her expectations are raised to impossible heights. Yet those who talk endlessly of rights have always led society to some sort of disaster. One only has to think of Robespierre on the French Revolution, or of Marx's influence, to know that this is true.

Most of us gain happiness from a satisfactory life of give and take. There are memorable moments. There are sad and desolate moments. There are testing moments. We all have moments of glory; we all have moments of hope, but our best moments at the end of it all will be those where we have helped one of our family to succeed—those are the rewarding moments that when we come to the end of our lives we look back on and treasure.

It is here, in this world, with our friends and family, that we must all find happiness and fulfilment. As Wordsworth wrote:

> Not in utopia—subterranean fields or some secreted island—but in the very world, which is the world of all of us—the place where in the end we find our happiness, or not at all.

## Mother Teresa

Jesus came to give us the Good News that God is love and that He wants us to love one another as He loves each of us. To make is easy for us to love one another, Jesus said, 'Whatever you do to the least of my brethren, you do it to me. If you give a glass of water in my name, you give it to me. If you receive a little child in my name, you receive me'. What a wonderful tenderness of God's love, to make it so easy for us to love one another.

When Mary received Jesus in her womb, she went in haste to share the joy of the presence of Jesus with her cousin Elizabeth, for she was with child and she wanted to serve and help her. And something very strange happened when Mary came into the home of Elizabeth. When they greeted each other, the little unborn child in the womb of Elizabeth leapt with joy at the presence of Jesus—very, very strange that God used an unborn child to proclaim the coming of Jesus.

Let us thank God for His great love in giving us so many beautiful occasions to prove our love for Him. In India we have leper families. But the child born of a leper mother does not have the disease, so I have made children's homes in every possible place so that as soon as a child is born we can take him there and save his life. There is great suffering for the mother, that she cannot keep her child. But she makes the sacrifice with so much love, for so much of that child is of her very life. This is a beautiful thing, this love in the heart of a mother for her child, that she makes a sacrifice so that the child will be saved.

I beg you, if any of you ever find children that nobody wants, please give them to our sisters. We now have our sisters in ninety-five countries, so you can always find where the sisters are. It is something beautiful for the love of God, to help and protect a little child, a loved one, a child that has been created for greater things.

Today there is so much trouble in the world and I think much of it begins at home. The world is suffering so much because there is no peace. There is no peace because there is no peace in the family. We must make our homes centers of compassion.

Thoughtfulness is the beginning of great sanctity. If you learn this art of being thoughtful, you will become more and morer Christlike, for His heart was meek and He always thought of the needs of others. If we also have that kind of thoughtfulness for each other, our homes would really become the abode of God most high.

Do you know the poor of your own home first? Maybe in your home there is somebody who is feeling lonely, very unwanted, very handicapped. Maybe your husband, your wife, or your child is lonely. Do you know that?

Today we have no time even to look at each other, to talk to each other, to enjoy each other... And so less and less we are in touch with each other. The world is lost for want of sweetness and kindness. People are starving for love because everybody is in such a great rush.

Be happy... and make it a special point to become God's sign of happiness. Joy shows from the eyes; it appears when one speaks and walks. It cannot be kept closed inside us. When people find in your eyes that habitual happiness, they will understand that they are the beloved children of God. Joy is very infectious. We shall never know all the good that a simple smile can do. Be faithful in little things. Smile at one another. *We must live beautifully.*

If we bring prayer into the family, the family will stay together. They will love one another. Just get together for five minutes. That is where your strength will come from. The time we spend in having our daily audience with God is the most precious part of the whole day. I want you all to fill your hearts with great love.

Make your house—your family—another Nazareth where love, peace, joy and unity reign, for love begins at home.

God be with you and God bless you.

# Biographical Notes

## Dr Melvin Anchell

Dr Melvin Anchell is a neuropsychiatrist as well as having a private practice consisting of General Medicine and Psychiatry since 1948. He is an active member of numerous American medical associations and is a Fellow of the American Society of Psychoanalytic Physicians. His list of books includes *Sex and Insanity* and he has written an account of modern sex education from the psychoanalytical viewpoint. He has written articles for magazines and professional journals on pornography, homosexuality and sex education and wrote the *Effects Report* critique for President Johnson's Commission on Obscenity. He is frequently called on to be an expert witness in pornography and obscenity cases at Federal and State levels.

## Dr Digby Anderson

Dr Anderson is Founder Director of the Social Affairs Unit, an independent charitable trust and social policy research institute. Previously he was a Research Fellow at Nottingham University and has lectured in higher education in both the university and public sector. He holds a PhD, M.Phil and BA in sociology. He is author or contributing editor of 16 books and has published some 50 chapters in collections or papers in learned journals. He is or has been a regular columnist in *The Times*, *Sunday Times*, *Sunday Telegraph* and *The Spectator*. Since 1987 he has served on the Health Studies Committee of the Council for National Academic Awards and is a member of the Council of the Economic and Social Research Council.

## Dr Peter Benton

Peter Benton has been Director-General of the British Institute of Management since 1986. Formerly Managing Director and Deputy Chairman of British Telecom, he is Chairman of the Englefield Health Authority and was previously Chairman of the North London Hospice Group. He is Chairman of the World Bank's research programme on catastrophes and is an Independent Member of the British Library Advisory Council. His new book *Riding the Whirlwind* has recently appeared.

## Mrs Lynette Burrows

Lynette Burrows is a graduate teacher with teaching experience in English and Law. She is also a registered childminder and ran a playschool for seven years. She now teachers university students on summer courses and writes articles on education and family related matters for the *Sunday Telegraph*, *The Times* and *The Independent* as well as appearing on many television programmes on social affairs and family matters. She is married with six children and published *Good Children* in 1986.

## Rev Dr Nigel de S. Cameron

Rev Dr Cameron has been Warden of Rutherford House since 1981 and is a member of the Church of Scotland. He is editor of *Ethics and Medicine* and author/editor of several books on medical ethics including: *Abortion: the Crisis in Morals and Medicine* (with Pamela S. Sims); *Embryos and Ethics: The Warnock Report in Debate*; *Medicine in Crisis* (with Ian Brown); *Is Life Really Sacred?*; *The New Medicine* (Hodder, forthcoming 1991).

## Mr and Mrs Paul Danon

Paul and Helen Danon are married with four children. Paul Danon worked for a number of years as a journalist and now works in the computer industry whilst continuing to write. Helen Danon trained in music and taught and performed. She is a teacher in Natural Family Planning and is a Breast-feeding Counsellor with the National Childbirth Trust.

## Rev Peter Elliott

The Rev Peter J. Elliott, an Australian, studied at Melbourne University and Oxford and was ordained in 1973. While active in parish work he also became a popular religious writer. In 1984 he went to Rome to study at the John Paul II Institute for Studies on Marriage and the Family at the Lateran University. He currently works at the Pontifical Council for the Family and his latest book is *What God has Joined—the Sacramentality of Marriage*.

## Dr Otto von Habsburg MEP

The eldest son of the last Emperor of Austria and King of Hungary, Archduke Otto (who prefers Dr von Habsburg) is a member of the European Parliament for Bavaria. His family was exiled from Austria in 1919 (right to return only granted in 1966). The family lived in Switzerland until 1922 when they moved to Madeira where the Emperor died leaving a widow and eight children, with Archduke Otto the eldest at 10. Dr von Habsburg actively opposed the Nazi regime from 1933 and after the occupation of Austria in 1938 there was a warrant for his arrest. After the war he returned to Austria but was banished at the order of the Soviet occupation forces. He holds a Doctorate in Political and Social Sciences from Louvain University in Belgium and is the President of the Pan European Union. In 1951 he married Regina, Princess of Saxe-Meiningen and they have seven children.

## Dr Jacqueline Kasun

Professor Jacqueline Kasun is Professor of Economics at Humboldt State University, California. She gained her PhD from Columbia University and had research positions with the Standard Oil Company and the Haynes Foundation. She has written many books and articles, amongst which are included *The Real Population Explosion*, *Inflation and Unemployment*, *Population Myths and Realities* and *The War on Population*. She is married with three children.

## Mr Michael Keating

Michael Keating, Bachelor of Arts (History), Master of Arts (History and Sociology of Education); University of Michigan (Ann Arbor). Author of numerous books, notably *The Stolen Generation*, *Highway to Hell*, *More Than Meets the Ear*, *Pastoral Renewal*. He is currently International Director of University Christian Outreach, an interdenominational, international Christian movement among university students. He has been involved in this work for twelve years.

## Prof Thomas Langan

Professor Langan has been Professor of Philosophy at the universities of St Louis, Indiana, and Toronto. He has lectured all over the world, most recently at universities in Africa, South America and Asia. His subjects include metaphysics, the family and world economic relations. He is currently involved in marriage preparation work for young people in Toronto.

## Prof Jérôme Lejeune

Professor Jérôme Lejeune is currently Professor of Fundamental Genetics at the Faculté de Médicine Necker–Enfants Malades, Chief of the Department of Cytogenetics at the Hôpital des Enfants Malades and Director of the Institut de Progenese, Paris. He is a member of various Academies of Science (Boston, London, Rome, Stockholm) and has received many awards for his work on human chromosomal diseases (Kennedy Award 1962, William Allan Memorial Award 1969). After the discovery of trisomy 21 (Down's Syndrome or 'mongolism'), the first chromosomal disease discovered in man (1958 and 1959) and the first example of a translocation (1960), he described many chromosomal diseases (e.g. Cri du Chat syndrome) in collaboration with workers in the Institut de Progenese. After publishing a new model on the possible role of the one carbon cycle in the cause of mental retardation, especially in trisomy 21, he worked on clinical studies and metabolic trials. His work as a specialised consultant in the Hôpital des Enfants Malades, for Down's Syndrome, is extremely active (nearly 3000 individual records). Beside his work on trisomy 21, he has made contributions to mathematical genetics, radiation genetics, chromosomal evolution of species and molecular biology.

## Dr Patricia Morgan

Dr Patricia Morgan has worked in university research at the interface between sociology and law. An experienced author, she is married with two young children, one of whom has been handicapped from birth.

## Dr Kongolo Mulumba

Dr Kongolo Mulumba holds a Doctorate in Economics, Social and Political Sciences. She is at present, since 1980, Head of Research at the University of Kinshasa. She is a consultant on matters concerning the social welfare of women in Zaire, notably for USAID and UNICEF. She is responsible for many publications on the condition of women in Africa. She is married and has seven children.

## Professor Seyyed Hossein Nasr

Professor Seyyed Hossein Nasr was born and brought up in Iran. He has a PhD in Philosophy and in History of Science from Harvard University, and a BS in Physics from MIT. He is presently Professor of Islamic Studies at George University in Washington. He was Dean of the University of Teheran, Head of the University of Aryamehr and founder of the Islamic Academy of Philosophy. He is an active lecturer, has contributed many articles and is the author of several books, in particular *The Encounter of Man and Nature*, *The Spiritual Crisis of Modern Man*. Presently also President of the Foundation for Traditional Studies and supervising the creation of a major TV film series *Islam and the West* being produced by the Foundation and the Maryland Public Television.

## Dr Bernard Nathanson

Professor Bernard Nathanson is Assistant Professor of Clinical Obstetrics and Gynaecology at Cornell University Medical College and Associate attending obstetrics and gynaecology at the New York Hospital. He is the author of seventeen books. He is the author of the film *The Silent Scream* and *The Eclipse of Reason*.

## Professor Erik Odeblad

Professor of Medical Biophysics and Chairman of the Department of Biophysics at the University of Umea, Sweden, Erik Odeblad has many medical qualifications in obstetrics, gynaecology and endocrinology. He is a world authority on research concerning the cervical mucus, and has directed seminars in many countries on this subject. He is also Chairman of the Umea Biophysical Society since 1975, and a member of the Committee for Environmental Protection and Health, University of Umea, since 1983. He was awarded the Eberling Prize in Medical Physics in 1978 and the Mangberg Prize in Neurological Sciences in 1985.

## Mr Robert Parsons

Robert Parsons, Director of CARE for the Family, is a qualified solicitor and teacher. A senior partner in a legal practice, he has just completed a short radio series for BBC Wales, *The Family Starting Again* and is currently producing a series of vignettes entitled *Family Matters* in conjunction with local radio stations. Robert is married to Dianne and they have two children. They are both currently in the middle of a series of seminars called *Marriage Under Pressure* which in the past year have been attended by over six thousand delegates.

## Rev Mario Picchi

Father Picchi, founder and President of the Italian Solidarity Centre of Rome, has been treating drug addicts and their families with great success for twenty years. It was his activity and his style of understanding and rehabilitation of youth which turned the attention of religious, civil, medical and health-care authorities toward a more positive approach to the care of drug addicts. Don Picchi was the very first in Italy to believe firmly that the therapeutic community would make a profound cultural change in attitudes towards drug addicts. The therapeutic programme of the ISC, *Project Man*, treats about ten thousand young people each year, with outstanding success. Don Picchi attributes much of this success to the application of Logotherapy, taught originally by Professor Viktor Frankl.

## Mrs Veronica Pierson

Veronica Pierson is a teacher of Natural Family Planning. Married, with two sons, she is a regular speaker at London schools, pioneering new programmes of family life education aimed at teenagers. Her centre in South London offers counselling and practical courses in the Billings' Method of natural family planning.

## Dr Myriam Puig

Dr Myriam Puig is a paediatrician, Doctor of Biochemistry in Nutrition and Metabolism (Massachusetts Institute of Technology). She was formerly Assistant Paediatrician at Harvard University (1975–1977) and Professor of

Paediatrics at the University of Navarra (1978–1985). Myriam Puig has been a member of the New York Academy of Sciences since 1981.

## Mrs Suzanne Rini

Mrs Rini is a freelance journalist. She wrote for a number of publications in her native Pittsburgh before founding, in 1978, her own newspaper there. Her articles covered care of the mentally handicapped, teenage alcoholism, and domestic violence among other issues. Her book, *Beyond Abortion: A Chronology of Fetal Experimentation*, was published last year. She is married with three children.

## Mrs Katarina Runske

Bachelor of Arts of the University of Stockholm, Mrs Katarina Runske, who has a diploma for History of Arts, is president of several associations occupied with families. Member of the Institute for Public and International Law (Stockholm), she published articles in many European and American newspapers about human rights and about the law concerning families.

## M and Madame Guy Scheen

Christiane and Guy Scheen are respectively nurse and social worker, aged 35 and 39 years. Married since 1974, they had one healthy child, and one severely handicapped, who has since died. They adopted three other children through *SOS Emmanuel*. Since March 1988, Guy Scheen was closely involved with the work of *SOS Emmanuel* as a social worker.

## Dr Philippe Schepens

Dr Schepens is an ear, nose and throat specialist. He is editor and publisher of the medical journal *News Exchange*. He is a member of the board of consultants of Human Life International, Washington DC. Since April 1987, he has been President of the Association of Doctors Who Respect Human Life in Belgium, and Secretary of the World Federation of Doctors Who Respect Human Life.

## Dr Michael Schluter

Dr Michael Schluter has an MS and a PhD in Agricultural Economics from Cornell University. He is Director of the Jubilee Centre, a Christian research and campaigning group based in Cambridge, and Director of the Keep Sunday Special campaign. He has been a consultant to the World Bank on agricultural policy analysis, as well as compiling a working paper for the International Food Policy Research Institute to the European Parliament. He is married with three children.

## Professor Julian Simon

Professor Simon teaches business and social science at the University of Maryland. His Doctorate in Business Economics is from Chicago University and his BA in Experimental Psychology from Harvard. He is the author of over a hundred lead articles and twenty books in a great variety of subjects dealing with economy, sociology, consumerism; the latest book *Man, Our Last Chance* is a coast to coast best-seller. He is married and the father of three.

## Dr Susan Stanford

Dr Susan Stanford, a native of Montreal, received her PhD degree in Counselling Psychology from Northwestern University. She has extensive experience in university teaching and counselling, and held positions as Assistant Vice-President for Human Resources at Wayne State University and Dean of Unity College. Her book *Will I Cry Tomorrow?* offers women who suffer from post-abortion trauma hope and a pathway to healing.

## Miss Rachel Tingle

Rachel Tingle is an economist and journalist. She has a BA in Economics from the University of Exeter, and an MSc in Economics from the University of Surrey. She was an economics research fellow at the University of York investigating the provision of care for the mentally ill before working for some years in economic consultancy. More recently she has worked as an advisor to various senior politicians and in newspaper and television journalism. She writes a regular column on Church affairs for *Freedom Today* since 1977 and other articles have appeared in the *Daily Telegraph*, the *Economist* and the religious press. Her booklet *Gay Lessons* was published by Pickwick Books in 1986.

## Dr Niklaus Waldis

Dr Waldis is Swiss and studied Medicine at the Universities of Fribourg and Berne. He later undertook postgraduate studies in Surgery, Internal Medicine, Gynaecology, Obstetrics and Tropical Medicine. He has worked as a GP and at the Mission Hospital in Lesotho. He is currently at the Department of Internal Medicine of the Cantonal Hospital in Frauenfeld, Switzerland. He is married with three children.

## Mrs Valerie Riches

Mrs Riches worked as a social worker with unmarried mothers and became the secretary of what was to become Family and Youth Concern in the 1970s. She has since lectured all over the world on topics relating to family life and the pressures on young people. Her subject of feminism is covered widely in a recent paperback *Feminism Against Mankind* to which she is a contributor—she is also the author of a number of other publications including *Sex and Social Engineering*. She is married with two children.

## Rt Hon Angela Rumbold PC CBE MP

Member of Parliament for Mitcham and Morden (Surrey), Mrs Rumbold is a former local councillor in the Royal Borough of Kingston upon Thames, and a founder of the National Association for the Welfare of Children in Hospital. She is currently Minister of State at the Home Office, having held office in the Departments of Environment and Education.

## Dr Zhang de Wei

Dr Zhang de Wei, obstetrician and gynaecologist, is director of the Communal Commission of Shanghai for Family Planning. She is editor in chief of the medical journal *Reproduction and Contraception*.

## Richard Whitfield PhD

Professor Richard Whitfield was Director of Studies at Cambridge University for 9 years for BA (Ed) and BEd and was later Dean of Social Sciences and Humanities at Aston University for 3 years. He has been Director of UK Child Care for the Save the Children Fund and is the founding Chairman of the National Family Trust. He is married with four children.

## Mrs Mercedes Arzu Wilson

Mercedes Wilson was born in Guatemala and is married to an English oil company executive. She lives in Louisiana with her husband and two children. She is co-founder of World Organisation for the Family and Executive Diretor of Family of the Americas Foundation. She is author of the book on the ovulation method *Love and Fertility*. She organised the 1st International Congress for the Family in her native Guatemala City, inspiring and guiding others to accomplish a further fifteen Congresses.

*Appendix*

# World Organisation for the Family
## International Alliance for the Family

**President:** Christine de Marcellus Vollmer
**Vice President:** Mercedes Arzu Wilson
**Secretary:** Jose Carredano
**Executive Director:** Anne Higgins

**International Board:**
Sybille Le Hodey, *Belgium*
Rosario Gortazar de Oraa, *Spain*
Princesse de Bourbon Lobkowicz, *France*
Antoinette Göess, *Austria*
Myriam Puig, *Venezuela*
Carlos Casares, *Uruguay*
Robert de Marcellus, *USA*
Jorge Gonzalez, *Mexico*
Leonardo and Martha Casco, *Honduras*
Hernan Fernandez, *Chile*

The World Organisation for the Family (International Alliance for the Family) is a non-profit, non-sectarian, non-political, educational and service organisation which believes that strong families result not only in happy, productive individuals, but also strong communities and nations.

The World Organisation for the Family is working to counter the current threats to family life and human life by promoting progressive solutions to human problems.

The World Organisation for the Family
... serves as a research and resource centre for demographic, social, economic, ethical, and political issues that affect the family and the right to life.
... networks with existing pro-family groups on both national and international levels, promoting the creation of such associations where none exist.
... sponsors leadership conferences and public awareness programmes, including high-visibility international Congresses.
... develops and distributes printed and audiovisual educational materials.
... monitors government activities that impact on the family and the right to life.
... promotes proper understanding of sex and marriage, thereby helping adolescents to adopt a lifestyle which enhances physical, emotional and spiritual health.
... promotes marriage preparation, marriage enrichment and parenting skills.

# XVIth International Congress for the Family

## Patrons

General Eva Burrows
  Salvation Army.
Most Rev The Lord Coggan of
  Canterbury and Sissinghurst PC.
Rev Dr Donald English
  President, Methodist Conference.
Most Rev Cardinal Basil Hume OSB,
  Archbishop of Westminster.
Lord Jakobovits,
  Chief Rabbi.

Rt Rev Dr Eric Kemp
  The Bishop of Chichester.
Rt Rev Cormac Murphy-O'Connor,
  Bishop of Arundel and Brighton.
Most Rev Dr Robert Runcie,
  The Archbishop of Canterbury.
Rev Prof Tudno-Williams
  President, Free Church Federal
  Council.

## XVIth International Congress for the Family (UK) Ltd

Directors: Michael Pinkess, Esq.
  Mrs P.D. Riches
  Mrs Madeline M.H. Sanne
  Robert Standing, Esq. (Chairman and Treasurer)
  Mrs Christine de M. Vollmer (President)
  Mrs Mercedes A. Wilson
Office: James Bogle, Esq. (Secretary-General)
  Miss Tatiana Holstein–Ledreborg (Assistant)

# XVIth International Congress for the Family

# Council of Reference

David Alton MP
Donald Anderson MP
Nicholas Baker MP
William Benyon MP
Alan Beith MP
Nicholas Bennet MP
Mrs Phyllis Bowman MP
Sir Bernard Braine MP
John Branagan FRSA JP
Rev Clive Calver
Sr Jose Carredano
Bryan Cassidy MEP
Roy and Fiona Castle
Gerald Coates
Charles Colchester
Neville Cooper
Patrick Cormack MP
Baroness Cox of Queensberry
The Lord Craigmyle
Veronika, Countess Czernin
Baron Joseph Doblhoff
Monika, Countess Draskovich
Sarah Drummond
The Baroness Elles
Frank Field MP

Roger Forster
Lady Grantchester
Lynn Green
Lt Col Mrs Muriel Holdstock
Simon Hughes MP
His Honour Alan King-Hamilton QC
Mme Sybille le Hodey
Dame Jill Knight DBE MP
Angela, Countess de Malherbe
The Baroness Masham of Ilton
The Duke of Norfolk
Sir John Peel KCVO DM FRCOG FRCP
Gabrielle, Countess of Plettenberg
Irina Ratushinskaya
The Lord Rawlinson of Ewell PC QC
Sir Hugh Rossi MP
David Sala
Sir Jack Stewart-Clark MEP
The Lady Torphichen
Sir Gerard Vaughan MP
Rosario, Duchess de la Victoria
Joanna, Countess of Westphalia
Nicholas Winterton MP
Mrs Ann Winterton MP
Rt Rev Bishop Maurice Wood DSC

The Mayor of Brighton is welcomed to the XVI International Congress for the Family by the Secretary-General Mr James Bogle

HRH the Princess of Wales meets Congress speakers including Prof Richard Whitfield (left) and Mrs Valerie Riches

*HRH the Princess of Wales is welcomed to the XVI International Congress for the Family by Mr Robert Standring (Chairman) and Mrs Christine de Marcellus Vollmer (President – centre).*
*Pictures: Terry Chambers – Photographer*

*HRH the Princess of Wales greets members of the organising team of the International Congress of the Family.*

*Mr Michael Keating.*

*Mr Peter Benton.*

*Prof Jerome Lejeune.*

*The Chief Rabbi, Rev Lord Jakobovits.*

*Mrs Christine Vollmer and Mrs Mercedes Wilson.*

*Singer Dana brought her own message to the Congress in song.*

*A bouquet for the Mayor of Brighton from young Congress delegate Abigail Orr (4).*

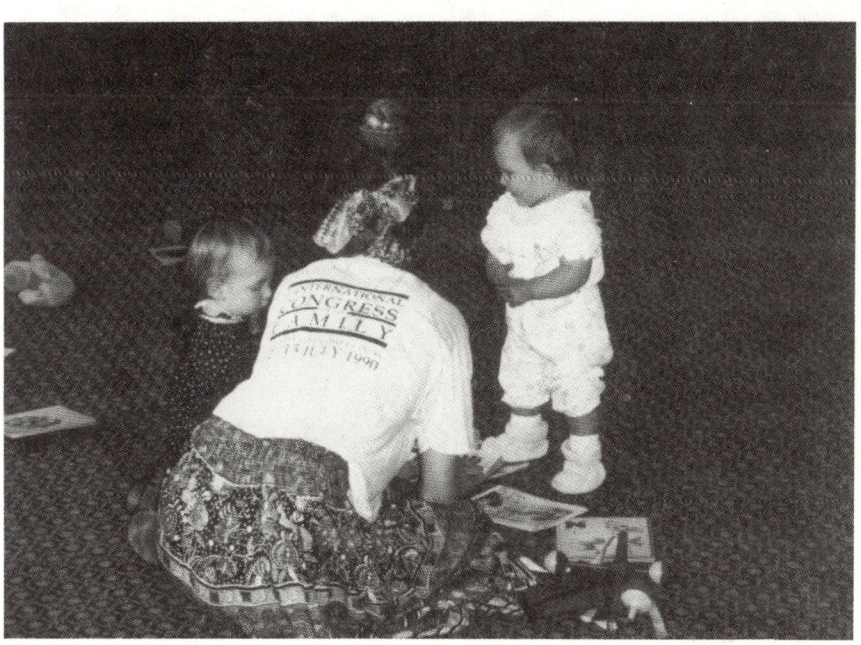

*Children are at the core of family life–a scene at the Congress creche.*